China's State Ideology and the Three Gorges Dam

This book uses the case of the Three Gorges Dam project to explore the Chinese state's use of ideology, namely the political theodicy of development, as a governing tactic in the reform era.

Presenting observations from fieldwork collected after the dam's completion, it reveals communities who not only embraced their improved livelihoods but also expressed support for the mega-project and the Party's leadership. However, the research also indicates that the effects of the ideological dissemination surrounding the project were not monolithic, with the development process involving extensive struggles and contradictions, including locals facing unemployment and the fragmentation of their social networks. This disjuncture between the state ideology and social reality thus revealed flaws in the official imperative of political theodicy.

Displaying how the authoritarian rule of the Chinese state can be adaptive in modifying its mode of governance, especially when faced with the unintended consequences of failures, this book will be a valuable resource to students and scholars of Asian environment; development politics; and Chinese politics, history, and society.

Yuen-ching Bellette Lee teaches Chinese politics under reform and international relations of East Asia at the University of California, Los Angeles. She obtained her PhD in political science from the University of Chicago.

Routledge Contemporary China Series

259 Modernization in Eastern Tibet
Leviathan the Forager
Su Hu

260 Inside The Expressive Culture of Chinese Women's Mosques
'This Turmoil of the Soul'
Maria Jaschok

261 Exploring China's Religious Sites
Digital and Spatial Insights
Zhaohui Hong

262 Cultural Bifocals on Chinese TV Series and Diaspora Fiction
Sheng-mei Ma

263 Chinese Educated Youth Literature
Ambivalent Bodies and Personal Literary Histories
Gabriel F. Y. Tsang

264 Performance Across Chinese Borders
Wei Zhang

265 Heritage, Homemaking, and Identity Formation in Migrant Workers
An Ethnographic Study of Yi Migrants in Shenzhen
Junmin Liu

266 China's State Ideology and the Three Gorges Dam
The Political Theodicy of Development
Yuen-ching Bellette Lee

For more information about this series, please visit: www.routledge.com/Routledge-Contemporary-China-Series/book-series/SE0768

China's State Ideology and the Three Gorges Dam

The Political Theodicy of Development

Yuen-ching Bellette Lee

Routledge
Taylor & Francis Group
LONDON AND NEW YORK

First published 2025
by Routledge
4 Park Square, Milton Park, Abingdon, Oxon OX14 4RN

and by Routledge
605 Third Avenue, New York, NY 10158

Routledge is an imprint of the Taylor & Francis Group, an informa business

British Library Cataloguing-in-Publication Data
A catalogue record for this book is available from the British Library

ISBN: 978-1-032-87108-0 (hbk)
ISBN: 978-1-032-87219-3 (pbk)
ISBN: 978-1-003-53149-4 (ebk)

DOI: 10.4324/9781003531494

Typeset in Times New Roman
by Apex CoVantage, LLC

For Yuhki

Contents

Figures

Preface and Acknowledgments

The Three Gorges Dam project first came to my attention in the early 1990s. Following decades of debate, the project was tabled at the National People's Congress (NPC) in 1992 for approval. This was three years after the Tiananmen crackdown, and the Chinese economy had just come out of retrenchment with a new phase of reform. The public attention the project proposal drew, the number of vetoes and abstentions on the project at the NPC meeting, and the intensity of debate both inside and outside the assembly hall injected a breath of fresh air into the somber post-suppression sociopolitical atmosphere. As I looked deeper into the dynamics of the project, I became captivated by its complexity and multidimensionality in the economic, social, and environmental, not to mention political, realms. In the past twenty-odd years, as the construction got into full swing and also after it was completed, I visited the gorge area as well as resettlement villages outside the river valley, witnessing the process of displacement and the change in the life of those who were relocated far away from their hometowns and struggled to strike a foothold in the new land. Resistance and criticism have been well known. But what struck me during those visits, especially after the dam's completion, was certain people's support for the project and embrace of the Party's decision, to the extent that some of my hosts, who were ordinary folks, including my own cousin, tried to steer my research to the direction of a favorable view about the dam, insisting that "people in the West, particularly those from the United States, should look more at the bright side of our society." Inasmuch as I sought to be informed about the opposition, I was happy to listen to people's stories that recounted positive outcomes. It was striking to me that they had an assumption, which was my intent to dig up the dirty side of their system, and they were eager to expose me to the favorable aspects of the dam scheme and the Party's rule in general. Their stance bore resemblance to the views of quite a number of my interviewees inside and outside the gorge area. This got me thinking: why is it so? How did these folks, who were perfect strangers to one another, come to share such a similar view about the dam project, the Party, and the West? I started to wonder if the answer might lie beyond the abstract idea of nationalism and propagandistic indoctrination, and that led me to the theme of this book.

This work would not have been possible without the encouragement and support of various teachers and friends. I am indebted to William Sewell, who patiently guided me through the writing and research at the University of Chicago. Valuable input and help were also provided by Prasenjit Duara, as did Lisa Wedeen and Dali Yang. Katsuya Hirano and Ching Kwan Lee read the introduction and gave me insightful comments. I thank them all for inspiring me to think harder on various parts of my analysis. My special thanks are due to Kwai Ng, who read through the draft and helped me bring my argument into focus. I am also grateful to Nicholas Sharifi, who generously created the artwork and made the preparation of this manuscript an easier process. Any mistakes and shortcomings, of course, are mine alone.

My fieldwork and interviews were facilitated by Chinese intellectuals and gorge resettlers alike. I am deeply thankful to my informants, who nevertheless cannot be named here. Dai Qing, Fan Dainian, and others provided me with information and gave me valuable insights about the dam debate in the earlier stages of my research. I am grateful to them all. In addition, I owe this book to my sister, Karen, who, without knowing it, has been motivating me with her unconditional support. My husband, Katsuya, has been a delightful companion on my intellectual journey. Finally, I would also like to thank my daughter, Yuhki, for being the reason for me to finish this work. I dedicate this book to her.

Introduction

Large-scale engineering projects have been embraced by modern states as an embodiment of modernity and national power. However, the financial costs and social disruptions caused by such projects often engender public opposition. In many nondemocratic states, governments use their authoritarian might to push through such projects with few constraints from legal norms and political accountability. The Three Gorges Dam is no exception. In my over two-decade-long study of the mega-scheme, I witnessed how local villagers, journalists, and Chinese intellectuals, some of whom collaborated with transnational activists from Western countries, opposed the construction. However, after the completion of the dam, I conducted further fieldwork in and outside of the Three Gorges area and found that many people embraced their new life and expressed willing support for the Party's decision. This finding is not all-encompassing – inasmuch as not all the villagers were defiant toward the construction when the project was launched, not every resident who had gone through resettlement was happy with the outcome of the displacement. Yet the willingness and even eagerness of many people to support the Party's act was remarkable. I put the dam in the context of China's broader scenario of reform and found a congruent pattern: despite many people's disenchantment (as manifested in "mass incidents") with the widening wealth gap, environmental degradation, and corruption, the Dengist and post-Dengist regimes have remained firmly in power. The validity of the party-state system has rarely been challenged. Most of all, reform as the desirable politico-economic orientation of China has maintained widespread acceptance among the populace. In this context, how do we explain the Three Gorges resettlers' active embrace despite the severe disruptions incurred to their lives? What can we learn from the case of the Three Gorges Dam about the Party's governing strategy in the reform era?

This book argues that the state uses ideology – developmentalism or, more precisely, what I conceptualize as the *political theodicy of development* – as the governing tactic. The analysis does not stop at the point of conceiving ideology as a set of ideas or beliefs. It examines the material existence of ideology and how it gets reproduced through everyday practices, including those of working and living. In the case of China, the Party's monopoly on violence operates alongside the ideological persuasion of progress (under the name of reform), which assures people of the regime's exclusive capacity to realize a better livelihood, to reorganize society

DOI: 10.4324/9781003531494-1

in the direction of modernization, and to bring China onto the path of national rejuvenation. It appeals to those who gained in the reforms that the status quo has to be maintained with political stability ensured by one-party dominance, and to those who lost out in the reforms, the "poor," through the hope of material betterment and the promise that existing defects of the reforms will be remedied under the imagined scenario of "common prosperity."

Development has been comprehensively studied in developing countries and the politics of modernization. However, what is specific about China's developmentalist aspiration is its affinity to the logic of redemption, which is reminiscent of what I call *political theodicy*. Throughout Chinese communist history, from the point of Mao Zedong leading the peasants to found the People's Republic to Deng Xiaoping launching the reforms amid lingering hardship following the Cultural Revolution and, more recently, Xi Jinping's pledge of national rejuvenation to avert the malign intervention of Western powers, the regime has built its power upon a theodicy of suffering. I draw from the Weberian idea that "[t]he annunciation and the promise of religion have . . . been addressed to the masses of those who were in need of salvation . . . from sickness, poverty, and from all sorts of distress and danger,"[1] and argue that the theodicy in the Chinese case is not religiously spiritual but *political*. In place of the god in Christian faith, the Party is the "savior" of the Chinese community, substituting the god-individual relationship with a state-subject pact. From the rubble of socioeconomic crises, whether as a result of the civil war in the 1940s, the campaigns of radical mobilization such as the Cultural Revolution, or the real and imagined threat from Western powers pronounced by leaders including Xi, the Party has emerged as the "redeemer," proclaiming to pull people out of the abyss of misery and onto the road of perceived progress – whether in the form of a "new China," "China under reform," or the "China century." The political theodicy of development as an ideology is not simply rooted in the mindset of "catching up" with advanced nations. Rather, it is built upon the specific historical narrative of China, in that past events have consistently been framed as intrusions, atrocities, and, most of all, humiliation, which is considered the major source of suffering. The savior, the Party, is there to lead the people out of their state of distress and forge a path toward the utopian projections of "poverty elimination," "common prosperity," and the "ascendancy of a powerful China."

In congruence with religious rationalism,[2] the political theodicy in China comes with the principle of reward and punishment. "Good deeds" conforming to Party directives are recompensed with the promise of hope for salvation. On the contrary, "sins" committed as a result of breaking away from state-prescribed orthodoxies are penalized with not only coercive retribution but also the threat of falling – into unfathomable material dispossession and social disintegration, in a word, chaos. Accordingly, people are purported to benefit from the chance of redemption if they follow the Party with absolute faith.

The logics of misery and redemption, and of reward and punishment, apply both collectively and to individuals. As much as the *hope* for salvation and the *fear* of destruction are profound for individual social members, the same holds true for the Chinese nation as a whole. Developmentalism touches on both individuals and the collective body, and binds them together under the rhetorical banner of a common destiny, in the sense that rectifying the distressing conditions of individuals adds up to the salvation of the nation as a whole.

The political theodicy of development, as illustrated in the Three Gorges case, is twofold and consists of a series of binary components – suffering and redemption, sacrifice and reward, present and future. First, the socioeconomic conditions of the gorge area before the dam have been framed in official narratives as being poor and backward. The project would thus relieve the villagers from the suffering of poverty and backwardness and lead them toward the bright prospect of modernity and prosperity ("Casting off poverty and getting rich" (*tuopin zhifu*)). Second, the political theodicy represents a promise of development that any sacrifice an individual makes today (the pain of displacement) will be rewarded tomorrow – with wealth as a resettler, and with national glory as a Chinese ("Sacrificing one's [short-term] interests for the [long-term] collective good" (*shexiaojia weidajia*)). The vessel transporting the individuals and nation from suffering to this prospective future would be the Party, which is supposed to deliver salvation, redemption, and reward (or punishment) under the condition of conformity.

The Three Gorges Dam offers a lens through which we can explore the ideological reproduction of political theodicy as the Chinese state's governing tactics.[3] For its multifarious illuminating points, ranging from the social impacts of resettlement to the political implications of massive economic reordering and the people's responses to them, the project is exemplary of the Party's ideological workings of development both under and after Deng. Today, the Three Gorges Dam study continues to carry significance. As what Arif Dirlik calls the "global economic horse race" continues to prevail, China's Party-led developmentalism and the idea of political theodicy underpinning it remain a robust tactic of Xi Jinping's governance.[4] As the Chinese economy is showing signs of fragility and the unemployment rate of young people has risen to an all-time high, the state highlights the drive for technological innovations – this time focusing on AI and microchips – as the way to achieve China's long-term progress. In particular, this is conceived in connection with the "rise of China" vis-à-vis the Western powers' purportedly sustained efforts to thwart China's claim of national supremacy.

The Dam

The Three Gorges Dam is located in Hubei Province on the middle reaches of the river and is by far the biggest dam in the world (Figure 0.1). It has a height of 185 meters with a water level of 175 meters, and its width of 2,316 meters is equivalent to the span of the Golden Gate Bridge. The official cost of the project was $25 billion. It took sixteen years to complete and relocated a historic number of 1.3 million people from 20 cities and counties, 116 townships, and 1,711 villages to make way for the construction and the reservoir.

While some villagers were resettled in new urbanized towns built on high ground within the gorge area, many others were displaced to regions as distant as Guangdong, which is hundreds of miles away. The inundation of the villagers'

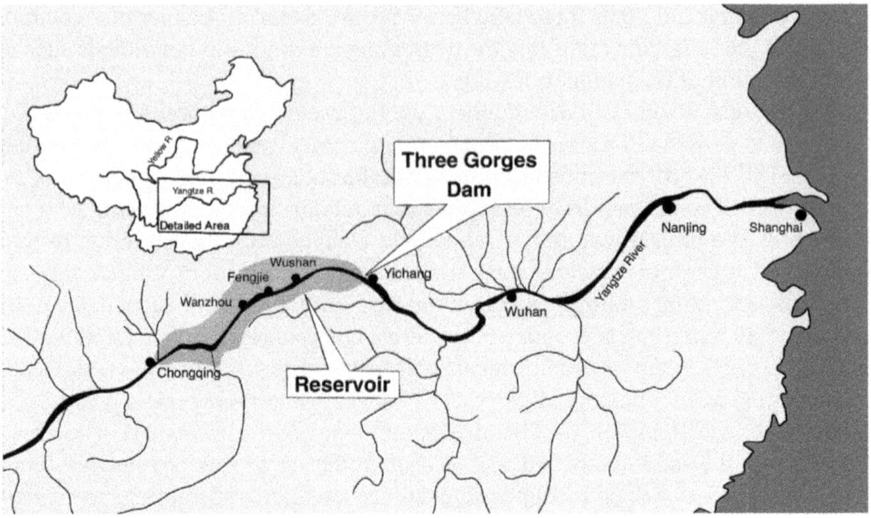

Figure 0.1 Location of the Three Gorges Dam (Provided by Nicholas Sharifi)

residences and the destruction of their kinship networks have changed not only the people's lifestyle but also their social relationships. The transformation of the natural landscape was accompanied by a reformulation of the economic structure, which entailed a change in the people's work from farming to factory manufacturing, entrepreneurship, or agribusiness. Numerous cultural relics, ranging from a few hundred to thousands of years old, including temples, rock inscriptions, and remains of ancient battles, were removed or submerged. The negative environmental impacts of blocking the second-largest river in China have included landslides, siltation, and the endangerment of rare species. Moreover, throughout the construction process, the project was plagued by scandals, including substandard structures, violations of villagers' entitlements, and officials' embezzlement of public funds that had been allocated to relocatees. The scale of resettlement and historic preservation, unprecedented in the history of dam building, as well as the social disruptions and injustices, induced resistance not only from local villagers and Chinese intellectuals but also from transnational environmental groups, which conducted a worldwide campaign against the dam builders and global financiers who funded the dam. Yet the project was completed in 2012, with all the mechanics fully operational and resettled people living their lives in the new space as planned.

Harnessing the Yangtze by building a dam at the Three Gorges area in central China had been on the modernization agendas of leaders from different generations ever since China became a nation-state in the early 1910s. It has been a focus of debate throughout the communist history of China because of its technical complexities, social disruptions, and financial as well as environmental implications. The dam that ultimately came to fruition has created a reservoir of 635 square kilometers, which is as big as Lake Superior. The technology employed in the structure, including a five-tier ship gate and twenty-six 700-megawatt turbines, is unprecedented in hydropower generation. The dam is designed to produce 84.7 billion kilowatt-hours per year, which is the capacity of 18 nuclear plants, to hold back floods from the upper and middle reaches of the river, and to facilitate the navigation of 10,000-ton ships to the inland.

Despite the costs and disruptions, proponents consider it justifiable given the proclaimed "comprehensive benefits" the dam brings. Besides the aforementioned functions, officials maintain that the construction scheme is a cornerstone for gorge residents to break the age-old poverty cycle and "get on the way to becoming rich." Moreover, as the discourse on the dam evolved through the 1990s, the project came to assume the new task of helping to fulfill the urbanization of southwestern China, which is a strategic part of the Chinese hinterland that lags behind the industrialized seaboard. The dam, conceived as part of the nationwide marketization program, is intended to pull resources, including capital and production know-how, from the coastal area to form regional hubs of economic exchange inland. It is designed to generate electricity for the fast-growing urban and industrial centers in the east and bring economic opportunities to the southwestern corner of the country as part of the "Great Western Development Drive" through construction projects and capital investment.

The conceived significance of the Three Gorges project, in other words, lies not only in its modernizing role in the Yangtze Valley but also in China's national development. The channeling of economic resources by integrating the activity of bureaucratic units, research institutes, and companies all over China is envisaged to form a market that consolidates a national economy and enriches the overall population (thereby purportedly evening out the distribution of wealth). Furthermore, these productive operations are connected with activities in the global community through capital flows, the transactions of machinery and technological knowledge, the exchange of information, and the circulation of ideas such as those regarding the environment. The interweaving social practices on the three spatial scales – local, national, and global – converge at the site of the dam, both in the Yangtze Valley and beyond, daily instantiating and reproducing the ideology of development in signification and in practice.

To better understand the operational dynamics of political theodicy, I define "development" at three levels, each of which is connected with the others. First and most basic of all, harnessing the river (building the dam) for various utilitarian purposes is meant to develop a natural resource, the water, for human consumption. The development of the Yangtze Valley entails the application of capital and technologies to generate electricity and facilitate an improved navigational channel.

The technologies and knowledge thus introduced also effect change in the social community, which brings us to the second understanding of "development." This involves a meaning of material transformation in which living standards are expected to improve as modern (often seen as coterminous with Euro-American or, until three decades ago, Soviet) techniques are introduced to populations that previously lived without them.[5] Such a chance of improved livelihood means that hardship is transient. In addition to explicitly material or economic matters, this book also argues that development refers to transformations in the ways in which people live and see their world. Ways of life, people's states of mind, and the configuring of social relations are changed along with their material conditions. People leave their country houses and move into urban high-rises, for example, and have fewer extended family relationships. Artisans and peasants sometimes become factory workers, undergoing a transformation of subjectivity as laborers of an industrial order.

The third meaning involves an understanding of political theodicy on a collective level – the cultural belief in national progress. It builds on the aforementioned definitions of resource development and elevated socioeconomic conditions. Modernization, industrialization, and economic growth are common keywords adhering to development, which suggest an overall progressive trajectory charted by the path of change in a community, oftentimes a nation. The function of the Three Gorges Dam as an engine to propel capital investment to the inland and assist in the urbanization of central and southwestern China is a part of market formation and people's enrichment on a national scale envisioned by the Party. Developing the water resource becomes a means of advancing the material conditions of not only the Three Gorges area but ultimately also the whole of China. "Development" here takes on the meaning of national progress on the path of redemption, revival, and ascension, a concept that is in congruence with the discussion of the "rise of China" and the "China century" emerging in recent decades.

For its (re)ordering of nature and society in accordance with the principles of rationalism, the Three Gorges Dam fits snugly into what James Scott calls a "high modernist" project.[6] Scott identifies the combination of three elements in the making of a state-initiated engineering act that often results in disasters – the ideology of high modernism, the unrestrained use of the authoritarian might of a modern state, and a prostrate civil society.

> At its center [of high modernism] was a supreme self-confidence about . . . the development of scientific and technical knowledge, the expansion of production, the rational design of social order, . . . and, not least, an increasing control over nature (including human nature) commensurate with scientific understanding of natural laws.[7]

While the high-modernist ideal provides the will, the authoritarian state offers the politico-economic capacity to push through the feat of engineering, and an incapacitated civil society is too weak to mount an effective resistance. Some examples of such utopian schemes include Le Corbusier's city designs, the Soviet collectivization of agriculture, and Tanzania's village settlement campaign.

The large-scale comprehensive ordering that is characteristic of Scott's high-modernist schemes is not unlike the "hydraulic society" that Karl Wittfogel analyzes in *Oriental Despotism.*[8] But what distinguishes the modern manifestations of rational planning from the imperial configurations, according to Scott, is the "*administrative technology* and *social knowledge* that make it plausible to imagine organizing an entire society"[9] with the goal of creating realizable utopias. The Three Gorges project, with its transfiguring of the riparian topography, the reorganization of family patterns, and the orchestration of institutions in the displacement of people, among other phenomena, is symptomatic of a high modernist project accomplished through the mastery of technological knowledge. While the dam itself is a local project, what it manifests, however, is a crystallized version of the rationalist organization of a nation's social order under modernization.

The hegemonizing potential of Scott's social engineering schemes is reminiscent of Michel Foucault's "governmentalized" form of power, which is:

> an ensemble formed by the institutions, procedures, analyses and reflections, the calculations and tactics that allow the exercise of . . . power, which has as its target population, as its principal form of knowledge political economy, and as its essential technical means apparatuses of security.[10]

Foucault's concept of "governmentality" is developed from Guillauma de La Perrière's idea that "government is the right disposition of things," in that "things" denote not only objects including humans but also their relations, and:

> their imbrication with those other things which are wealth, resources, . . . the territory with its specific qualities, climate, irrigation, fertility, etc.; men in their relations to that other kind of things, customs, habits, ways of acting and thinking etc.; lastly, men in their relation to that other kind of things, accidents and misfortunes such as famine, epidemics, death, etc.[11]

The end of government, in other words, is the effective management of the territory-bound population, including their productive activities, land use, capital flow, and people's work habits, to make sure that the economy is thriving, people are healthily reproducing, and the country is secure from internal and external threats. The way to attain that goal, for Foucault, is to employ "tactics" – the methods and means by which a modern state governs. These may include bureaucratic mechanisms, economic policies, legal instruments, and most of all, sets of knowledge encompassing techniques, statistics, and scientific analyses. Wrapping up all these, in a nutshell, is what Foucault calls the "reason of state" or "state rationality."

If we combine Scott's high-modernist thesis with Foucault's governmentality to look at the Three Gorges Dam, we see a picture whereby the state's ambitions to transform nature for the perceived benefits of the Yangtze Valley economy and, more broadly, the Chinese nation's development would entail the mobilization of a host of party organs, state decrees, companies, and scientific experts to formulate, plan, and execute the mega engineering work. In the process, the river course is altered, the buildings are removed (or submerged), and the people are relocated to new urban towns. The river, the people, and the economic organizations, among others, are "things" that are reordered for the utopian vision of regional and, furthermore, national modernization. More significantly, what is being reorganized are not simply the physical objects, but the relations among them – the severing of kinships that have family members resettled in disparate places, the change of people's productive work from farming to becoming employees of new companies, and, most of all, the transposing of connections between humans and their land, which is now mediated by the built urban space. The rearrangement of "things" and their relations is conducted according to statistical calculations and experimental modeling informed by scientific knowledge, with the faith that the latter can bring a rational social order to this rural area and will continue to expand its production as a new economic engine. Given the complexity of the project, the number of people resettled, and the scale of socioeconomic reorganization, a strong, centralized state is required to effectively coordinate the official agencies, financial institutions, and other non-state actors for the hydraulic work. Few states are better candidates than the Chinese Communist Party, and the weak civil society in China provided the soil for the authoritarian state to act upon, although the latter was not completely devoid of the will to resist, as we shall see later in the book.

The Three Gorges Dam epitomizes the high modernist ambitions of planners who, in Scott's accounts, fail to fulfill the goal of improving the human condition because of their willful negation of practical knowledge. But the Three Gorges scheme did not fail like the projects Scott studied. This is not to say that it succeeded in a functional sense; it survived, instead, by two means. One is the justification that suffering caused by the resettlement and social disruptions is simply a transition to the envisaged prospects of poverty elimination and national reinvigoration. Here we see the ideology of political theodicy at work. Another means involves how the project underwent modifications, incorporating adaptive strategies that state actors devised in the face of contingencies arising out of the development process, such as political malpractices, popular protests, transnational social groups' opposition, and environmental fallout. By examining the political effects a high modernist design produced, we gain a glimpse of how an authoritarian regime persists and what strategies are employed toward this end.

The high-modernist ideology that Scott propounds in his book is definitely a pertinent theoretical supposition for the analysis of the Three Gorges project, but the "uncritical, unskeptical, and thus unscientifically optimistic"[12] faith in comprehensive planning has left out the human dimension of a development process. That is to say, the *subjectivity* or, more precisely, the change in the subjectivity of human agents in the process of social, economic, and environmental transformation. Borrowing the legitimacy of science and technology to reconfigure the natural order and engineer a new social design is one thing; persuading the people to believe in progress and give up their time-honored kinships and living habits for proclaimed improvements in a newly built environment is quite another. Yet both are central to the task of rational reordering. Moreover, both, for the purpose of the existing work, are to be investigated in terms of *ideological practices* that manifestly represented the Party's governing strategies. The use of political theodicy as ruling tactics does not simply involve a set of beliefs and desires for material advancement; it also entails the *act* of social transformation informed by such beliefs.

Defining Ideology

Some scholars consider ideology to be a system of ideas, beliefs, and values expressed in primarily linguistic modalities. For John Thompson, language in the forms of utterances, expressions, and spoken or inscribed words is the medium through which ideology is translated into social action. It is a "social-historical phenomenon which is embroiled in human conflict," a "means of action and interaction, a medium through which history is produced and society reproduced."[13] To study ideology, he argues, is to conduct "depth hermeneutics," which interprets the discursive meaning or signification that sustains relations of domination in a specific social and institutional context. Thompson's emphasis on the contextuality of language use is akin to Terry Eagleton's conception of ideology as "discourse." For Eagleton, what differentiates an ideological utterance from an ordinary expression is the context in which the piece of language is articulated. However, Eagleton sets himself apart from Thompson in that, for him, ideology does not necessarily serve the power of a dominant social or political group. Loaded with power interests, Eagleton's discourse-ideology involves the "actual uses of language between particular human subjects for the production of specific effects."[14] From socialism to feminism to the ideas of the Levellers, Diggers, and Suffragettes, the belief systems that do not entail relations of domination are considered ideological in Eagleton's "discourse."

A conception of ideology as a system of discursive representations is certainly applicable to this work. Deng's idea of "socialism with Chinese characteristics," the envisaged scenario of "common prosperity," and the "developmental mode of resettlement" in the Three Gorges project – narratives that are invested with a promise of political theodicy – call for a hermeneutical reading into the deep-seated cultural meanings of the semantics of words. The social contexts in which these concepts were enunciated, the power relations embedded in them, and the political interests they have served come to the surface as we decipher the significations of tropes.

However, discourse analysis suffers from the limitation of placing its primary focus on language use. This is particularly problematic when the subject matter touches on nonlinguistic objects such as human constructions or artifacts, the physical landscape, and moving debris of natural disasters. This has specific import for the current work, which covers nonlinguistic and yet significant matters, including the Yangtze River, the gorges, ancient temples, floating garbage, landslides, and, most of all, the dam itself. Like the mosquitoes in Timothy Mitchell's *Rule of Experts*, these objects are speechless.[15] But with their visual attributes (like the dam's), their motion (the landslides), and their sheer presence (the four-meter-high floating garbage behind the dam), they *tell* "stories" of a nation's collective resolve to achieve unsurpassed technological advances under the Party's leadership, a civilization redefined, and an answer from nature about the physical consequences of the regime's developmentalist ideal. They speak without utterances; they emit meanings without linguistic signals. Some of them – the river, the relics, and the dam – are embodiments of significations encoded by social agents who have various interests to pursue and power to defend. Others – the landslides and earthquakes – are material objects and occurrences in the nonhuman world that do not simply act as a medium of meaning-making. They convey messages about the workings of nature – the balance between water and soil, the geological stability of the landmass, and the consequences of the loss of these as a result of human intervention – with their sheer kinetic power.[16]

Linguistic expressions and meaningful physical objects are important media of ideological representation, but what makes the development ideology potent, I should like to emphasize, is its instantiation and thereby reproduction in material practice. It pertains to the nonlinguistic aspect of the social world – the daily actions and activities of human subjects who experience economic development as *real*. Going to work in a commercial hotel built in the place of a demolished historic temple, no longer walking on the hillside with back-borne baskets as a primary means of transportation and instead riding in motor vehicles on highways, leaving aside earthen-walled hamlets and inhabiting multistory houses equipped with gas ranges and telecommunication facilities, or having one's child educated in a school with language laboratories updated with computerized equipment: these are daily enactments of development as lived experiences – the signifying practices inscribed with meanings of a life under modernization. Parallel with the gain in modern living, as registered in the quotidian acts of progress, is also a meaning of loss – of physical objects such as historical artifacts and villages, and local knowledge as well as customs accumulated over generations. The hardship of enduring the loss, however, is justified with a promise of wealth and plenitude in the future. The conception of ideology – the political theodicy of development – as inscribed in material practice is best illustrated in Louis Althusser's "Ideology and Ideological State Apparatuses,"[17] to which the analysis will now turn.

Dissemination of Political Theodicy

Althusser argues that ideology has a material existence: it resides in everyday practices and is reproduced in the actions of subjects as their real experiences. For Althusser, ideological outlooks do not simply constitute an illusion; they also make an *allusion* to the real world.[18] What makes Althusser's theory pertinent, particularly when it comes to the analysis of development politics, is this idea of "allusion." Illusory representations of the real world may carry little political potency as they fall in line with a borderline lie that entails a disconnect between people and the authority's imaginary representations. Allusion to the real world, on the contrary, enables ideology to gain traction as a political instrument by virtue of its materiality in quotidian life. The experience of "ideas" as *real* leads human subjects to believe that what they live is not entirely an illusory distortion.

Althusser distinguishes between two kinds of state institutions that serve to reproduce state power – repressive state apparatuses (RSA) and ideological state apparatuses (ISA). The former, which include the army, police, courts, and prisons, primarily operate "by violence."[19] The latter, which mainly function "by ideology," can be found in media, trade unions, religious and cultural organizations, schools, and even families. Althusser does not define the limits and capacity of what ISAs do "by ideology," as opposed to how RSAs sustain state power through the monopoly of means of violence ("by violence"). However, from his theory, one can infer that ISAs do not only *maintain* power in the way that RSAs do; they also *generate* power and create new possibilities for dominance. In other words, ISAs play a reproductive and, further, generative role for authority and are crucial for the sustenance of state power. "No class," wrote Althusser, "can hold State power over a long period without at the same time exercising its hegemony over and in State Ideological Apparatuses."[20] For this reason, Althusser believes that ISAs are not only the stake but also the *site* of class struggle. In the case of China, repression in terms of military crackdown and police surveillance is not a sufficient condition for regime durability; ideological persuasion plays an important and enduring role, with the persuasiveness here rooted in the materiality of daily actions.

With its omnipresence in material practices in both the public (RSA) and largely private (ISA) domains,[21] the Althusserian ideology constitutes concrete individuals as subjects "naturally" and "spontaneously," to the extent that one lives in that subjectivity with "obviousness." "You and I are *always already* subjects," he asserts, "and as such constantly practice the rituals of ideological recognition."[22] Insofar as ideology exists in the activities of the plethora of institutions one lives in, whether this is the church or school and family, an individual is "hailed" through everyday practices as a subject in the act of "interpellation," be it a believer of a certain religion, a rule-abiding student at school, a citizen following the law, or a laborer performing prescribed routines at the workplace.

In the case of the Three Gorges, the resettled villagers underwent a process of what I call *double interpellation*. They were first hailed as "agrarian" subjects who led a "backward" life, inhabiting earthen-walled huts, for example, and then interpellated into the position of "modern" citizens who have taken up an "advanced" way of working and commuting. The "imaginary" part of the ideology here is not the "dreaming up" of a new lifestyle. It is rather like the "imaginary" that Althusser argues to be pertaining to an "image"[23] – the recognition of one's "hailed" identity borne out by one's material conditions of living in the process of subject formation. According to official Chinese narratives, the Three Gorges residents have experienced a transformation from agrarian subjects to modern workers. Effectuating the transfiguration is the set of practices that people conduct in, for example, their living, schooling, and working environments – routines that they repeat daily as a part of their everyday life.

Althusser argues that "men *live* their actions . . . in ideology, *by and through ideology*; in short, that the 'lived' relation between men and the world . . . passes through ideology, or better, *is ideology itself*."[24] If ideology is inscribed in specific meaningful practices that constitute humans as social subjects, what is represented in the ideological "imaginary" – one's subjectivity – is not simply the conditions of existence one lives in, but also the *relation* between the human subject and the real world. Hailing a social member as "backward" and "poor" does not register if it is not made in reference to the living conditions of their fellow compatriots in the urban coastal area. By the same token, transforming oneself into a "modern" subject through the act of "casting off poverty and getting rich," purportedly made possible by the dam project, denotes a change in one's social position from a rural context in the direction of the world lived by an urban folk. Ideology here serves as a representation of *imagined* social relations that power defines as inferior or superior and what is less or more desirable. Upon this order of differences, the transition of one's subject position in a preexisting set of social relations to the other is promoted as a celebrated change in the development process.

During my field research, particularly in the Three Gorges valley after the dam's construction, I was struck by the "naturalness" with which people recounted their experiences of living through the change before and after the project's completion. A common evaluation that the resettlers made was infrastructural development that replaced their original means of transportation, from walking and low-horsepower boats to ferries, cruise ships, and high-speed trains. Time and again, I was told how much time was being saved with the new modes of transport, how much closer they felt to Chongqing (a major inland city at the western end of the reservoir), and how "backward" their towns had been before such developments were put in place. The manner in which people *live* their changed environment conjures up the Althusserian idea of a "noncognitive and unconscious process"[25] that escapes the human subject. By engaging in quotidian socio-practical activities, the resettlers live their relations to the (transforming) social world "pre-reflectively" in an apparently natural and spontaneous fashion, which manifests and reproduces the idea of double interpellation.

Yet how can something real – our lived experience and our real condition of life – be untrue? And how can something true be ideological? The questions themselves imply two assumptions: first, that if something is real, it is necessarily true; second, that ideology is bound up with falsehood and illusion. The list of people's lived experiences under the reforms can go on and on. Outside my Three Gorges research, I witnessed how a relative of mine with prostate cancer uses the money he makes as a private entrepreneur to purchase expensive injections that maintain his health. Another relation of mine, who became a furniture manufacturer together with his sons, gathered sufficient wealth to tear down their rat-ridden farmhouse and replace it with a bungalow furnished with up-to-date appliances. Their new occupation also enabled them to quit their hard labor in rice paddies, which had exposed them to the predation of leeches, and to gain sufficient leisure time for the singing of Cantonese opera. Yet another cousin of mine has sent her son abroad to receive a college education so that he does not suffer from the prospect of failing in an intensely competitive educational system. These experiences are *real*. To the extent that some people's living conditions, including health, sanitation, and physical comfort, have changed for the better since Dengist times, it is *true* that economic development under the reforms has brought an improvement in their livelihoods.

However, when the issue involves "political stability" as an assumed imperative of the material achievements, as official narratives hold, the "trueness" becomes less transparent. The political theodicy on hardship, a chance of change for the better, is only presumed to work when the Party enjoys absolute power. "Political stability," as understood in Dengist discourse, necessitates the maintenance of the one-party monopoly and the suppression of free speech despite public discontent over social injustices. This was the rationalization the leadership put forward as it imposed a military crackdown on the pro-democracy protests in 1989.[26] The scenario of political "instability" portrayed by the authorities is essentially chaos – disabled infrastructural systems, dysfunctional official institutions, and disrupted economic activities – which would, as the official argument goes, wipe out the fruits of the reforms and jeopardize the prospects of material advancement and, further, of national redemption. The possibility of a more competitive representation system, an independent judiciary able to redress power imbalances such as those between corrupt officials and the people, and institutionalized channels of pluralistic articulation – changes that do not necessarily endanger the country's economic development but nevertheless point to the severing of the Party's monopolistic control – have rarely been part of the ideological imaginary. Some Beijing leaders, such as the deposed party chief Hu Yaobang, ousted premier Zhao Ziyang, and, more recently, the former premier Wen Jiabao, did take initial steps toward possible political liberalization, but they were either persecuted (as in the cases of Hu and Zhao) or obstructed by factional opponents.[27] In effect, the projection of "political instability" in official accounts inspires *fear* – an emotion of loss and of falling into a void of material dispossession. It operates on the assumptions and deductive connections that a change in or any questioning of the existing political system will inevitably lead to chaos, which in turn will halt people's experiences of material attainment, thereby destroying their chance of redemption from poverty. Its *logical* plausibility, despite the lack of *empirical* testability, and its link to one's actual life chances make this ideology robust. As a matter of fact, the assumption has been embraced by certain Chinese public figures across time, including the Qing reformer Liang Qichao, who in his later years opted for enlightened despotism over republican democracy for fear of public disorder should the people be given institutionalized freedom.[28] In my encounters, I have been told by more than a few Chinese that the status quo has to be maintained if China wishes to sustain its prosperity.[29] To this day, despite discontent with inequality and injustice, the premise of "political stability" has rarely been questioned.

Another unspoken imperative of the development ideology that is no less potent than the fear of falling is the *hope* for elevation. From the official aspirations for "common prosperity" to the yearning for sustained growth among the private entrepreneurs I met, to some farmers' wishes that the fruits of development that have so far eluded them will eventually come in their lifetime, the scenario of a realizable dream is vivid. I was told by some Three Gorges resettlers during my fieldwork how they set their hopes on their younger generations despite the hardships they were facing in the new location, hundreds of miles from their birthplace. The hope for a better livelihood, for themselves and their young ones, was not pure imagination. The material attainments of one's relatives, neighbors, and fellow countrymen are real and concrete. The rootedness in social reality of this dimension of the development ideal – *hope* – lends vigor to the ideology. For the sake of realizing the dream, one is motivated to endure the hardships caused by development, to convince oneself of its positive effects, or to simply work harder to make a new life for oneself and one's family according to the rules laid down by the authorities.

Insofar as the idea of the political theodicy of development has a material existence and economic growth does improve certain people's lives, the ideology is not illusory – the thesis I am exploring has little bearing on "illusionary distortion." But if we take into consideration the "imaginary" character of some of the constitutive dimensions of this ideology, such as *fear* and *hope*, we will argue that lived experiences rooted in social reality can be ideological. The "imaginary" in this sense is somewhat different from an individual's "image," which I expounded earlier. To the extent that the "imaginary" is related to one's subject position, discursively formed and practically produced (be it a "backward" agrarian farmer or a "progressive" urban dweller, or the celebrated transposition from one to the other), I concur with Althusser's formulation of "imaginary misrecognition." But when it comes to his view of it "not correspond[ing] to reality,"[30] which is the second meaning of his "imaginary," there is a qualification I attach to the applicability of his theory to my thesis. For the "imaginary" I am addressing here involves a person's *envisaged* real-life chances in the broad scenario of a reforming China. The projected attainment of improved health, sanitation, and physical comfort for a relocated farmer or the possibility of losing those qualities of life for a Three Gorges resident who has managed to establish a new life, the sources of their fear and hope are not mere erroneous mystifications. They are not illusory because the probabilities of "political instability" and a better material life, as aforementioned, are logically plausible even though they are empirically untestable and unverifiable, or not yet verified. So setting my argument apart from the Althusserian "imaginary distortion," I rather suggest that the projected milieus are *elusive, unascertained*, and *unknown*: the chances are they may be realized, or they may not, ever, in certain places and for certain people. The ideology of political theodicy in the Chinese case works in such a way that the "real" – the *lived*, and the "imaginary" – the *elusive*, are ingrained in each other in the operations of institutions, in the unfolding of daily routines, and in the significations of symbols in material life. Together they form the rhythm of social action, organically reproducing the ideal of personal and, in turn, national progress under the Party's dominance. The political theodicy of development, as a result, enables power to effectively incorporate the uncertainties of sociopolitical affairs and of life in general for the maintenance of control.[31]

The view that ideology exists in material practice provides us with a cipher with which to reread Deng's idea of "practice as the sole criterion of truth." Contrary to many China specialists, who hold that under Deng the country has experienced an "ideological vacuum," this book argues that Deng's "practice" is ideological through and through. I agree on the sinologists' view of "pragmatism" to the extent that the "practice" trumpeted by Deng at the end of the 1970s can be understood as an emphasis on practical situations and contingent circumstances vis-à-vis the dogmatism and veneration of Maoist thought. I also concur that Deng's "connecting theory with practice" can be made sense of as underscoring the use of practice to unpack theory, including testing, verifying, and falsifying it (in the manner of "crossing the river by groping the stones"). However, if we probe deeper into his idea, "practice" is essentially productive action as a cumulative process: it refers to a particular economic setup configured by a specific set of policy initiatives pertaining to accelerating efficiency, increasing productivity, and quadrupling the GDP. "Practice" is purported to be the means by which "truth" is arrived at – the truth of industrial progress under a restructured socioeconomic order through capital accumulation and the production of new relations of production fulfilled by the reforms. Here, ideology does not merely inform practice, in the way that Marxism-Leninism-Mao Zedong Thought did, but is registered in practice, or resides in practice. The Chinese people, assuming new subject positions of "household responsible" farmers, factory managers, or private entrepreneurs, for example, strive to "get rich" under the new ruling principles of a reformist party leadership that has sought to reformulate a political, economic, cultural, and social structure redefined by a new technical civilization.

To sum up, the Dengist and post-Dengist ruling ideology of political theodicy through development is organized around a core set of values, ideas, and beliefs which acquire a concrete form of existence through linguistic articulations, signified physical objects, and, most of all, semiotic practices. Through them, the sanctioned ideals get instantiated, actualized, and regenerated as a natural(ized) part of the material world. The ideology we are looking at is at once concrete and elusive, real and imaginary. As a cultural system, in the sense that culture denotes "practices of meaning-making,"[32] it entails a systematic network of norms, activities, and classified categories that effectuate the aforementioned rationalist organization of a modernizing nation's social order. This organization not only involves spatial reordering, transmutation of the natural landscape, and the transformation of people's subjectivities, but it also arranges society, in a cultural sense, into what William Sewell calls a "semiotically and politically ordered field of differences"[33] between present and past, new and old, science and nature, modernity and traditions – dichotomous relationships that are symptomatic of the binary separation between subject and object in modern times. The state's development discourse seeks to homogenize, and it does so by discriminating, hierarchizing, and prioritizing people's experiences vis-à-vis the endorsed values, relegating the latter element of the dichotomous pairs to the position of inferiority, and thereby setting limits on what values are politically endorsable, culturally relevant, and socially appropriate. The authorities' ruling strategies, or what I argue as the *ideological practices of development*, at once homogenizing and differentiating, seek to produce the effects of a social order coalesced around the core beliefs of human superiority over nature, national redemption through progress, and the insurmountability of the Party's power.

Adaptability of Power

The mode of developmentalist tactics, however, does not remain static. They are modified along with changing historical contexts and sociopolitical scenarios, demonstrating the Party's resilience in adjusting to differing circumstances and governance needs. Development as a set of ideological practices does not unfold in a unilinear trajectory, as the authority would have people believe, but is full of contradictions, disruptions, and change. The execution of a development act, be it the promotion of scientific knowledge or solicitation of capital on the global financial market, not to mention the construction of a mammoth dam on the country's second-largest river, is met with resistance, contestation, and negotiation.

Confronted with the punctures of the development process, the authority devises new tactics, thereby altering the course of "progress" and in turn the mode of governance.

In the Three Gorges area, the impacts of the dam have been much more diverse than the singular picture that official ideology prescribes. Some people acknowledge improvements in their livelihood, expressing explicit support for the dam and reform in general. Others made use of the newly relaxed boundary, as in the 1980s, for dam-related public articulations to push for a more democratic say in other government policies. Still others experienced social injustice in the implementation of construction projects and queried the significance of development or sought ways to redress the problems, including bringing in foreign activist groups for help. The political strategies of development, themselves a dependent variable of authoritarian domination, are at the same time an independent variable causing variegated effects.[34]

The ideology of political theodicy, in other words, is never totalizing. The causality between developmental culture and political control is neither transparent nor unidirectional. Far from being the neat, clear-cut, and smooth progression of economic advancement – like the dualistic configurations from poverty to wealth, backward to advanced, and nature to science that Deng and other political elites represented in their ideas – the process of development as epitomized by the Three Gorges Dam is messy, uncertain, and conflict-ridden. It is full of negotiations, struggles, and contradictions. Aside from the example of relocated villagers refusing to accept their new life and moving back to the gorge area, collapsed bridges in the process of construction and landslides as a result of the weight of the massive reservoir injured and killed people instead of bringing increased efficiency. Local officials embezzled funds rather than spending them to enrich people with the "developmental mode of resettlement," and the double-digit unemployment rate that resulted from economic restructuring in the gorge area defied the official rhetoric of "eliminating poverty and getting rich." Moreover, the government's development plan was challenged by the global environmental campaign, and the picture was further complicated by the defiance of nature – the Sichuan earthquake – in 2008.

The disjuncture between ideology and a significant part of social reality reveals fundamental flaws in the official imperative of political theodicy. The state, faced with the unintended consequences of miscalculations, failures, and resistance, constantly adapts its development strategies to uphold its political persuasiveness. It thereby opens up the possibility of change and transformation in the mode of governance. The form of authoritarian rule this book examines is adaptive and flexible: it constantly undergoes modifications amid contingencies, be they objections from social agents, political crises, or challenges from the global community. The book covers this change in the ideological practices of development from the 1980s up until the point of writing. The chapters are arranged in a way that illustrates particular configurations of discourse, institutions, and practices transforming along with the mutating ideology of political theodicy in specific time periods – the 1980s up to the Tiananmen protests, the 1990s, and from the late 1990s until the early 21st century.

Chapter 1 provides an overview of the historical background of the dam. It surveys the modernist development visions of Chinese historical leaders before Deng: Sun Yat-sen's aspirations to conquer the Yangtze River as a part of his grand nation-building blueprint; the Nationalists' preliminary work on a Three Gorges dam in their alignment with American engineering elites, including John Savage; and Mao Zedong's imagination of utopian national modernization through the conquest of nature by megaprojects. In the history of 20th-century China, Sun and Mao occupy important positions: though headed in different directions, one the republican and the other communist, both of them built a new polity upon the ruins of war and destruction, with the ideal of reversing abject poverty and social disintegration according to their modernization designs. In the official dam discourse during the reform period, Sun's nation-building blueprint, Savage's exclamation over the Three Gorges, and Mao's Yangtze poem are often invoked. They are constitutive of a narrative, or what John Thompson calls a "tissue of tales," which provides a cultural text legitimating the Yangtze's exploitation and, more generally, national development.

Chapter 2 covers a key moment of political theodicy in Dengist China: the launch of "reform and opening" as an answer to the Party's legitimacy crisis, along with the collapsing socioeconomic order in the aftermath of the Cultural Revolution. The study engages the discourse of the reformist state's development ideology through a close reading of Deng's "socialism with Chinese characteristics." It is a textual analysis of the dichotomies of capitalism and socialism, egalitarian distribution and modernization, and backward and advanced in Dengist thought. These semiotic relationships of contrast shoot through the ideological practices of development in Dengist and post-Dengist China. The dichotomies, which constitute the conceptual trajectory of official development discourse in the reform era, have simplified the complexities of the real world and concealed the contradictions inherent in the process of economic progression. Hu Jintao's "scientific concept of development" lays bare the contradictions of wealth distribution and social injustice as reform unfolded, while Xi Jinping's "China dream" highlights the nationalist dimension of China's modernization drive.

Chapter 3 begins the examination of the political theodicy of development in action – the official use of "socialist democracy" and "scientific decision making" as governing tactics in the 1980s to repair the devastated condition of society after the Cultural Revolution and to reestablish the Party's credibility. The experimental mode of development in this first decade of reform involved the inclusivity of pluralistic voices that were mushrooming in the public sphere. Dissidents working against the Three Gorges Dam proposal rode on the state's promotion of "democratic and scientific decision making" and effectively launched an opposition campaign through publications, open debate in public forums, and coalition-building among intellectuals, journalists, and scientists. The official agenda of reform and opening brought about political effects that spread across segments of society. What had been meant as a prescription of political "salvation" from the collapsing socioeconomic order turned into people's uncontrollable quest for rights and freedoms. Liberalization culminated in the pro-democracy demonstrations in Beijing in 1989, which extended to other parts of China and became across-the-board popular unrest. The military crackdown on June 4, 1989, shut down all articulations of dissent, including those relating to the Three Gorges Dam proposal. It marked what Michel Foucault calls a "threshold of transformation" in China's development practice, which shifted from inclusive participation to a muted, depoliticized formulation of progress.

Chapter 4 explores the adjusted tactics of the 1990s following the "threshold of transformation" – the fully fledged formation of markets, reversing the previous strategy of liberalization and "democratic and scientific decision making." The focus was overwhelmingly on economic development, representing a shifted and reinforced emphasis on wealth-building and shared material pursuits. It purported to achieve "common prosperity" to narrow the increasing wealth gap between the coastal cities and the rural hinterland.

This chapter illustrates the thesis of political theodicy on both the collective and individual levels. The new development strategy entailed the conception of a nationwide developed space, the construction of a modern national infrastructural system connecting urban centers in the east with economic backwaters in the West, all to be mediated by a new, urbanized space in the Yangtze Valley in central China. Linking the growth of national strength with the life chances of individuals, the Three Gorges Dam project promised to bring people "out of poverty and [allow them to] get rich" through the "developmental mode of resettlement." The analysis introduces the human dimension to the examination of discourse. My fieldwork data illustrate the ways in which people conduct their new lives in the resettled areas, manifesting the process of *double interpellation* in which people's subjectivities were transformed from "poor," "agrarian" individuals to "enriched," "modern" citizens through the quotidian activities of their everyday life, thereby reproducing the ideology of political theodicy in progress.

The development act successfully rallied the support of certain people who found their life in the newly built environment improved, and they willingly embraced the Party's leadership in bringing about the change. That said, the research findings also indicate that the promised "redemption" for current suffering (poverty and/or sacrifices inflicted by displacement) was punctured by the reality of unemployment, declining living standards for some, and environmental fallout, resulting in public frustrations expressed in petitions and protests.

As a continuation of Chapter 4, Chapter 5 examines the incorporation of nonhuman objects – historical relics and the natural landscape, including the river and land – in the ideological practice of political theodicy, with a particular goal of national rejuvenation. It analyzes how the civilizational outlook of culture (regarding the past and the "ancient civilization") became subsumed by development discourse through the cultural re-encoding of the Yangtze. The river has been represented in official narratives as China's "mother river" and the "second cradle of Chinese civilization." With the imposition of a world-leading technological structure – the dam – the river took on the meaning of a forward-looking, futurist nation. Developmentalism, as illustrated in the Three Gorges case, is thus bound up with techno-nationalism, in that the dam, as an embodiment of the futurist nation, has severed the understanding of a civilizational past in favor of technological supremacy.

Predicated on this new meaning, a revamped tourist industry emerged, selling a combination of commercialized displays of historical relics and technological showcases of China's modernization (such as the dam, the reservoir, and agribusiness). The semiotic representation of "national redemption" through the achievement of the world's largest dam merges with the material practice of money-making through tourism. Historical artifacts are incorporated into the touristic activities and are turned into embodiments of a new culture of material accumulation. The reformed tourist industry also promises new jobs and increased income, purportedly contributing to the "elimination of poverty and getting rich," in a process that has destroyed villagers' habitats and their time-honored customs.

Chapter 6 examines another threshold of transformation in China's developmental path. At the turn of the 21st century, the political theodicy of material elevation took a transnational course as the Chinese economy embraced the global market and became a major player in the cross-border milieu. China's new tactic of development changed from the high-modernist mode of social engineering in a local setting to a neoliberal form of calculated progress on a global scale. This chapter uses the dam to illuminate how the country incorporated global resources, including capital, technical expertise, and ideas of river-harnessing, into the national strategy of economic development. However, the enabling factors of globalization also came with constraints: in joining the global community and gaining access to new resources, China also opened itself up to intervention by transnational actors. The Three Gorges Dam project encountered resistance from a cross-border environmental campaign that questioned the official claim of poverty elimination by highlighting human rights abuses that left many displaced villagers impoverished. Unfolded in the analysis are the tensions and clashes between global capital, national government, and transnational civil society.

In Epilogue, I examine how Chinese dam technocrats turned the tables on the cross-border anti-Three Gorges activists and formed what I call a new "hydropower discourse." They achieved this by appropriating the principles of environmental protection and sustainable development to justify dam building when a convergence of circumstances pointed to an urgent need to tap into energy alternatives to fossil fuels. This was a time when the world was wrestling with ways to curb the effects of climatic change caused by excessive greenhouse gas emissions. Moreover, China was faced with the problem of an energy shortage in powering its expanding industries and sustaining its economic growth. These problems coincided with a worldwide oil supply shortfall. With "environmental protection" as a supporting postulate, hydropower advocates in China sidestepped assertions of social disruption, ecological damage, and human rights violations typically used in the anti-Three Gorges campaign and pushed for an accelerated pace in river exploitation.

From the argument of this book, there emerges a picture of dialectical change in the state's form of power, which is constituted by an open-ended bilateral causal chain of action and reaction, tactics, and (unintended) consequences. At every "threshold of transformation," the state responds to social contentions (which are themselves reactions to its development strategies) or contingencies and devises new ruling tactics. The ideological structure, at once a medium and outcome of development practices, mutates with political crises, the intervention of social actors, or discursive change in the global community.[35] The dialectical transformation illuminates alterations of the Dengist and post-Dengist state's mode of governance, encompassing modifying ideological strategies. This transmutation capacity demonstrates the artificiality of the development vision: what the reformist state represents to its people as transparent, indubitable, and morally desirable in material progress are politically motivated constructs subject to prescription and re-prescription according to the needs of the regime and power configurations. It also demonstrates the Party's adaptability despite social crises and contentions, providing an explanation for the conundrum of the durability of the authoritarian regime.

This book is a result of research that spans more than two decades. The first site visit took place in 2001 when my cousins who were living in Guangzhou took me to two resettlement villages in the rural part of Guangdong Province, which is hundreds of miles away from the dam site. There, I met people who had just moved from the Three Gorges area. They told us their stories of resettlement, the life they had had before the move, and what they encountered in the new community. At that time, the Three Gorges Dam resettlement was underway in full swing. The news I received outside China was mostly negative – about, inter alia, collapsed bridges, official embezzlement of funds, and suppression of villagers who protested over inadequate compensations. I visited the river valley and witnessed the massive displacement alongside the dotted structures of modern bridges, new towns, and the dam, which was in the early stage of construction. My interest in the project led me back to the Three Gorges area after the dam was completed. In 2015–2016, I visited Wanzhou, Fengjie, Wushan, and Yichang and conducted interviews with people who had settled upslope in the newly built environment and were having a life drastically different from before. I also went back to the two villages I had visited in 2001, and in this field trip, I added three other resettlement villages to the list, all of them in Guangdong Province. These were displacees who had undergone "outward relocation" (*waiqian*). I interviewed residents in those settlements, ranging from retired elders and working-age men to stay-at-home mothers. Our conversations covered the experiences they and their children had in the new places – their jobs, income, schools, living conditions, social networks, leisure activities, and ingredients of daily meals, among others. The relocatees talked about the improvements as well as difficulties they encountered, in comparison with the livelihoods they had experienced in the Three Gorges.

Reading meanings in the resettlers' practices and verbal utterances, I also conduct discourse analysis of textual materials expressed in different institutional settings. The methodology entails an interpretative reading of state and non-state actors' articulations in the forms of speech and publication, with the support of news sources and academic materials. These texts are not mere written representations – they inform practices in their respective contexts, which instantiate and in turn reproduce the ideas underlying the linguistic terms. Reading into the meanings of texts, therefore, helps us decipher the ideologies of actors in different socio-political positions. Moreover, to understand the mode of governance specific to each period under study, I identify tropes, such as "scientific decision-making" and "common prosperity," that the state employed to guide our reading of the ideological tenets embedded in the development practice of the time.

Notes

1 Max Weber, "The Social Psychology of the World Religion," in *From Max Weber: Essays in Sociology*, ed. H. H. Gerth and C. Wright Mills (New York: Oxford University Press, 1975–2), 272.
2 Weber, "Social Psychology."
3 Anders Sybrandt Hansen uses the concept of "theodicy" to examine the issue of corruption within the Party. See "Purity and Corruption: Chinese Communist Party Applicants and the Problem of Evil," *Ethnos* 78, no. 1 (March 2013): 47–74.
4 Arif Dirlik, "Developmentalism," *Interventions* 16, no. 1 (2014): 32.
5 Various scholars have critiqued the idea of development or developmentalism. See Wolfgang Sachs, ed., *The Development Dictionary: A Guide to Knowledge as Power* (Witwatersrand University Press, 1997); James Ferguson, *The Anti-Politics Machine: "Development," Depoliticization, and Bureaucratic Power in Lesotho* (Minneapolis: University of Minnesota Press, 1994); Arturo Escobar, *Encountering Development: The Making and Unmaking of the Third World* (Princeton: Princeton University Press, 1995); and Dirlik, "Developmentalism," 30–48.
6 James Scott, *Seeing Like a State* (New Haven and London: Yale University Press, 1998).
7 Scott, *Seeing Like a State*, 89–90.
8 Karl A. Wittfogel, *Oriental Despotism: A Comparative Study of Total Power* (London: Oxford University Press; New Haven: Yale University Press, 1957).
9 Scott, *Seeing Like a State*, 378, n 11 (italics added).
10 Michel Foucault, "Governmentality," in *The Foucault Effect*, ed. Graham Burchell et al. (Chicago: The University of Chicago Press, 1991), 102.
11 Foucault, "Governmentality," 93.
12 Scott, *Seeing Like a State*, 4.
13 John B. Thompson, *Studies in the Theory of Ideology* (Berkeley: University of California Press, 1984), 2.
14 Terry Eagleton, *Ideology: An Introduction* (London and New York: Verso, 2007), 9.
15 Timothy Mitchell, *Rule of Experts: Egypt, Techno-Politics, Modernity* (University of California Press, 2002), 19–53.
16 For a theoretical explication of an articulated form of diverse semiotic modalities, a "language game," see William H. Sewell Jr., "Refiguring the 'Social' in Social Science: An Interpretivist Manifesto," in *Logics of History: Social Theory and Social Transformation* (Chicago and London: The University of Chicago Press, 2005), 318–372.
17 Louis Althusser, "Ideology and Ideological State Apparatuses," in *Lenin and Philosophy and Other Essays* (New York: Monthly Review Press, 2001).
18 Althusser, "Ideology and Ideological State Apparatuses," 110.
19 Althusser, "Ideology and Ideological State Apparatuses," 94–100.
20 Althusser, "Ideology and Ideological State Apparatuses," 98.
21 Althusser, "Ideology and Ideological State Apparatuses," 97.
22 Althusser, "Ideology and Ideological State Apparatuses," 117 (original emphasis).
23 See Eagleton, *Ideology*, 142.
24 Louis Althusser, *For Marx* (London and New York: Verso, 2005), 233 (original emphasis).
25 Althusser, *For Marx*.

26 See "*Bixu qizhi xianming de fandui dongluan*" *[A Resolute Objection to the Turmoil]*, *Renmin ribao [People's Daily]*, April 26, 1989.
27 Willy Lam, "Premier Wen's 'Southern Tour': Ideological Rifts in the CCP?" *China Brief* 10, no. 18 (September 10, 2010), https://jamestown.org/program/premier-wens-southern-tour-ideological-rifts-in-the-ccp/; "People's Daily Stresses Step-by-step Political Reform," *People's Daily Online*, October 27, 2010, http://english.people.com.cn/90001/90776/90785/7178352.html; "Chinese Leadership Meeting Squashes Talk of Political Reform," *World Socialist Web Site*, October 26, 2010, https://www.wsws.org/en/articles/2010/10/ccpm-o26.html; and "Hopes of Political Reform Hit Brick Wall," *South China Morning Post*, October 20, 2010.
28 Andrew Nathan, *Chinese Democracy* (I.B. Tauris, 1986), 58–63.
29 The view came up recurrently in my interviews with informants and casual conversations with, for example, taxi drivers and restaurant owners, summer 1991 – summer 2015.
30 Althusser, "Ideology and Ideological State Apparatuses," 110.
31 I am indebted to Prasenjit Duara for bringing this idea to my attention.
32 Lisa Wedeen, "Conceptualizing Culture: Possibilities for Political Science," *American Political Science Review* 96, no. 4 (December 2002): 713–728.
33 William H. Sewell Jr., "The Concept(s) of Culture," in *Logics of History*, 173.
34 For a conceptualization of culture and its methodological use in political science research, see Wedeen, "Conceptualizing Culture."
35 The concept of structuration is explored in William H. Sewell Jr., "A Theory of Structure: Duality, Agency, and Transformation," in *Logics of History*, 124–151.

Bibliography

Althusser, Louis. 2001. "Ideology and Ideological State Apparatuses." In *Lenin and Philosophy and Other Essays*. New York: Monthly Review Press.

Althusser, Louis. 2005. *For Marx*. London and New York: Verso.

Chan, John. 2010. "Chinese Leadership Meeting Squashes Talk of Political Reform." *World Socialist Web Site*, October 26. https://www.wsws.org/en/articles/2010/10/ccpm-o26.html.

China Daily. 2004. "Balanced Growth a Priority." March 31.

Dirlik, Arif. 2014. "Developmentalism." *Interventions* 16 (1): 30–48.

Eagleton, Terry. 2007. *Ideology: An Introduction*. London and New York: Verso.

Escobar, Arturo. 1995. *Encountering Development: The Making and Unmaking of the Third World*. Princeton University Press.

Ferguson, James. 1994. *The Anti-Politics Machine: "Development," Depoliticization, and Bureaucratic Power in Lesotho.* University of Minnesota Press.

Foucault, Michel. 1991. "Governmentality." In *The Foucault Effect*, edited by Graham Burchell et al. The University of Chicago Press.

Hansen, Anders Sybrandt. 2013. "Purity and Corruption: Chinese Communist Party Applicants and the Problem of Evil." *Ethnos* 78 (1) (March): 47–74.

Lam, Willy. 2010. "Premier Wen's 'Southern Tour': Ideological Rifts in the CCP?" *China Brief* 10 (18) (September 10). https://jamestown.org/program/premier-wens-southern-tour-ideological-rifts-in-the-ccp/.

Mitchell, Timothy. 2002. *Rule of Experts: Egypt, Techno-Politics, Modernity*. University of California Press.

Nathan, Andrew. 1986. *Chinese Democracy*. I.B. Tauris.

People's Daily Online. 2010. "People's Daily Stresses Step-by-step Political Reform." October 27. http://english.people.com.cn/90001/90776/90785/7178352.html.

Renmin ribao [People's Daily]. 1989. "Bixu qizhi xianming de fandui dongluan [A Resolute Objection to the Turmoil], editorial." April 26.

Sachs, Wolfgang, ed. 1997. *The Development Dictionary: A Guide to Knowledge as Power*. Witwatersrand University Press.

Scott, James. 1998. *Seeing Like a State*. New Haven and London: Yale University Press.
Sewell, William H. Jr. 2005. *Logics of History: Social Theory and Social Transformation*. Chicago and London: The University of Chicago Press.
South China Morning Post. 2010. "Hopes of Political Reform Hit Brick Wall." October 20.
Thompson, John B. 1984. *Studies in the Theory of Ideology*. University of California Press.
Weber, Max. 1975–2. "The Social Psychology of the World Religion." In *From Max Weber: Essays in Sociology*, edited by H. H. Gerth and C. Wright Mills. New York: Oxford University Press.
Wedeen, Lisa. 2002. "Conceptualizing Culture: Possibilities for Political Science." *American Political Science Review* 96 (4) (December): 713–28.
Wittfogel, Karl A. 1957. *Oriental Despotism: A Comparative Study of Total Power*. Oxford University Press, Yale University Press.

1 Historical Background of the Dam

In the official discourse on the Three Gorges Dam, the texts and poems of Chinese political leaders and Western experts who lived through the 20th century were recurrently invoked as part of the historical "lineage" of the water project. The nation-building blueprint of Sun Yat-sen, the exclamation clause of John Savage, and the poem written by Mao Zedong were all narratives used by the contemporary dam proponents to construct the authority of the development ideology that the Three Gorges project instantiated. Authors of these texts were portrayed as not only dam supporters but also champions of modernization, having the will to transform nature and reorganize society through human endeavor. In particular, Sun and Mao occupy important positions in the history of 20th-century China: though heading in different directions, one a republican and the other a communist, both of them built a new polity upon the ruins of war and destruction, with the ideal of reversing abject poverty and social disintegration according to their modernization designs. Together with Savage's, their narratives, using the words of John Thompson, are "stories" that make up a "tissue of tales that recapitulate the past and anticipate the future."[1] Such stories, Thompson argues, justify the exercise of power by individuals who possess it by situating themselves in the "tissue of tales." In the discourse on the Three Gorges Dam, power derived from the historical narratives was not exercised by the "individuals" per se – Sun, Savage, and Mao – but by those in contemporary times who deployed the "stories" as discursive threads to weave a fabric of modernization tales that legitimated the value of the dam. In what follows, we will examine the articulations of Sun at the point of nation founding, Savage in the Nationalist period, and Mao during the Communist era, and the practices inspired by as well as revolving around those articulations.

Sun Yat-Sen: Rescuing the Nation with Economic Construction

In 1911, revolutionaries under the leadership of Sun overthrew the Qing court, bringing the dynastic rule of thousands of years to an end and initiating an era of modern governance. Sun's conceptions of nation-building, which were spelled out in the late 1910s, consisted of a constitutional government inspired by Montesquieu's constitutionalism, which was modeled upon the Euro-American democratic systems. They also entailed a massive economic program of industrialization,

DOI: 10.4324/9781003531494-2

which incorporated western capital with Soviet ideals of state ownership and egalitarian distribution. His blueprint of economic reconstruction was the first full-scale exposition of a modern commercial and industrial structure envisioned to be established in China.

In Sun's proposition, the idea of damming the Yangtze at the Three Gorges was first conceived for an improvement of inland navigation and the generation of hydroelectric power. His vision, however, was not realized in his lifetime. It remained an imaginary, "dreamt" by successive leaders and a narrative appropriated by different governments. In the reformist period, it became a part of the rationalized industrial construction scheme under the Dengist regime.

The nation Sun envisioned was outlined in his *International Development of China* published in 1921.[2] It consisted of verbal and visual representations – in the forms of maps, drawings, and diagrams – of his conceived industrialization plans in geographical locations covering the whole of China. These constituted an integrated schema comprising the creation of major ports and harbors in the north, east, and south, the reformation of canal and waterway systems, the construction of railroads and highways extending to all corners of the country, and the building of telegraph lines along with telephone and wireless networks linking up different local communities. Alongside harbors and around railway termini, modern cities were to be built with public utilities, and industries ranging from iron and steel to car manufacturing and garment production would be established. To utilize the redundant labor of soldiers returning from the First World War and exploit natural resources, Sun also proposed the colonization of Manchuria, Mongolia, Xinjiang, and Tibet.

The schema Sun explicated constituted a nation-scale space implicating the coastal and inland areas of China in the east, south, north, northwest, and southwest. It was a conceptualized space envisioned to be modern, industrialized, and economically productive. His conceived space did not actualize in the form of material production in his time, but the blueprints were transmitted among leaderships under different political regimes in distinct forms of appropriation. This national space, moreover, was an aggregate of numerous local spaces like the one in the Yangtze Valley, and on a more micro scale, at the Three Gorges. In the section dedicated to the "improvement of the existing waterways and canals," Sun wrote,

> To improve the Upper Yangtze, the rapids should be dammed up to form locks to enable crafts to ascend the river as well as to generate water power. Obstructions should be blasted and boulders removed. Thus, a ten-foot channel right along from Hankow to Chungking could be obtained so that through the inland, water transportation could be established from Chungking to Peking in the north and to Canton in the south, as well as all navigable points in China Proper all year round.[3]

Sun's proposal to dam the Three Gorges for economic benefit was recurrently quoted in newspapers, books, magazines, and videos by dam supporters in Dengist times. The construction scheme materialized at the end of the 20th century with a significantly more complex configuration than the one Sun outlined: it involved not only navigation and hydroelectricity generation but also global capital, technological transfer, and the creation of a modern agricultural and urbanized regional community.

Despite the similar visions of economic construction between Sun and Deng on the basis of nationalist imperatives, what distinguished Sun's plans from those of the Communist reformists was their perceived role in determining the nation's "survival" in the context of China's semi-colonization and Western industrialization. Sun's idea of Chinese modernization was a nationalist appropriation of the globalizing discourse of progress and development disseminated before and during Sun's lifetime. By the middle of the 18th century, the concept of material progress had been established primarily in Europe as both possible and desirable. Classical economists from Adam Smith to David Ricardo agreed, by and large, with the French encyclopedists and the English utilitarians that the most desirable outcome of government was people's happiness. For that to be achieved, they believed economic development was a necessary means.[4] An increase in wealth became the aspiration of statesmen and industrialists alike, not only for national power but also for the general prosperity of society. In practice, modernization in the form of industrial organization spread from Britain to other European countries and, further, to non-Western parts of the world through colonial expansion. Sun's ideas of Chinese economic construction emerged in the context of this globalized discourse of progress and modernization. His thesis was a national incorporation of the global discourse, including its moral presupposition of teleological advancement.

The destination of this projected teleology, for Sun, was the developmental level of Europe and North America. "Let us all unite with one heart and one mind," he said, "adapt ourselves and *catch up* with the world trends, and build a most politically enlightened country where people enjoy the greatest happiness."[5] In a striking resemblance to Deng's objective of "catching up," which will be discussed in the next chapter, Sun put his envisioned modern Chinese nation on a standardized temporality, which is characteristic of modernity, that embraced the decline of the dynastic era and the emergence of a thorough socioeconomic reconstitution in the post-revolution age.

> If this new-born Republic of China should hope to come up to the standing of the Western Powers, it will have to work hard for several decades. During these decades the Western Powers will continue to advance along newer and better lines. It will be necessary, therefore, for us to make ten paces of progress in knowledge while they make one pace. Only in this manner can we rank China among the civilized nations of the world.[6]

Sun's projection of China's development in relation to Western countries bore an almost uncanny resonance to the development narratives of the Communist reformist leaders, in particular, Deng himself.

John Savage: Rest My Soul at the Three Gorges

Another historical figure ubiquitously invoked in the contemporary Three Gorges discourse was John Savage, the chief designing engineer of the American Bureau of Reclamation, who conceived the structures of many major hydraulic projects in the United States, including the Hoover Dam, and around the world in the first half of the 20th century. To him, a great dam like Grand Coulee is "a monument to all persons who are a part and parcel of their country."

In 1944, he was invited to China by the Nationalists to study the feasibility of another possible "monument" at the Three Gorges. It was a time of war between the Chinese and the Japanese. At the age of sixty-four, Savage traveled down the Yangtze by sampan in an area that was partially occupied by the Japanese military. Among the five alternatives he proposed for the dam site, which were located within a ten-kilometer section of the gorge area upstream from the city of Ichang, he personally surveyed one of the sites, which was within two miles of the Japanese lines. There, he conceived a dam that would carry enormous economic and engineering possibilities: it was to be a massive concrete straight gravity structure around 738 feet high and 2,493 feet long, being taller and bigger than the Hoover Dam and producing five times the electrical power of the Grand Coulee power plant. It would also set itself apart from comparable American structures, with most of its vulnerable features, such as the electricity generators, housed underground to make the project "100 percent bomb-proof."[7]

This proposal was contained in the Preliminary Report on Yangtze Gorge Project that he presented to the Nationalist government in November 1944. In the report, he acknowledged the feasibility of a dam to be built at the Three Gorges for the purposes of hydropower production, irrigation, flood control, navigation, domestic water supply, and recreational resources. The dam, as he conceived it, would be constructed with cooperative assistance from the Bureau of Reclamation and the Tennessee Valley Authority, which would prepare the designs, supervise the construction work, and train Chinese technical personnel in both the United States and China. Describing the study of the Yangtze Gorge as "extremely interesting," given the "unprecedented magnitude" of the engineering challenge, and as "one of the greatest pleasures in my forty years of engineering experience," Savage concluded his report as follows:

> The Yangtze Gorge Project is a "CLASSIC." It will be of utmost importance to China. It will bring great industrial developments in Central and Western China. It will bring widespread employment. It will bring high standards of living. It will change China from a weak to a strong nation. The Yangtze Gorge Project should be constructed for the benefit of China and the World at large.[8]

Savage's vision was about to be realized when the Bureau of Reclamation and the National Resources Commission of China signed a contract right after the end of the Pacific War, in October 1945, to proceed with the design of the Yangtze

Gorge Project. Chinese technicians were sent to the United States to work with the Bureau's engineers on the dam blueprint. Progress was made on the location of the dam, the design of the dual power plants, methods for moving ocean-going ships around the dam with a series of eight locks, and a general scheme of construction. What remained undecided was the height of the dam and the design of the coffer-dams.[9] The work and the vision of building the world's largest hydraulic engineering project were, however, halted when the Chinese Civil War broke out between the Nationalists and Communists, which resulted in a suspension of the scheme in June 1947, amidst military and financial uncertainties in China.

The story of Savage was turned into a fabric for the "tissue of tales" and became a part of the "Three Gorges dream" (*sanxia meng*) conjured up by contemporary dam proponents through numerous Chinese publications. In some of them, Savage was quoted as saying regarding his sentiments about the envisioned dam:

> If God gives me time and allows me to witness the realization of the Three Gorges project, I will rest my soul at the Three Gorges after my death![10]

Similar statements were not found in English sources covered by the present study, but Savage as an important component of the Three Gorges "lineage" was visible in various Chinese texts. On February 20, 1998, full-page coverage, titled "The Legendary Savage, the Greater Three Gorges will Never Forget," appeared in the *Three Gorges Weekend*, a daily newspaper published by the China Three Gorges Project Company, reporting a Chinese visit to Denver, where Savage lived and died. Shortly before the Yangtze River was blocked at the end of 1997, a group comprising a representative of the Three Gorges Company, an engineer from the Yangtze River Water Conservancy Committee, and crew members of China Central Television (CCTV) visited places where Savage had worked and lived. They went to his office at the Bureau of Reclamation and the Julia Temple Nursing Home, where he spent the final years of his life. The crew also dedicated flowers and a segment of granite mined at the Three Gorges Dam site to Savage's grave, "to console the soul of Dr. Savage with the good news of the upcoming blockage of the Yangtze River," and "to express the respect and memory we and the Chinese people have for you."[11] Besides the newspaper story, which came with photos of different sites, the visit was also made into an episode of CCTV's "Three Gorges Memorandum" series, which, according to the newspaper report, would "remind Chinese posterity of you as the pioneer who developed the Three Gorges water resources, and have them bear in mind the life energy you dedicated to the cause and the achievement you made on hydropower works around the world."[12]

Savage's footprints in China and his study of a Yangtze Gorge dam were real, but with the discursive reinvention, his experience became mythicized and turned into a "legend." His contact with the Chinese technicians during the research, the formulaic calculations he laid down in the *Preliminary Report* for the engineering details, and the construction costs he estimated based on the actual economic conditions at the time were all grounded in real-life experiences. Yet in the official discourse of the dam, this reality was abstracted both temporally and spatially to become a component of the "Three Gorges dream" – an imaginary that the dam proponents repeatedly invoked to give meaning to the contemporary structure. In various Chinese sources during Dengist times, Savage was portrayed as a "legendary" figure who "constructs the eternity of history with the ephemerality of life." More mention was made of his alleged exclamations such as "[T]his (the Three Gorges hydro resources) is a blessing from God" and "rest my soul at the Three Gorges" than the practical projections he made in the *Preliminary Report*.[13]

In the report, Savage conceived in the Yangtze Gorge Project values that he outlined in the short paragraph in his conclusion: it would bring great industrial developments in Central and Western China; it would create job opportunities, raise people's living standards, and change China from a weak to a strong nation. His estimations dovetailed with every single argument dam proponents made in the Dengist and post-Dengist periods. Moreover, the hope of modernization set on dams in Savage's times resonated in different corners of the world, particularly before and after the Second World War.

If we connect the two points – the Three Gorges scheme's perceived value in the reformist era and the economic modernism aspired for through dam-building earlier in the century – we discern the continuity of a developmentalist ideal that permeated national and regional sociopolitical agendas in much of the 20th century, one that James Scott characterizes as the "high modernist" vision of the world. From the Tennessee Valley Authority (TVA) in the United States[14] to the Sloy project above Loch Lomond under the "TVA for the Highlands" in Scotland through to the Damodar Valley Corporation in India, large dams were venerated as an embodiment of a new order that set people "free" by releasing "individual resourcefulness and inventiveness."[15] In China, the TVA symbolized not only the ontological superiority of the human spirit but also the definition of civilization in modern times. Hu Shih, a prominent Chinese writer, philosopher, and ambassador to the United States between 1938 and 1942 under the Nationalist government, had the following rebuke to views about the "materialistic" detriments of development on human civilizations:

> For to me that civilization is materialistic which is limited by matter and incapable of transcending it; which feels itself powerless against its material environment and fails to make the full use of human intelligence for the conquest of nature and for the improvement of the conditions of man. Its sages and saints may do all they can to glorify contentment and hypnotize the people into a willingness to praise their gods and abide by their fate. But that very self-hypnotizing philosophy is more materialistic than the dirty houses they live in, the scanty food they eat, and the clay and wood with which they make the images of their gods.
>
> On the other hand, that civilization which makes the fullest possible use of human ingenuity and intelligence in search of truth in order to control nature and transform matter for the service of mankind, to liberate the human spirit from ignorance, superstition, and slavery to the forces of nature, and

> to reform social and political institutions for the benefit of the greatest number – such a civilization is highly idealistic and spiritual.[16]

From China and India to the United States, Europe, and other continents, the call for development echoed around the world for a good part of the 20th century, resonating with the "haunting" chimes of Sun's industrialization and Deng's socialist modernization. Nationalism, developmentalism, and modernism coalesced into an ideological triad in which the nation-state (with the right- and left-leaning alike) stood at the center, with a vanguard charging into the futurist scenario called progress. After the Second World War, amidst the wave of nation formation and the establishment of communist systems, dams took on new significance as a practical and symbolic representation of national power.

Mao Zedong: Man Must Conquer Nature

The founding of the People's Republic of China under the leadership of Mao Zedong, after the civil war between the Communists and Nationalists, came in the wake of the Second World War to become a major socialist power on the international scene. Mao, armed with his ruling doctrines of Marxism-Leninism-Mao Zedong Thought, was determined to reconstitute China into a country that could shake off its long history of "humiliation by imperialist powers" and become self-reliant despite international isolation. China, as Mao envisaged, would regain its strength and be able to measure up to Western European and North American states as a new political, social, and cultural entity. Mao's vision of change, however, followed an extreme form of utopianism, which was ready to knock down any obstacle and transform any element in the natural environment to create new social relations conducive to his envisioned mode of production.[17] The Three Gorges project came into the picture of Mao's new China as a manifestation of his determination to achieve increased productivity and social stability through the overcoming of all material conditions, including those in the natural world, with human will.

In the narrated historical lineage of the Three Gorges scheme, Mao was the most prominent figure frequently invoked as the icon of the proposed dam. The portrayed commitment of the supreme leader was represented in numerous books and articles, which carried accounts of the words or conversations he had with technocrats on the issue. According to the official narratives, his interest in damming the Yangtze dated back to the early 1950s, soon after the founding of communist China. His meeting with Lin Yishan in 1953, the former head of the Yangtze Valley Planning Office, was described as follows: Mao asked Lin if a Three Gorges dam could replace the aggregated effectiveness of all the dams built on the upstream tributaries. When told that a dam at the Three Gorges would surpass the total flood control capacity of all the structures constructed upstream, Mao said, "Why don't we set the priority on a Three Gorges dam, so that we put a blockade [of the water] at that key point and accomplish the whole task at one stroke?"[18]

But the most commonly cited text on Mao's depicted enthusiasm about a potential Three Gorges dam was a poem he wrote in June 1956, after touring the Yangtze and swimming in the river. The poem was written in the aftermath of a historic flood in the middle and lower reaches of the river, in which more than 32,000 people drowned and at least 21 million mu of farmland was inundated. The flood also caused the major railroad connecting Beijing in the north and Guangzhou in the south to be suspended for 100 days, bringing about great economic loss. The poem, titled "Swimming – to the Tune of Shui Tiao Keh Tou," was also written at a time when the Soviet Union was providing aid to China for the planning of a Three Gorges dam. This entailed the deployment of 140 surveyors, dozens of experts, and more than ten aeroplanes to China within five years after 1955. In the poem, Mao expressed his vision of a Yangtze tamed through engineering technology and modern infrastructure.

> I have just drunk the waters of Changsha
> And come to eat the fish of Wuchang.
> Now I am swimming across the great Yangtze,
> Looking afar to the open sky of Chu.
> Let the wind blow and waves beat,
> Better far than idly strolling in a courtyard.
> Today I am at ease.
> "It was by a stream that the Master said –
> 'Thus do things flow away!'"
> Sails move with the wind.
> Tortoise and Snake are still.
> Great plans are afoot:
> A bridge will fly to span the north and south,
> Turning a deep chasm into a thoroughfare;
> A wall of stone will stand upstream to the west
> To hold back Wushan's clouds and rain
> Till a smooth lake rises in the narrow gorges.
> The mountain goddess if she is still there
> Will marvel at a world so changed.

The poem betrayed a romantic juxtaposition of legendary tales and modern technology, incorporating Chinese cultural symbols into his vision of "a world so changed" by human endeavors and scientific techniques. The "mountain goddess" at Wushan, one of the Three Gorges, who is believed to be capable of summoning the "clouds and rain" to nourish the farmland for good harvests or create downpours for destructive floods, would marvel at the human inventions of "bridge" and "wall of stone." This "wall of stone" – the imagined Three Gorges dam – was no ordinary wall. It could "hold back Wushan's clouds and rain" and form a "smooth lake" that "rises in the narrow gorges." The implicit logic was that with the employment of modern knowledge and technology, powerful forces in nature such as those mobilized by the Wushan goddess – or she herself as that force in nature – could be overcome and brought under the heel of human power and engineering.

The idea of "overcoming" or "conquering" was ubiquitous in Mao's conception of the relationship between humans and nature in his envisioned scenario of China's progress. In this picture, not only scientific knowledge and modern technology but also human will, essentially that of communist resolve, would bend the rhythms of nature and put them in the service of mankind, or more precisely, the Chinese community. This spirit was demonstrated in the ideas of "Men Must Conquer Nature" (*Ren ding sheng tian*) and the "Foolish Old Man Who Removed the Mountains" (*Yugong yi shan*), which were advocated by Mao and turned into slogans during moments of mass mobilization from the Great Leap Forward to the Cultural Revolution. In a somewhat poetic statement quoted as referring to the Yangtze, Mao stated, "Water overcomes me, I overcome water. If I don't control water, it will control me. I ought to control water!" (*Shui zhi wo, wo zhi shui, wo ruo bu zhishui, shui jiu yao zhi wo, wo bizu zhishui!*)[19] The idea of "overcoming" or "controlling" water (*zhi shui*) was central to the conceived relationship between humans and rivers in traditional Chinese thought. From Yu the Great, a legendary figure who lived four millennia ago and has remained famous to this day for his achievement in tackling floods, to Mao, who led China through the construction of numerous dams – in success or failure – and left his discursive mark in the Three Gorges "tissue of tales" with his poem, humans have consistently been placed in an oppositional position to nature. What set Mao apart from Yu the Great, however, was the mobilization of modern technology and heavy machinery and his propagated ability to envisage the "comprehensive functions" of river harnessing, namely, power generation, flood control, irrigation, navigation, and fish farming. This capability, it was claimed in the book written by Lin, warranted Mao's position as "exceeding the achievement of Yu the Great."[20]

Underlying the conceived relationships between humans and nature, the Foolish Old Man and the Mountains, and Mao and water was the dichotomous opposition between subject and object characteristic of modern times. In this dichotomous alienation, the subjects – nature, mountains, and water – were rendered objects in their relations with the purported *authentic* subjects – humans, the Foolish Old Man, and Mao. The subject and object were conceived as fundamentally distinct and external to each other, with the former assuming a superior position in the power hierarchy, harnessing or controlling the latter. The separation between subject and object was not unique to Mao's time and ideas; it was also found in Sun's nation development blueprint, Savage's hydraulic engineering plans, and David Lilienthal's vision of river exploitation.

The binary tension between the subject and object, and in this case, the (communist) human and nature, is a constituent dimension interweaving the conceptual triad of nation-state – development – modernism. While Mao was contemplating his "wall of stone" that would "hold back Wushan's clouds and rain," Jawaharlal Nehru conceived a "New India" that would be built upon modern technology and the "scientific temper."[21] Dams, considered a manifestation of techno-economic power and a means of national empowerment, were famously described by Nehru as "modern, secular temples"[22] of the newly independent India. From the Bhakra project under Nehru to the Aswan High Dam in Egypt to the Three Gorges scheme in China, dams in postwar years represented the endeavors of postcolonial nation-states that strived to break free from imperialist influence and embark upon the path to modernity through the embrace of science and mastery of nature.

Conclusion

The tale of the Three Gorges dream was a story of China's modernization as much as that of the world in the 20th century. Development as the agenda of nation-states occupied the minds of policymakers and engineers alike not only in developing countries but also in industrialized powers. From the Tennessee Valley Authority in the United States to the Damodar Valley Corporation in India, and from Sun to Mao and through to Deng in China, the quest for economic progress in the form of the reorganization of the natural and social worlds reached across space and time. The improvement of people's livelihoods and the consolidation of national power became inseparable and indistinguishable goals of statesmen in their socioeconomic designs. These goals often involved nature in the reordering and reformulating of the relationship between the human community and the natural environment. Through the Three Gorges proposal and more broadly dams in general, we discern the human yearnings to conquer nature, the faith in modern scientific knowledge, and the redefinition of a techno-mechanical civilization. The Three Gorges tale of harnessing the Yangtze, as manifested by the "stories" of Sun, Savage, and Mao, linked up the 20th-century aspirations for controlling the natural environment, modernization, and the striving for a nation-state's power and glory in the enunciations and practice of river development. This tale continued to the end of the century and beyond and was articulated with different ideological propositions by leaders under the reforms.

Notes

1 John B. Thompson, *Studies in the Theory of Ideology* (Berkeley: University of California Press, 1984), 11.
2 Sun Yat-sen, *The International Development of China*, 2nd ed. (New York and London: G.P. Putnam's Sons, 1929).
3 Sun, *The International Development of China*, 74.
4 H. W. Arndt, *Economic Development: The History of an Idea* (Chicago and London: The University of Chicago Press, 1987), 1–8.
5 Sun Yat-sen, *Jian guo fang lue* (Shanghai: Min zhi shu ju, 1925), Preface, 3 (emphasis added).
6 Sun Yat-sen, *Fundamentals of National Reconstruction* (Taipei, Taiwan: Chinese Cultural Service, 1953), 94.
7 John L. Savage, "Preliminary Report on Yangtze Gorge Project," presented to the Government of China, Ministry of Economic Affairs, National Resources Commission, Chungking, China, November 1944; and Benjamin D. Rhodes, "From Cooksville to Chungking: The Dam-Designing Career of John L. Savage," *The Wisconsin Magazine of History* 72, no. 4 (Summer 1989): 266–272.
8 Savage, "Preliminary Report," 6.
9 Rhodes, "From Cooksville," 269.

10 See, for example, Lu Jianglin et al., *Fengliu xiagu [The Distinguished Story of the Yangtze Valley]* (Zhongguo qingnian chubanshe, 1993), 45. Also published as *Zhongguo mengxiang [A Chinese Dream]* (Zhongguo qingnian chubanshe, 1996).
11 Lu Chen and Ning Ma, "Zhuanqi de Safanqi, da Sanxia buhui wangji" [The Legendary Savage, the Greater Three Gorges Will Never Forget] *Sanxia zhoumo [Three Gorges Weekend]*, February 20, 1998, 1.
12 Chen and Ma, "Zhuanqi de Safanqi, da Sanxia buhui wangji" [The Legendary Savage, the Greater Three Gorges will Never Forget], *Sanxia zhoumo [Three Gorges Weekend].*
13 Chen and Ma, "Zhuanqi de Safanqi, da Sanxia buhui wangji" [The Legendary Savage, the Greater Three Gorges will Never Forget], *Sanxia zhoumo [Three Gorges Weekend]*; and Lu et al., *Fengliu xiagu.*
14 David Lilienthal, *TVA: Democracy on the March* (New York: Harper & Brothers Publishers, 1953), and *The Journal of David E. Lilienthal* (New York: Harper & Row, 1964).
15 Lilienthal, *TVA: Democracy*, 77–81.
16 Quoted in Lilienthal, *TVA: Democracy,* 221.
17 Judith Shapiro, *Mao's War Against Nature: Politics and the Environment in Revolutionary China* (Cambridge, UK: Cambridge University Press, 2001).
18 Yishan Lin and Malin Yang, *Gong gai dayu [Exceeding the Achievement of Yu the Great]* (Beijing: Zhong yang dang xiao chu ban she, 1993), 101; and Lin Yishan, "Sanxia beiwang" [Three Gorges Memorandum], *Zhongguo sanxia gongcheng bao [China Three Gorges Project News]*, September 25, 1999.
19 Lin and Yang, *Gong gai dayu*, 96.
20 Lin and Yang, *Gong gai dayu*, from the title of the book.
21 Daniel Klingensmith, *One Valley and a Thousand: Dams, Nationalism, and Development* (New Delhi: Oxford University Press, 2007), and "Building India's 'Modern Temples': Indians and Americans in the Damodar Valley Corporation, 1945–60," in *Regional Modernities: The Cultural Politics of Development in India*, ed. K. Sivaramakrishnan and Arun Agrawal (Stanford, CA: Stanford University Press, 2003).
22 Klingensmith, *One Valley*, 263.

Bibliography

Arndt, H. W. 1987. *Economic Development: The History of an Idea*. The University of Chicago Press.

Chen, Lu, and Ma, Ning. 1998. "Zhuanqi de Safanqi, da sanxia buhui wangji" [The Legendary Savage, the Greater Three Gorges Will Never Forget]. *Sanxia zhoumo [Three Gorges Weekend],* February 20.

Klingensmith, Daniel. 2003. "Building India's 'Modern Temples': Indians and Americans in the Damodar Valley Corporation, 1945–60." In *Regional Modernities: The Cultural Politics of Development in India*, edited by K. Sivaramakrishnan and Arun Agrawal. Stanford University Press.

Klingensmith, Daniel. 2007. *One Valley and a Thousand: Dams, Nationalism, and Development*. New Delhi: Oxford University Press.

Lilienthal, David. 1953. *TVA: Democracy on the March.* New York: Harper & Brothers Publishers.

Lilienthal, David. 1964. *The Journal of David E. Lilienthal*. New York: Harper & Row.

Lin, Yishan, and Yang, Malin. 1993. *Gong gai dayu [Exceeding the Achievement of Yu the Great]*. Beijing: Zhongyang dangxiao chubanshe.

Lin, Yishan. 1999. "Sanxia beiwang" [Three Gorges Memorandum]. *Zhongguo sanxia gongcheng bao [China Three Gorges Project News]*, September 25.

Lu, Jianglin et al. 1993. *Fengliu xiagu [The Distinguished Story of the Yangtze Valley]*. Zhongguo qingnian chubanshe.

Rhodes, Benjamin D. 1989. "From Cooksville to Chungking: The Dam-Designing Career of John L. Savage." *The Wisconsin Magazine of History* 72 (4) (Summer): 266–72.

Savage, John L. 1944. "Preliminary Report on Yangtze Gorge Project." Presented to the Government of China, Ministry of Economic Affairs, National Resources Commission, Chungking, China, November.

Shapiro, Judith. 2001. *Mao's War against Nature: Politics and the Environment in Revolutionary China*. Cambridge University Press.

Sun, Yat-sen. 1925. *Jian guo fang lue*. Shanghai: Min zhi shu ju.

Sun, Yat-sen. 1929. *The International Development of China*.2nd ed. New York: G.P. Putnam's Sons.

Sun, Yat-sen. 1953. *Fundamentals of National Reconstruction*. Taipei: Chinese Cultural Service.

Thompson, John B. 1984. *Studies in the Theory of Ideology*. University of California Press.

2 From "Socialism With Chinese Characteristics" to "China Dream"

The Concept of Development Under Reform

Deng Xiaoping: "Four Modernizations"

The 3rd Plenum of the 11th Central Committee in 1978, which marked the beginning of the reform era, has been regarded both within and outside China as the third great turning point of the country's 20th-century history, after the 1911 republican revolution and the 1949 communist takeover. While the meeting itself was not a revolutionary event, the policy decisions it made effectuated a significant break from the Maoist-fashioned socioeconomic structure and laid down the groundwork for new initiatives that would increasingly deviate from the communist prescription. Four decades after that meeting, the Chinese economy and society look more capitalist than communist, to the extent that China is recognized as a powerful player in the global neoliberal economy.[1]

At the apex of the reform initiatives was Deng, who had been purged three times before he came to the center stage to carry out his plans of modernization. Widely regarded as the architect of the reforms, Deng laid down the framework of China's economic transformation in the 3rd Plenum and sketched the directions that the country's developmental orientations were to follow. His approach to economic reconstruction, "practice as the sole criterion for testing truth," is regarded by many scholars as "pragmatist," which puts emphasis on material results devoid of ideological concepts. However, this view is contested by scholars like Stuart Schram, who argues that Deng was primarily a Marxist, essentially Leninist, in that he was a "veteran revolutionary who believes in the dictatorship of the proletariat, the vanguard role of the party, and a certain number of moral values he learned during the Yan'an period."[2] Marxism, Schram believes, was consistently the source of learning for Deng in adapting it to China's circumstances to find a way to modernize.

Schram's ideology-as-guide perspective clashes with the ideology-vacuum approach, which holds that what informed the reforms were pragmatic and eclectic ideas that had very weak roots in ideology. Whatever yielded economic results, scholars holding this view argue, would be considered desirable and compatible with socialism. "[T]he policies now evolving in China and the systemic changes taking place in the system," Doak Barnett argues,

DOI: 10.4324/9781003531494-3

> have relatively little to do with Marxism-Leninism, whether in its original, its Stalinist, or its Maoist forms. . . . What is occurring in China is a dramatic decline and secularization of ideology – not simply another stage in its adaptation to changing local conditions.[3]

For both groups of sinologists, the debate over "pragmatism" and "ideology" rests upon the assumed definition of ideology as a set of ideas that claims universal applicability to human society, and hence validity, as a source of political action. Ideology denotes, for them, rather narrowly, Marxism-Leninism and, in its variegated form, Maoism, which is to be extracted and understood from a reading of the respective doctrines given.

However, as this book argues, ideology may also be embedded in discourses as a "deep" level of meaning that cannot be deciphered with the literal understanding of texts. It exists as a connotative discourse that derives its meaning from particular historical, social, and political contexts.[4] Viewed from this angle, Deng, indisputably a pragmatic political strategist, is also, and perhaps more importantly, an ideologist. His speeches and advocacies of "reform," "modernization," and "socialism with Chinese characteristics" were all framed in economic terms or Marxist-styled economic-determinist political phraseology. Yet beneath such words, there lies a latent discourse of party supremacy, the nation's power and glory, and, most of all, a society's fundamental transfiguration into the modern.

Understood in this way, China under Deng did not experience a decline in ideology, let alone an abandonment of ideology. It was rather governed by a *new* ideology that took the place of Marxism-Leninism-Mao Zedong Thought and which was loaded with the ideas and visions of capital accumulation, material abundance, and the life of a modern Chinese subject. In a word, it was developmentalism – as a doctrine of his reform initiatives and the defined practice of people's everyday life. Deng's ideas of development were not only expressed in the 3rd Plenum – they were extended and elaborated after the Plenum, and also before. The political implications of his thoughts, which were framed in economic terms, can be deciphered in his speeches in the late 1970s and 1980s.

"New Long March"

The *political theodicy* in Deng's development ideology surfaced in December 1978 when he announced his plans for economic reconstruction on the heels of the destruction that had been caused by the Cultural Revolution. Describing the modernization project as a "New Long March," Deng emphasized that it was to be a "great turning point" and a new phase of social, political, and economic development in the history of communist China.[5] The introduction of reform, which he projected would quadruple China's GDP within twenty years, marked the initiation of a redemptive moment that promised to rescue China from abject poverty and social disintegration.

The original Long March, in which Deng himself participated, is a legendary event in the Party's history, described by Edgar Snow as "an odyssey unequalled in modern times."[6] It took place at the most critical point of the Party's survival in 1934 when the Communists were besieged by Chiang Kai-shek's troops, who had been given the mission of annihilating them. With their size reduced to almost half after battles of "encirclement" under Chiang's campaigns, the 90,000 remaining Red Army forces trekked 6,000 miles – about twice the width of the American continent – climbing some of the world's most difficult trails, unfit for wheeled traffic, and crossing mountain passes of 16,000 feet and more, far above the snow line, where "we kept reaching down to pull men to their feet only to find they were already dead" of cold and exhaustion, and wading through swamps where men "had to sleep standing in pairs or groups of four, back to back" to prevent drowning in mud.[7]

The march took around one year to complete. Only about one-tenth of those who participated survived it and the battles involved in its course. To the survivors, the march was a symbol of their indestructibility.

To the communists like Deng, the Long March was also a symbolic trajectory of the Party's life path – its near demise, survival, subsequent revival, and eventual spectacular rise to power. To them, it was a result of undefeated determination and utmost commitment, a possibility born out of the impossible. In the eyes of Deng, the Four Modernizations project, like the Long March, was to be a formidable task that required a comparable level of resolve and dedication. It was conducted at a time when the Party was also at its lowest point of morale and organizational integrity as a result of the Cultural Revolution, which left the people utterly alienated and the Party's credibility severely jeopardized. Deng's introduction of reforms and his "New Long March" discourse emerged against the backdrop of an imperiled party facing a precarious prospect, not unlike the circumstances that had motivated the Red Army to embark upon the Long March forty years earlier.

Both the Long March and New Long March were conceived as a path to progression: they were forward-looking and moved toward the better. But while the original one was an actual trek performed by a particular group of people, the Red Army, the contemporary one acted as a metaphorical trajectory of communist China's development process. Talks of "lagging behind" other industrialized countries were common in Deng's speeches. The modernization program was considered by Deng as the only hope to resuscitate the country from severe "backwardness" resulting from the political and socioeconomic disasters brought about by Mao's revolutionary campaigns. The "New Long March" discourse, in this context, acted as a rallying cry for the Chinese people to support the reforms and in turn the Party's leadership. "Whether or not we can achieve the Four Modernizations," Deng asserted,

> will determine the destiny of our country and the destiny of our nation. . . . Today, every member of the Communist Party and the Communist Youth League and every patriotic citizen must devote all his energies to the modernization drive and do all he can to overcome every difficulty under the unified leadership of the Party and government.[8]

The point in focus was the issue of survival (and therefore salvation). Inasmuch as forty years ago the Long March had been a move that preserved the Party, the Four Modernizations in the late 1970s were considered the only chance for the survival of the Party and indeed communist China. These tasks, according to Deng, were to be accomplished by the Party that he aimed to sustain and revitalize – its legitimacy, its authority to govern, and its capacity to restore order and lead China out of the state of "poverty" and "chaos."

"Socialism With Chinese Characteristics"

When Deng first proposed the Four Modernizations concept in 1975, one year before the end of the Cultural Revolution, his blueprints were branded by the Gang of Four as "poisonous weeds."[9] "The day the Four Modernizations program is realized," they said, "will be the time capitalism is restored."[10] They were particularly concerned that the incentive system Deng proposed to stimulate economic production was the "thin edge of the wedge as far as the dilution of socialism and its replacement by capitalism were concerned."[11]

There is no intention here to explore the Gang of Four's ideology as a critique of Deng's policies. What is intriguing to the present work is the perceived dichotomy between socialism and capitalism, between egalitarian distribution and modernization in the deliberations about China's socioeconomic transfiguration. The Gang of Four's rhetoric died out as the articulators exited the political scene with their deaths in prison. However, the ideological struggle between socialism and capitalism persisted and indeed permeated through Deng's reforms, this time carried by Deng the statesman himself, until the very end of his life. His insistence on the socialist path while advocating the borrowing of capitalist practices from Western countries was echoed in various parts of his discourse. But what did he mean by "socialism?" What implications or ramifications did such an ideological tension within his thoughts lead to? To find an answer, we will explore his "socialism with Chinese characteristics," a concept that lies at the core of his Four Modernizations and that puzzled the world upon its introduction.

To Deng, "socialism with Chinese characteristics" is a localized version of Marxism that combined the Marxist principle of economic development with the Chinese reality he discerned. In his scanty explication of theories, Deng defined communism, also Marxism to him, and a communist society as "one in which there is no exploitation of man by man, there is great material abundance, and the principle of from each according to his ability, to each according to his needs is applied."[12] Before attaining the communist stage, which involved overwhelming material wealth, Deng believed China had to first realize socialism, whose fundamental task was to develop society's productive forces and provide the material basis for communism. In other words, in a major departure from Mao's thought, the transition to the communist utopia was made indefinite. The Dengist leadership argued that despite the structural reformations under Mao, socialism in China remained in its "initial stage" and that in order to complete the transition from capitalism to communism, China would have to progress from the existing "undeveloped" to a "developed" socialist stage before arriving at the communist phase.[13]

Rhetorically, Deng's definition of socialism was essentially the development of productive forces with the attainment of even wealth distribution as the end goal. Yet, with a closer look, his "socialism" has a second-layered meaning derived from two dichotomies – that lie between "socialism" and "capitalism," and between communist China and the "developed" world. In a conversation with Kim Il Sung, the then-aspiring head of North Korea, in 1982, Deng noted,

> In a country as big and as poor as ours, if we don't try to increase production, how can we survive? *How is socialism superior, when our people have so many difficulties in their lives?* The Gang of Four clamored for "poor socialism" and "poor communism," declaring that communism was mainly a spiritual thing. That is sheer nonsense! We say that socialism is the first stage of communism. When a backward country is trying to build socialism, it is natural that during the long initial period its productive forces will not be up to the level of those in developed capitalist countries and that it will not be able to eliminate poverty completely. *Accordingly, in building socialism we must do all we can to develop the productive forces and gradually eliminate poverty, constantly raising the people's living standards. Otherwise, how will socialism be able to triumph over capitalism?* In the second stage, or the advanced stage of communism, when the economy is highly developed and there is overwhelming material abundance, we shall be able to apply the principle of from each according to his ability, to each according to his needs. *If we don't do everything possible to increase production, how can we expand the economy? How can we demonstrate the superiority of socialism and communism?* We have been making revolution for several decades and have been building socialism for more than three. Nevertheless, by 1978 the average monthly salary for our workers was still only 45 yuan (US$5.6), and most of our rural areas were still mired in poverty. Can this be called the superiority of socialism? That is why I insisted that the focus of our work should be rapidly shifted to economic development.[14]

Why is it the case that "socialism" is necessarily considered inferior when the people of the country embracing it are "poor"? What are the implications when we say that a certain ideology is superior when the country that adopts it has higher economic production? Running through the aforementioned passage is a tension between "socialism" and "capitalism." However, the dichotomous comparison Deng was making was not between two sets of competing ideas per se. Nor was he addressing the issue in terms of political structure, social practices, and cultural values that an ideology defines and directs. Apparently, he was placing an emphasis on the economic side of the ideological manifestations. Yet his distinction between the "inferior" and "superior" did not stop at the level of the economic system. Rather, he was pointing to *relative political power* in the international hierarchy – the power of socialist and capitalist states in the names of "socialism" and "capitalism" – measured by the criterion of economic production. Deng criticized the Gang of Four for rendering socialism or communism as belonging to the "spiritual" or superstructural realm. To him, it had to be understood in material terms and derive its primary meaning from the base, with its vitality evaluated according to the state's economic power – productivity, general living standards, and workers' income levels.

In a separate speech, Deng approached the relative strength of "socialism" and "capitalism" from the perspective of people's livelihood in China:

> The purpose of our struggle over the last few decades has been to eliminate poverty. Our first objective is for our people to lead a fairly comfortable life by the end of this century, that is, to reach a level that is neither rich nor poor. Our second objective is to approach the economic level of the developed countries in another three to five decades, so that our people become relatively well-off. This is the overall interest of the country.[15]

If the previous passage illuminates what he meant by "socialism" involved a socialist state's economically derived political power in general, this passage elaborates his thought of "socialism triumphing over capitalism" as a dichotomous competition between communist China in particular and the developed world. Here China was compared to not only the Western capitalist countries and Japan but also the advanced socialist state of the Soviet Union. In his speeches, Deng repeatedly emphasized that China was a "poor" and "backward" country in need of modernization. He estimated that China was at least one century – or even up to two to three centuries – behind the industrialized countries in the cultural, economic, and technical arenas (in the field of science and technology, he said, China was at least twenty to thirty years behind).[16] His goal of "catching up" was to turn China into a "well-to-do" society, with a GNP of one thousand dollars per capita by the end of the 20th century and ultimately "approach the economic level of the developed countries" by 2030 to 2050. The timeline, as we shall see in the upcoming section, resonates with the projected target of Xi Jinping's "China Dream," which, nevertheless, focuses on a different purpose.

Putting together the two dichotomies of "socialism" and "capitalism," and communist China and the "developed" world, we see a logical progression in Deng's argument from "developing the productive forces" to the expansion of economic power to the exercise of political power and further to the manifestation of ideological supremacy. Emerging from the triumphing ideology is China, which, if it succeeded in pursuing the hypothetical line of progression, would be the representative, the crusader, or the exemplary embodiment of "socialism." It would be a state that demonstrates the capacity to approximate the capitalist state, and to narrow the gap between the "rich" and "poor," the "advanced" and "backward" countries vis-à-vis the "hegemonism," in the words of Deng, of the United States and the Soviet Union. Standing at the center of this envisioned aggrandizement is the Party, which, with its manifested governing capability, would lead the nation along the "New Long March" out of poverty and onto the road of wealth and power.

To many observers, Deng's policy prescription of modernization centered upon the principle of "practice as the sole criterion of truth" is straightforward and without complex ideological underpinnings. Underneath the semantics of reform and economic growth in his enunciations, however, there lies a latent discourse of a nation's rejuvenation, a socialist state's ascendancy, and the aspirations for a party to recapture its power. These ideological propositions cut through the policy formulations of the Dengist government, defining a new phase of politics that sets itself apart from the Maoist-styled revolutionary governance.

Nonetheless, the manifested tension between "socialism" and "capitalism" in Deng's rhetoric is infused with his ambivalence toward the value of the capitalist experience. This ambivalent position was ubiquitous in his reform policy, and it became a major fault line in his development ideology. Despite his recognition of the danger of capitalist influence on the Chinese system, Deng was adamant that the country's political infrastructure and socialist economic setup would stand this test. At the same time, he was eager to "make use of the science and technology they [the capitalist countries] have developed and of those elements in their accumulated knowledge and experience which can be adapted to our use."[17] In the initial reform years, restructuring might not go as far as deregulation. However, it paved the way for subsequent initiatives that would incrementally move toward the capitalist scenario. Polarization between the rich and poor, the coastal and inland, and the urban and rural became increasingly difficult to bridge, to the extent that China's Gini coefficient rose to a peak of 49.1 in 2008.[18] It was in this context that Hu Jintao's "scientific concept of development" came into being, tracking a new path of modernization with a modified meaning of progress.

Hu Jintao: "Scientific Outlook on Development"

The concepts of "science" and "development" embedded in Deng's modernization, which he did not elucidate explicitly, came to the forefront in Hu's political doctrine. "Science" or "scientific" was recurrently invoked in Hu's speeches outlining his socioeconomic policy and governance agendas.

> The formation and implementation of the Scientific Outlook on Development have to be closely combined with the scientific way of thinking. The Scientific Outlook on Development is a scientific thinking that directs development. Only when we pragmatically identify and master the regularity can we understand the essence [of the concept].[19]

The use of "science" had not been new in the reform era. In the 1980s, under the principle of "scientific and democratic decision making," the reforms opened up a sanctioned space of anti-leftist radicalism that emphasized scientific methods in policy formulation with purported impartiality. Science was privileged as an instrument with which economic production and technological innovation would be advanced through the application of objective, positivist knowledge. Scientism, the belief that science carries universal validity not only in solving problems in the natural world but also in the human community, became a driving force for the relentless exploitation of natural resources and ambitious construction of social engineering projects that in part defined the reform era.

The "scientific way of thinking" Hu espoused is distinct from the positivist universalism that his predecessors embraced in the implementation of reform. In his speech, Hu emphasized a "regularity" that was closely connected with the "scientific concept of development." Yet the regularity Hu referred to was not the calculable consistency and procedural predictability of a scientific method that informs the uninterrupted progression of a modernization drive. Rather, it was the studied prescription (under his auspices) that would purportedly remedy a deflected and potentially punctuated path of development China was traversing.

The "development" Hu propounded is fundamentally a projection of incremental socioeconomic change. But unlike what his reformist predecessors had envisioned and directed, Hu's view of development was not a linear trajectory that extended on a levelled field into indefinite progress and growth. Rather, it was defined and characterized by *disjunctures*. Despite exponential economic growth after China entered the World Trade Organization in 2001, to the point where the country overtook Japan to become the second-largest economy in the world in 2010, China was entering a phase of developmental disjuncture under Hu in terms of income distribution, utilization of natural resources, and, most of all, the Party's capacity to deliver an evenly rising standard of living. The "big *gaps* between regions, between urban and rural areas, and between different social strata and social groups"[20] were increasingly unbridgeable and became an urgent issue to be addressed by the government.

This is the kind of scenario that Deng would be most disenchanted to see – the irreconcilable tension between socialism and capitalism, and the unhappy marriage between economic liberalization and Leninist power monopolization. Hu time and again reiterated Deng's words that "development is the absolute principle (*yingdaoli*)." He also emphasized that "development is the solution to all the problems in China" and that it was the "key to the party's capability to govern and rejuvenate the nation."[21] Yet under Deng's ideology of modernization, everything was subordinated to economic imperatives – the country's mode of production, people's life goals, and the leadership's policy orientations. "Getting rich is glorious" and "letting a group of people get rich first" were unquestioned dictums that motivated a generation of Chinese to embark on relentless entrepreneurship and capital accumulation. The pursuit of growth-above-all left China in a perverted shape of environmental degradation, socioeconomic inequality, and a society that skewed toward the rich, the urban, the eastern coast, and humans (in relation to nature), at the expense of the poor, the rural, the western inland, and the natural environment.

Hu's emphasis on the urgency to identify and master the "scientific regularity" of development was symptomatic of the problems China was facing in the course of modernization. His introduction of the "scientific outlook on development" can be read as a recognition of the *contradictions* the Chinese economy and society had built up after years of reform. Hu's development, in contrast to Deng's understanding of the concept, took on a somewhat different meaning: it was conceived as a process that incorporated deflected dimensions of change – the haves over the have-nots, winners over the disenfranchised, and industrialized techniques over ecological integrity. The "regularity," in this context, is a logical schema that would bridge the irreconcilable and reunify the fragmented, to the point where China would attain a "harmonious society."

The idea of reunifying or mending was expressed in official discourses in terms of "change" and "coordination." Restructuring the mode of economic development, according to Hu, was high on his leadership's strategic agenda. This would involve the change from being export-oriented to domestic consumption-oriented, from the focus on manufacturing to a diversified model including the primary, secondary, and tertiary industries, and from a structure driven by high natural resource exploitation to one supported by improved technology and refined labor skills, as well as managerial methods.[22] To bridge the *gaps* of developmental discrepancy, Hu promoted "coordination" and "sustainability," which involved the "coordinated development of the urban-rural socio-economic setup, the complementary co-development of the eastern-central-western regions, a sustainable development strategy, and harmony between humans and nature."[23]

The Scientific Outlook on Development, in short, is a *remedial reconciliation* of the contorted offsprings of the development process given rise by the reform. Whether it is comprehensive, coordinated, or sustainable, as the official narratives express, the crux of the agenda is, in the words of Premier Wen Jiabao, raising the Party's "governing ability."[24] In other words, the program of "putting people first" is just another way of re-rallying popular support and sustaining the regime's legitimacy.

Xi Jinping: "China Dream"

If Deng's modernization is a catch-up game in the re-ranking of great powers and Hu's scientific development is the antidotal repair for the fallout of reform, Xi's "China Dream" is the ultimate hail for a promised political theodicy. While the champion of both Deng's and Hu's development is the *socialist state* of China, the protagonist of Xi's "dream" is the *rejuvenated nation* of China, which is projected to attain supreme power and glory with an identifiable timeline. In his speeches on the "China Dream," Xi made a rallying cry to his people by singling out their conceived commonality of culture and appealing to their desires for a historic redemption. "The Chinese Dream," he said,

> pertains to the past and the present, but also the future. It is the crystallization of the tireless efforts of countless people with lofty ideals, embraces the yearnings of all the sons and daughters of the Chinese nation, and reveals the prospect of a bright future, when our country will be prosperous and strong, the nation will be rejuvenated, and the people will enjoy a happy life.[25]

In place of "socialism" or China as an exemplary communist entity in Deng's prescription of modernization, Xi put in the "great Chinese nation" (*weida de zhonghua minzu*),[26] a polity that has a prospect to not only harmonize the uneven forces of development but also forge a formidable position in the ranks of global powers.

The desire for national redemption has run through the political blueprints of various communist leaders, tracing it back to the founding point of the Chinese republic under Sun Yat-sen. The use of nationalism as an instrument of governance under the Communist Party was particularly prominent after the military crackdown on the pro-democracy protests in the spring of 1989, with the then party general secretary, Jiang Zemin, launching a series of measures ranging from patriotic education to rhetorical indoctrination, which reconstructed the country's historical narratives.[27] With these efforts, the Chinese Communist Party was reconceived from a revolutionary vanguard to a patriotic figurehead, and China, portrayed as having been victimized at the hands of Western powers since the late 19th century, including in particular Japan, would see the chance of coming back as a great power.

Throughout the reform period, the focus of political theodicy changed from alleviating the misery of material dispossession at the onset of Deng's modernization to the avenging of Western "humiliation" through the attainment of national supremacy. From Jiang to Xi, the Party has been placed at the center of official patriotic narratives – it has not only been represented as a perceptive leader but also as a steadfast crusader capable of leading the Chinese community through a tunnel of darkness to an esteemed future of global eminence. At the point of assuming power in 2012, Xi made a speech reiterating:

> Since the advent of modern times, our nation has gone through untold tribulations and faced its greatest perils. Countless people with lofty ideals rose up for the rejuvenation of the Chinese nation, but each time they failed. After it was founded in 1921 the Communist Party of China rallied and led the Chinese people in making great sacrifices, forging ahead against all odds, and transforming poor and backward China into an increasingly prosperous and strong nation, thus opening completely new horizons for national rejuvenation.[28]

Xi's conception of national rejuvenation is a successive note on the continuum of the Chinese nationalist discourse that cuts through the 20th century (from Sun Yat-sen to the May Fourth Movement through to the various communist leaders, the lamentation of the Chinese civilization's decline and the concomitant aspirations for a nationalist restoration have been prevalent). Linguistically, Xi's speeches may appear to deploy wordings not quite different from Jiang's and those who preceded him. What distinguishes Xi's "China Dream" from the others, however, is a concrete sense of prospective *realization* that comes with a clear timetable.

2050: A Convergence of State Goals

Unlike his predecessors, Xi offered a strikingly concrete temporal estimation of China's development, which he laid out with a clear timeline of progressive stages.

The concept of "double centenary" (*liangge yibai nian*) was recurrently used in his official articulations to represent the country's material progression with an identifiable scenario of national redemption in sight.

> We have set the goals of completing the building of a moderately prosperous society in all respects by the centenary of the CPC in 2021 and building China into a modern socialist country that is prosperous, strong, democratic, culturally advanced, and harmonious by the centenary of the People's Republic of China in 2049 so as to realize the Chinese Dream of the rejuvenation of the Chinese nation.[29]

The "Two Centenary Goals" as outlined by Xi encompassed the "three-step strategic plan for modernization,"[30] with the first two steps basically echoing Deng's prescription, namely doubling China's 1980 GNP by the end of the 1980s to provide adequate food and clothing for the people and, as a second step, doubling the 1990 GNP by the end of the 20th century to ensure a "moderately prosperous life." Xi added a third step, aiming to raise China's per capita GNP by the middle of the 21st century to the level of "moderately developed countries," packaged with a "relatively affluent life" for the people and the accomplishment of modernization for China.[31]

Noteworthy is that 2050 is also the time when China is projected to attain the "primary stage of socialism," which is defined in official discourse as a "particular historical stage in the building of Chinese socialism." "It refers to," as the explanation goes,

> the historical stage in which China has gradually *come out of underdevelopment* and will have by and large *realized socialist modernization*. It will take at least 100 years to take shape from the completion of the socialist transformation of the private ownership of the means of production in the 1950s to the completion of socialist modernization.[32]

The concept of the "primary stage of socialism" was first introduced at the end of the 1970s – the starting point of the reforms – under the term "undeveloped socialism."[33] The idea was popularized by the Marxist theoretician Su Shaozhi in the 1980s and became a major doctrinal support for the economic reforms of the then party general secretary Zhao Ziyang under the auspices of Deng.[34] To go through the primary stage of socialism, it was argued, China had to develop its forces of production with the support of the market mechanism through, inter alia, price deregulation, changes in property ownership, and the expansion of the private sector. The primary stage of socialism was meant to be a transition for China to attain full socialism before it would be ready for communism.

However, Xi's end goal of the primary stage of socialism is the rejuvenation of the nation. While Zhao had stated that this transitional period would last an indefinite time, Xi set the envisaged duration to around hundred years, from the Party's social transformation in the 1950s to the middle of the 21st century, when China would "come out of underdevelopment" and achieve modernization.

Piecing together the projected targets that Xi has put forward – the completion of the "primary stage of socialism," the "third step" of an affluent society at the level of a "moderately developed country," the accomplishment of modernization, and a China that is "prosperous, strong, democratic, culturally advanced, and harmonious" – we see a picture that shows the state goals converging in the year 2050, or sometime around that point. "In this new historical period," said Xi, "[we will] realize the Chinese Dream of the great renewal of the Chinese nation."[35] 2050 is to be the time when China has been "rejuvenated," to be "prosperous and strong," and it will be the year when the Chinese Dream is consummated.

To get there, according to Xi, "the only path" (*biyou zhi lu*)[36] is "socialism with Chinese characteristics." Like many of his utterances, the terms Xi used are nothing new. What is striking, though, is the new content or modifications that he added to the established significations already invested in the concepts. Like Deng's, his "socialism with Chinese characteristics" is centered upon economic development as its core and the one-party rule as its guide. However, instead of counting on Deng's "superiority of socialism" as the validating supposition of China's new status in the international community, Xi focuses on the ascendency of China, the *nation,* and wraps it in rhetorical trappings of "socialist" doctrines.

Foregrounding a rising Chinese nation with the support of a "socialist" system, Xi portrays the centrality of the Party, rationalizing the validity and significance of its dominance. "[T]he CCP," he said,

> has shouldered the historic mission of rejuvenating the Chinese nation ever since its birth. The very purpose of the Party in leading the Chinese people in revolution, development, and reform is to make the people prosperous and the country strong, and rejuvenate the Chinese nation.[37]

Through the articulations of the China Dream, the new role of the Party as a *nationalistic vanguard,* which was hardly mentioned before the Tiananmen crackdown, has now come into full force. The Party as the savior of socialist construction, highlighted in Deng's rhetoric, has now given way to the represented image of a "redeemer" capable of delivering the grand dream of a "prosperous and strong" nation, China, all with a realized scenario concretely in sight, that is, by 2050.

Having portrayed a grandiose picture of the China Dream, Xi further connected it to people's individual ideals. "[You] should," he said, "consciously assimilate [your] personal aspirations and family happiness into the great undertaking of national rejuvenation and making China prosperous and strong. [You should] closely tie your personal dream with the Chinese Dream."[38] The extension from the collective to the individual, from China the nation to people as citizens, represents a vivid moment of *interpellation.* It subjectivizes the individual to the position of a member of the modernizing China, calling on them to surrender their dream and life – as a Chinese national, a representative of their family, and a person with a particular social station – to participate in the overarching task of national renewal. Hailing the subjects, the interpellation also *incorporates* "you" into the collective, the Chinese, and subjugates "your" dream and life to the Chinese Dream, a purportedly higher order that is to elevate all members to a raised level of development in the world hierarchy.

The material entitlements a Chinese subject enjoys, or the raised living standards such goods and services embody, are the basis on which the Party relies for people's continuous support. So long as the Party delivers on development manifested in material terms, so long as it ensures the community's progression along the upward curve of national ascent, it can claim to be the country's valid and legitimate leader.

In over four decades of reform, under political leaders from Deng to Xi, the development ideal took on different forms of actualization under specific socioeconomic circumstances. At each threshold of transformation, China's development process altered its course as a result of unintended consequences. The trajectory of "progress," imbued with inherent twists and turns, manifested modifications in the form of power in different periods. In what follows, we will begin our analysis with "scientific and democratic decision-making" as the primary mode of governance in the 1980s.

Notes

1 David Harvey, *A Brief History of Neoliberalism* (New York: Oxford University Press, 2005).
2 Stuart Schram, "Deng Xiaoping's Quest for 'Modernization with Chinese Characteristics' and the Future of Marxism-Leninism," in *China in the Era of Deng Xiaoping – a Decade of Reform*, ed. Michael Ying-Mao Kau and Susan H. Marsh (Armonk, NY: M.E. Sharpe, 1993), 411.
3 Doak Barnett, "Comments by A. Doak Barnett," in *China in the Era of Deng Xiaoping – a Decade of Reform*, ed. Michael Ying-Mao Kau and Susan H. Marsh (Armonk, NY: M.E. Sharpe, 1993), 434.
4 Jorge Larrain, *The Concept of Ideology* (Athens: University of Georgia Press, 1979), 130–140.
5 Deng Xiaoping, "Emancipate the Mind, Seek Truth from Facts and Unite as One in Looking to the Future," in *Selected Works of Deng Xiaoping (1975–1982)* (Beijing: Foreign Languages Press, 1984), 151–165.
6 See Edgar Snow, *Red Star Over China* (New York: Grove Press, 1961), 211–238.
7 James Pinckney Harrison, *The Long March to Power: A History of the Chinese Communist Party, 1921–72* (New York: Praeger Publishers, 1972), 239.
8 Deng, "Uphold the Four Cardinal Principles," in *Selected Works of Deng Xiaoping (1975–1982)* (Beijing: Foreign Languages Press, 1984), 170–171.
9 David Goodman, *Deng Xiaoping and the Chinese Revolution: A Political Biography* (London and New York: Routledge, 1994), 77–89.
10 Deng, "Speech at National Science Conference," in *Selected Works of Deng Xiaoping (1975–1982)* (Beijing: Foreign Languages Press, 1984), 102.
11 Goodman, *Deng Xiaoping*, 83.
12 Deng Xiaoping, "Reform Is the Only Way for China to Develop Its Productive Forces," in *Selected Works of Deng Xiaoping III (1982–1992)* (Beijing: Foreign Languages Press, 1994), 141.
13 Lowell Dittmer, "Chinese Reform Socialism Under Deng Xiaoping: Theory and Practice," in *China in the Era of Deng Xiaoping*, 14–16.
14 Deng, "We Shall Concentrate on Economic Development," in *Selected Works of Deng Xiaoping III (1982–1992)* (Beijing: Foreign Languages Press, 1994), 21–22 (italics added).

15 Deng, "Reform of System for Science and Technology," in *Selected Works of Deng Xiaoping III (1982–1992)* (Beijing: Foreign Languages Press, 1994), 115.
16 Deng, "Jianchi sixiang jiben yuanze" [Uphold the Four Cardinal Principles], in *Deng Xiaoping wenxuan (1975–1982) [Selected Works of Deng Xiaoping (1975–1982)]* (Renmin chubanshe, 1983), 150 and 153.
17 Deng, "Jianchi sixiang jiben yuanze" [Uphold the Four Cardinal Principles], 175.
18 Statista, "Gini index: inequality of income distribution in China from 2008 to 2018," statista.com/statistics/250400/inequality-of-income-distribution-in-china-based-on-the-gini-index/#:~:text=This%20statistic%20shows%20the%20inequality
19 Hu Jintao, "Ba kexue fazhanguan guanchuan yu fazhan de zhengge guocheng he gege fangmian" [The Scientific Outlook on Development Runs Through the Process of Development and Its Various Aspects], in *Hu Jintao Wenxuan II [Selected Works of Hu Jintao II]* (Beijing: Renmin chubanshe, 2016), 185.
20 Quoted in Joseph Fewsmith, "Promoting the Scientific Development Concept," *China Leadership Monitor*, no. 11 (Summer 2004): 3 (emphasis added).
21 Hu Jintao, "Shenru xuexi linghui kexue fazhanguan" [Have an In-depth Study and Understanding of the Scientific Outlook in Development], in *Hu Jintao Wenxuan III [Selected Works of Hu Jintao III]* (Beijing: Renmin chubanshe, 2016), 3.
22 Hu, "Shenru xuexi linghui kexue fazhanguan" [Have an In-depth Study and Understanding of the Scientific Outlook in Development], 3–4.
23 Hu, "Shenru xuexi linghui kexue fazhanguan" [Have an In-depth Study and Understanding of the Scientific Outlook on Development], 5.
24 Fewsmith, "Scientific Development Concept," 6.
25 Xi Jinping, "Realize Youthful Dreams. May 4, 2013," in *Xi Jinping: The Governance of China* (Beijing: Foreign Languages Press, 2014), 53.
26 Xi Jinping, "Jinjin weirao jianchi he fazhan zhongguo tese shehuizhuyi xuexi xuanchuan guanche dang de shibada jingshen" [Study, Disseminate and Implement the Guiding Principles of the 18th CPC National Congress], in *Xi Jinping tan zhiguo lizheng [Xi Jinping on the Governance of China]* (Beijing: Waiwen chubanshe, November 17, 2012), 12.
27 See Zheng Wang, *Never Forget National Humiliation: Historical Memory in Chinese Politics and Foreign Relations* (New York: Columbia University Press, 2012), in particular 95–141.
28 Xi Jinping, "The People's Wish for a Good Life Is Our Goal," *Governance of China*, November 15, 2012, 3–4.
29 Xi Jinping, "Shigan caineng mengxiang chengzhen" [Hard Work Makes Dreams Come True], *Governance of China*, April 28, 2013, 47.
30 Xi, "Jinjin weirao jianchi he fazhan" [Study, Disseminate and Implement],12.
31 Xi, "Jinjin weirao jianchi he fazhan" [Study, Disseminate and Implement], 21, n 20.
32 Xi, "Jinjin weirao jianchi he fazhan" [Study, Disseminate and Implement], 11, n 18 (italics added).
33 Stuart Schram stated that "undeveloped socialism" was coined in 1979, while Richard Baum argued that the term was first used by Chinese academics in 1978. In either case, the concept was introduced at the starting point of the reforms. See Richard Baum, "The Road to Tiananmen: Chinese Politics in the 1980s," in *The Politics of China: Sixty Years of the People's Republic of China*, ed. Roderick MacFarquhar, 3rd ed. (New York: Cambridge University Press, 2011), 407–408, n 258.
34 See Baum, "The Road to Tiananmen: Chinese Politics in the 1980s," 404–410.
35 Xi Jinping, "The Chinese Dream Will Benefit Not Only the People of China, but Also of Other Countries," *Governance of China*, May 2013, 61.
36 Xi, "Shigan caineng mengxiang chengzhen" [Hard Work Makes Dreams Come True], 45.
37 Xi, "Jinjin weirao jianchi he fazhan" [Study, Disseminate and Implement], 12.
38 Xi, "Shigan caineng mengxiang chengzhen" [Hard Work Makes Dreams Come True], 45.

Bibliography

Barnett, Doak. 1993. "Comments by A. Doak Barnett." In *China in the Era of Deng Xiaoping – a Decade of Reform*, edited by Michael Ying-Mao Kau and Susan H. Marsh. Armonk, NY: M.E. Sharpe.

Baum, Richard. 2011. "The Road to Tiananmen: Chinese Politics in the 1980s." In *The Politics of China: Sixty Years of the People's Republic of China*, edited by Roderick MacFarquhar. New York: Cambridge University Press.

Deng, Xiaoping. 1983. *Deng Xiaoping wenxuan (1975–1982) [Selected Works of Deng Xiaoping (1975–1982)].* Renmin chubanshe.

Deng, Xiaoping. 1984. *Selected Works of Deng Xiaoping (1975–1982).* Beijing: Foreign Languages Press.

Deng, Xiaoping. 1994. *Selected Works of Deng Xiaoping III (1982–1992).* Beijing: Foreign Languages Press.

Dittmer, Lowell. 1993. "Chinese Reform Socialism under Deng Xiaoping: Theory and Practice." In *China in the Era of Deng Xiaoping – a Decade of Reform*, edited by Michael Ying-Mao Kau and Susan H. Marsh. Armonk, NY: M.E. Sharpe.

Fewsmith, Joseph. Summer 2004. "Promoting the Scientific Development Concept." *China Leadership Monitor* (11): 3.

Goodman, David. 1995. *Deng Xiaoping and the Chinese Revolution: A Political Biography.* Routledge.

Harrison, James Pinckney. 1972. *The Long March to Power: A History of the Chinese Communist Party, 1921–72.* New York: Praeger Publishers.

Harvey, David. 2005. *A Brief History of Neoliberalism.* New York: Oxford University Press.

Hu, Jintao. 2016a. *Hu Jintao Wenxuan II [Selected Works of Hu Jintao II].* Beijing: Renmin chubanshe.

Hu, Jintao. 2016b. *Hu Jintao Wenxuan III [Selected Works of Hu Jintao III].* Beijing: Renmin chubanshe.

Larrain, Jorge. 1979. *The Concept of Ideology.* University of Georgia Press.

Schram, Stuart. 1993. "Deng Xiaoping's Quest for 'Modernization with Chinese Characteristics' and the Future of Marxism-Leninism." In *China in the Era of Deng Xiaoping – a Decade of Reform*, edited by Michael Ying-Mao Kau and Susan H. Marsh. Armonk, NY: M.E. Sharpe.

Snow, Edgar. 1961. *Red Star over China.* New York: Grove Press.

Statista. n.d. "Gini Index: Inequality of Income Distribution in China from 2008 to 2018." statista.com/statistics/250400/inequality-of-income-distribution-in-china-based-on-the-gini-index/#:~:text=This%20statistic%20shows%20the%20inequality.

Wang, Zheng. 2012. *Never Forget National Humiliation: Historical Memory in Chinese Politics and Foreign Relations.* Columbia University Press.

Xi, Jinping. 2012. *Xi Jinping tan zhiguo lizheng [Xi Jinping on the Governance of China].* Beijing: Waiwen chubanshe.

Xi, Jinping. 2014. *The Governance of China.* Beijing: Foreign Languages Press.

3 "Science" and "Socialist Democracy"

A New Mode of Governance After Mao

In the first decade of reform, the official use of "socialist democracy" and "scientific decision-making" as major governing tactics signaled the beginning of the political theodicy of development in action. Objective scientific knowledge and the impersonal procedures of decision-making, which marked a radical shift in the mode of governance from the Maoist regime, were meant to reverse the devastating effects wrought by revolutionary extremism and bring China onto the track of rationalized productivity. The experimental mode of development involved the inclusivity of pluralistic voices, which were mushrooming in this most liberal decade of Chinese communist history. The terms "scientific" (*kexue-hua*) and "democratic" (*minzhuhua*) were frequently invoked in the Three Gorges Dam discourse, expressing the aspirations of technocrat proponents and intellectual dissidents alike concerning the project and the general political orientations at the time.

With the disruption of the educational routines and economic production during the Cultural Revolution, the level of science and technology in China by the end of the 1970s, as Deng estimated, was almost thirty years behind that of the developed world. The technical, educational, and economic systems were thus in need of serious restructuring. Deng came to the conclusion that if China were to "catch up" with the industrialized countries, the application of more advanced scientific techniques would be crucial. It was in the context of such a disjuncture that discourses of "science" and "socialist democracy" came into formation.

At the center was *science*, both as a method of producing knowledge and a procedure for making political decisions. In the reform program, the modernization of science and technology was considered crucial because this was fundamental to all the other three modernizations in industry, agriculture, and national defense. "[E]conomic strength, science and technology," Deng noted, "play an outstanding role in worldwide competition. Neither the United States and the Soviet Union, nor the other developed countries, nor the developing countries can afford to ignore this."[1] The Three Gorges proposal, a "key project" that was expected to play a significant role in energy production and in turn the national economic output, would be an emblem of China's capability to master the highest level of hydropower technology in the world.

DOI: 10.4324/9781003531494-4

"Science"

From the point when the Gang of Four lost power and Deng together with his reformist comrades gained a stable foothold in the Party's political core, the term "science" or "scientific" had been recurrently invoked in official narratives. In a conversation with other political leaders a year before the commencement of reforms, Deng pressed home his views that "[t]he key to modernization is the advancement of science and technology (*kexue jishu*), and in order to develop science and technology, we have to improve people's education. Modernization cannot be realized [without] . . . knowledge and talents."[2]

His words pointed to the first and the most basic definition of "science" under his leadership as a branch of knowledge. "Kexue jishu" can also be translated as "scientific techniques." The form of knowledge Deng was referring to was not simply "pure" science about nature for its own sake – it was also a utilitarian kind of knowledge that would enable China to overcome its "nature" of backwardness and elevate itself to a higher level of material attainment and national empowerment. It was a foundational resource for the Party to reform the country's socioeconomic structure in the direction of a viable industrialized entity. Knowledge was quantified in terms of the number of specialists who were considered the embodiments of scientific techniques. According to Deng, the United States had 1.2 million research personnel and the Soviet Union 900,000, while China had only over 200,000, including those who were old and sick, and therefore could not be "of much help." All in all, he estimated, China was twenty years behind in the fields of education in science and technology.[3]

The instrumentalist scientific techniques that the Dengist leadership espoused were not a general field of epistemological inquiry that post-Mao China sought after – there was a hierarchy of knowledge in which areas of scientific study were ranked according to their relative value for the new development strategy. Applied science was prioritized over theoretical research, and among applied sciences, focus was given to studies pertinent to industry, agriculture, and national defense. Cadres who did not possess scientific expertise, not to mention those who had little education, were marginalized at the bottom of the hierarchy, or outside of it, with a precarious prospect of sustaining the authority they had established in the Maoist days of populism.

The elevated status of applied science was connected in the general development scenario with economic growth and increased productivity. Under the reforms, every activity, including knowledge production, was geared toward market demands and production needs. To facilitate an integration between research institutes and production sectors, the government introduced regulations and a new remunerative contract system so that research initiatives would be more closely linked with enterprise objectives and more responsive to market changes. The leadership also cut back on allocations to science and technology units so as to compel them to seek funds from cooperation projects with enterprises.[4] Applied science, under these circumstances, became a dominant field of knowledge for its instrumental use.

However, scientific knowledge was not simply a resource in China's new modernization scheme; it was considered a productive force in its own right. Deng, invoking Marx's idea that "the development of mechanistic production requires the conscious application of natural science," argued that given the same amount of labor power and time, productivity could increase ten- or a hundred-fold with the utilization of science and technology.[5] Science as a productive force was also manifested in its combination with labor power. According to Deng, humans became an effective production factor when they were equipped with scientific knowledge, production experience, and manufacturing skills in the manipulation of tools and processing of raw materials.

By virtue of this conceived connection between science and labor, intellectuals were included in the sociopolitical category of workers under the new regime: if scientific knowledge was a force of production, the bearer of that knowledge was by extension also a productive force. This marked a radical departure from the anti-intellectual practice of "red versus expert" during the Cultural Revolution. In Deng's belief, scientific research and educational work involved mental labor, and "mental labor is also labor."[6] In the reformist mode of socialism under modernization, knowledge and manpower in the form of intellectual production were converted into economic factors and were in turn incorporated into the manufacturing process.

The utilitarian application of science to economic production points to the second meaning of "science" in the reform era, namely *scientism*, which believes in the universal validity of scientific knowledge in not only solving problems in the natural world but also those in the human community. In the context of communist China, and in part also during the Republican era, scientism acquired its theoretical foundation from Marxism-Leninism, which offers a revolutionary approach to social progress and national development. From Sun Yat-sen to Mao to Deng, scientific methodologies were considered powerful tools for their country's modernization. Science became an ally of technocracy in mastering the natural world to serve human purposes in the social, political, and economic realms. The Three Gorges Dam, with its unprecedented scale and technology, was an exemplar of the utility of science in altering the natural landscape and reformulating social communities for material progress.

Although the extension of scientific methods as a cumulative and linear procedure to tackle issues in the social and economic spheres was common to Sun, Mao, and Deng, the latter differentiated himself from the other two leaders in that he did not build his scientistic ideology upon liberalism or utopian fantasies. Rather, his test of "truth" with empirical "practice" set his party and its power apart from the Nationalist and in particular the Maoist doctrines of development. Deng staked the legitimacy of his party with his rational and practice-oriented policy upon the claim that his scientistic prescription would effectively reverse Mao's calamitous error and bring China onto the road of industrialization. This prescription would rest upon, as it claimed, a restoration of true Marxist-Leninist methodologies, an emphasis on pragmatic empiricism, and the universal laws of objectivity. If development is the governing ideological practice of the Dengist regime, scientism is the wellspring supporting and nourishing the progression along that trajectory.

In accordance with the new emphasis on science, the leadership wove a new structure of reformed institutions and social relations. Academic societies that had existed before the Cultural Revolution were reestablished. Technical professionals were encouraged to take the initiative in organizing specialized associations in various provinces and cities to mobilize human resources and special talents in the localities. At the central level, organizations such as the Chinese Academy of Sciences (CAS) were reformed. The academy's head was replaced by a chemist educated in the West, while its Scientific Council, which oversaw the organization's research planning and project evaluations, was enlarged to comprise 400 leading scientists and technical personnel. Twelve branch academies were added in provinces and major cities to increase efficiency through decentralization, and a "science fund" was established in early 1982 to introduce "peer review" into the process of research design.[7] Scientific journals, which had been suppressed during the Cultural Revolution, reappeared, while new ones were established. It was in this context that *Ziran bianzhengfa tongxun* (*Journal of Dialectics of Nature*) was founded and it became an active forum of the Three Gorges opponents in the 1980s.

Along with the technocratic ascendancy, a new set of norms and values coalesced. Intellectuals were no longer considered the "stinking ninth category" used during the Cultural Revolution. Improvements in the social status and living conditions of technical experts came along with the promotion of their positions within and outside the formal structure of the state. Scientists and engineers were moved into key posts in local and central government agencies. An increasing number of technicians and scientific personnel were recruited into the Chinese Communist Party to replace cadres who did not have the expertise. The post-Mao reformers' emphasis on scientific input was highlighted by a speech made by then Party General Secretary, Hu Yaobang, before the National Congress of the All-China Association for Science and Technology in 1980. He called on his colleagues to encourage specialists with administrative and organizational ability to take up positions of leadership in the Party, government, economic, scientific, and educational sectors. In the speech, he called for a collaboration between the scientists and his Secretariat, inviting the former group to be the latter's "teachers" (*laoshi*).[8]

The value the Dengist government placed on technical expertise was indicated in the consultative role it endorsed for scientists and engineers. Attempts were made to bring experts into the policymaking process as consultants on important technical issues. The Chinese Association for Science and Technology, for example, emerged as a key advisor for the political elite, offering the specialized knowledge of its 138 professional member bodies. This change was of particular importance to the Three Gorges debate. By virtue of the Party's recognition of the experts' consultative value, intellectual dissidents advocated their opposition from outside of the formal government structure or the decision-making core under the name of offering expert advice. They did this through institutions that were opened up under the reforms, which were in turn made possible by the policy of "socialist democracy," which will be explored in the next section.

The discussion of science was often linked to that of education. As illustrated in his quote earlier, the connection between "knowledge" and "talents" was commonly found in Deng's enunciations. In a speech titled "Remarks on the Work of Science and Education" ("*Guanyu kexue he jiaoyu gongzuo de jidian yijian*") made in 1977, Deng outlined an elaborate blueprint of educational reform, which entailed a systematic reorganization of the educational structure. It ranged from the designation of key universities to the rule allowing students to skip grades and the rewriting of textbooks to "reflect the progressive standards of modern science and culture."[9] In practice, entrance examinations were reinstated, new universities were established, and a system of postgraduate programs was formulated in cooperation with the CAS. These were intended to tackle the shortage of scientific manpower and achieve the goal of having 800,000 "research workers" by 1985. According to Richard Suttmeier, 1.02 million students enrolled in 633 institutions of higher education by the end of 1979, an increase of 164,000 students and 35 institutions compared to 1978. About 41 percent of all university students in 1979, it was estimated, were in areas of science and engineering.[10]

The leadership's emphasis on consultation and discussion with the intellectuals was related to the pragmatic empiricism Deng espoused as a new approach to decision-making after the Cultural Revolution. The idea that every aspect of social life is governed by *objective laws* is contained in what Tang Tsou called the "sociological postulate" underlying the post-Mao political logic. The concept obtained a theoretical content in the exposition of Hu Qiaomu, the then president of the newly created Academy of Social Sciences who reemerged after the Cultural Revolution as one of the most authoritative theoreticians for the reformist regime. In his interpretations of Marx, Engels, Lenin, and Mao, Hu argued that "economic laws" are like "natural laws," which cannot be changed at the will of society and the authorities. "Over and above the economic laws in objective existence," Hu claimed,

> politics itself cannot create other laws and impose them on the economy. In fact, insofar as the laws of economic developments are concerned, the mission of correct political leadership lies precisely in making the maximum effort to see to it that our socialist economic work operates within the scope of these objective laws.[11]

A misuse of political power to interfere with the operations of such laws, he added, would result in "enormous damage to economic development." The task of leaders, in other words, was to create the appropriate conditions for those laws to work to the advantage of desired development. Similar views, according to Tsou, had been expressed by the post-Mao leaders in all spheres of social life, including those in the areas of science and education. Taking into consideration this postulate, one may argue that the empiricist approach Deng propounded was to seek the truth of objective laws through practice. Under this concept, the pragmatic method of trial and error would enable the discovery of the true logic that underpins the operations of both the natural and human worlds and solves every problem contained within. Consultation with experts, in this sense, incorporated the knowledge needed for the exercise of technocratic inquiry in pursuit of the truth of these objective laws.

The idea of transcendent laws provided a logical root for the assumption that science is impartial, neutral, and impersonal regardless of human intervention and interpretation. The application of such an understanding of "science" to the political process of policy formulation, which is the third meaning of "science" that Deng's reforms embraced, was well publicized through the notion of "scientific decision-making." The concept was recurrently used by the authorities and dissenting intellectuals alike in the debate over the Three Gorges Dam in the 1980s and early 1990s. "Scientific decision-making" was espoused by Deng to counteract the leftist extremism that lingered in Chinese politics after the death of Mao. Its appeal to objectivity stood for a methodological procedure that disregarded the participants' political stands, ideological colors, and the personal preferences of leaders. A similar interpretation of "scientific" in decision-making was also embraced by the dissidents, albeit in a different direction. Anti-extremism was not the primary concern of the intellectuals. Rather, they believed that policy deliberations should be based on impartial facts that went beyond party lines and political biases, be they left or right.

"Scientific decision-making" also denoted, officially, the attainment of a breakthrough in epistemological inquiry and a higher level of human thought through the clash of ideas. The process of testing and falsifying could, it was believed, lead to the truth of the issue under study. In this way, Deng's pragmatic test of empirical practice was supposed to guide the Party to the best policy design. This idea provided sound support for the leadership to assign the Three Gorges proposal to feasibility studies and incorporate dissent into the debate. In practice, however, the "scientific" method that the government promoted was not based on pure objectivity. In fact, the composition of the feasibility study group demonstrates that the clash of ideas did not guide the inquiry to a neutral truth but oriented decisions toward the agenda of the Party, which clearly favored building a dam in the Three Gorges area. The impersonal use of scientific data, in this sense, was an inclusive utilization of knowledge but for an exclusive purpose. The procedure of decision-making was thus subordinated to politics, not in a personalized way, but rather in a manner that served the political purpose of revitalizing the Party, rationalizing its new political orientations, and legitimizing its policy objectives.

The persistence of official intrusiveness, albeit in a different manifestation, was what the scientists in the reform period objected to. They included not only those engaged in the Three Gorges polemics but also experts in the natural and social scientific fields. Through forums of articulation such as publications, mass media, and professional associations, which emerged under the sanctioned liberalization of public life in the 1980s,[12] they appropriated the regime's "scientific" claim of objectivity to resist authoritarian control. By virtue of the Party's recognition of the paramount importance of science and technology, technical experts gained autonomy as they constituted a social group that went outside and beyond the reach of the Party. The leadership's co-optation of science opened the way for technical elites to negotiate with the government according to the science principles that the regime officially embraced. The Party, at the same time, became sensitive to changes in interpretations of science's findings in not only the natural world but also the sociopolitical one. The result was an erosion of the Party's monopoly of *truth*. There emerged "clashes over who was competent to judge the validity of scientific argument, over the relationship between science and Marxism, and ultimately, over the relationship between knowledge and power."[13]

The conflict was reinforced by the diverse nature of the scientific discourse and the inherently unauthoritarian or anti-authoritarian character of the scientific disciplines. Practitioners in a field may agree on the goals and methods of research, but they often have different understandings about the significance of the inquiry they are engaged in, what science means to the modern world, and what values it offers to their surrounding society. Conflicts within the scientific community are mediated through the mechanism of the "invisible college," which is by nature pluralist and not authoritarian. Practitioners may also resort to public organizations and informal associations for the expression of their views. As a result, according to Lyman Miller,

> conflicts over scientific ideas and, especially, over the relevance of the values and methods of science beyond itself contribute to the assertion of a public sphere of political discourse and the erection of the institutions of civil society. Such pressures favor political pluralism and liberal politics and counter the totalizing tendencies of scientism and the authoritarian consequences of technocracy.[14]

Insofar as science was understood as a rationalized procedure through which *truth* emerged out of the collision of ideas, what both the official dam advocates and dissenting intellectuals engaged in was a competition over the truth. If being "scientific," moreover, entailed a scenario in which views interacted and results were concluded with purported transcendent neutrality and objectivity, both parties were involved in a contest over the actual meaning of the term "scientific." While dam technocrats emphasized the *product* of scientific data in the form of privileged knowledge in congruence with the Party's objectives as a result of research and experiment, the dissidents espoused the *process* of letting ideas and hypotheses freely collide in order to arrive at the best findings. "Science" and "scientific," in this sense, became a site of contestation and confrontation.

"Socialist Democracy"

In the debate over the Three Gorges Dam, the discussion of "science" was closely linked with the concept of "socialist democracy." "Democratic and scientific decision-making" was ubiquitous in the discourse of the dam in the 1980s, denoting a particular form of policy formulation in general in that period. This form of decision-making was part of the prescription of political theodicy meant to remedy the disastrous effects of personalized power exercised by Mao. In the official mouthpiece, *Liaowang*, Deng was quoted as saying that "for the people, socialist democracy is proletarian dictatorship." The author went on to explain:

> Without democracy, without an effective legal safeguard of democracy, proletarian dictatorship can evolve into feudal fascist dictatorship, and a

> proletarian revolutionary as great as Mao Zedong makes serious mistakes, which cause unassessable damages to the Party and the country. . . . Comrade Deng Xiaoping said: "In order to protect people's democracy, the legal system has to be strengthened to legalize and systematize democracy, so that such a system and laws will not alter according to the change of the leadership and the change in the leaders' stands and perspectives."[15]

"Democracy" in the context of the post-Mao period has a specific meaning in relation to the form of politics prevalent before the reforms. As the quote earlier indicated, "socialist democracy," which was represented in the terms of "proletarian dictatorship" under Deng, primarily denoted checks and balances within the Party, essentially the leadership, in the overarching framework of a one-party mechanism. It claimed to incorporate certain elements of "bourgeois democracy," not in the form of popular representation and competitive elections but rather in the possibility of "putting on rival shows" (*chang duitaixi*), that is to say, the articulations of dissent alternative to the sanctioned standpoints of the core power. The purpose was to limit the authority of the state and prevent one-man dominance in decision-making – a dominance that had been abused by even "a proletarian revolutionary as great as Mao Zedong" through his personality cult, which the Dengist leadership considered to be a primary factor leading to the Cultural Revolution. The "legalization" and "systemization" of "democracy," in this sense, was a routinization of policy objectives derived from inclusive deliberations and collective decision-making, which could withstand the biases of individual partiality and "politics in command" characteristic of the Maoist mode of power.

The checks and balances conceived to restrain the policymakers' behavior were also to be effectuated through a particular form of public participation. The emphasis the Dengist regime put on "practice as the sole criterion of testing truth" obliged the Party to take into consideration the "social practices of the masses, that is, the needs, the interests, the demands, the life situations, and the behavioral patterns of various social groups and individuals."[16] "Democracy" in this context constituted an institutional configuration that facilitated the inputs and feedback from different sectors of society, including scientists and specialists, in the form of *consultation* in the course of policy deliberations.[17] Like Mikhail Gorbachev's *Glasnost*, which was supposed to mobilize public initiatives to revitalize the Soviet Communist Party without forsaking political power, "socialist democracy" in China was purportedly a decentralization of authority while upholding the Party's dominance.

Deliberative consultation entailed a process of inclusion and incorporation. In a speech addressing "soft science research," which encompassed natural and social sciences, a Politburo member, Wan Li, pointed out that the wisdom and experience of leaders alone could not adequately tackle the complexity of issues in the contemporary world. To cope with problems emerging in the process of modernization amidst the ever-changing social and economic situations both domestically and internationally, Wan argued that the authorities had to incorporate not only specialists from various sectors but also intellectual tools, technical data, and knowledge systems for the analysis of the overall situation. "More importantly," he noted,

> systematic and multi-level study of complicated economic and social phenomena needs to be conducted for us to have a comprehensive grasp of the connections and mutual effects of the constituent components. This requires us to utilize various theories of the natural and social sciences, and advanced computational equipment and measurement methods, so as to enable us to combine static assessment with dynamic analysis, quantitative with qualitative study, and democratic with scientific decision-making.[18]

The process of inclusion, in this way, encompassed various analytical tools, knowledge systems, and scientific procedures of measurement, comparison, and evaluation.

The primary form of incorporation, nonetheless, was the involvement of scientific personnel. In the debate regarding the Three Gorges Dam, the concept of "drawing on collective wisdom and absorbing all useful ideas" (*jisi guangyi*) was recurrently invoked in the articulations of officials and dissidents alike. In an article echoing the views of Wan Li, Fei Xiaotong, a core figure of the "democratic parties" in China, argued that democratic decision-making was essentially a process of "centralization on the basis of democracy" through the solicitation of the wisdom of the masses. Intellectuals, he added, were in this sense given the socio-political role of offering ideas and becoming the advisers of the authorities.[19] Fei's argument fits into the concept of "socialist democracy," in that the intellectual capacity of the people – in this case, the scientists and technological professionals – was to be tapped and utilized through the exercise of what I consider *centralized incorporation.* Such a procedure was meant to compensate for the shortfalls of insufficient information in the decision-making process, and complement the inadequate experience and knowledge of leaders, thereby assuring the best possible policy design.

What characterized "science" and "democracy" in the 1980s and set them apart from a similar discourse in the May Fourth Movement seventy years earlier was the conceived circular relationship between science and democracy. Science was purported to improve the mechanism of decision-making by injecting impartial procedures and objective perspectives into the process of policy formulation, thereby ensuring an inclusive system that was able to resist leftist extremism. Democracy, at the same time, liberated science by distancing it from Maoist anti-expert ideologies and allowed the free collision of ideas to take scientific research to ever higher levels of inquiry. The resulting fruits of study would feed back into the political mechanism with new intellectual perspectives, analytical methods, and systematic technical knowledge. In the late 1970s and the 1980s, it was widely publicized that without democracy there would not be rapid development of science and, without science, there could not be true democracy.

Revolt of Experts

The inclusivity of perspectives under the *centralized incorporation* was meant to absorb the pluralistic voices that were mushrooming in the public sphere in the first decade of reform. What developed out of it, however, was an unleashed quest for freedom in not only scientific inquiry but also political exploration.

Democracy as limited government, which was meant ultimately to uphold the Party's control over society – albeit in a more pluralist way – was understood by the dissenting intellectuals as a broadening of freedom in technical research and, further, sociopolitical life. Their demands started with a separation of politics from academic study and extended to an assertion that true freedom of discussion in science and art was not possible without the broader freedom of expression in the political realm. The editor of *Historical Research*, Li Shu, wrote:

> To restrict freedom of speech on matters of politics is equivalent to endorsing political autocracy. Once an autocracy is established in political matters, it will definitely not be restricted to politics alone; freedom of speech in the sphere of science and art will also be written off by such an autocracy. This was precisely the case under the cultural autocracy established during the period when Lin Biao and the Gang of Four dominated over the people.[20]

In an article addressing democratic decision-making and the authority's leadership style, Chen Guojie argued that for intellectuals to participate in policy formulation, "in a political sense their creative labor has to be protected, individual rights to form independent opinions recognized, and their freedom of expression safeguarded."[21] In other words, opposing scientific views should be allowed to be freely articulated in the form of "letting a hundred schools of thought contend" (*baijia zhengming*) and clash without political constraints. This was important for the intellectuals, who believed that the "truth" of scientific inquiry would emerge from the "practice" of debate under the condition of respect for their creativity and freedom of intellectual pursuit.

The experts' quest for freedom of expression resonated with, and was indeed made possible by, the reformist leadership's recognition of open discussion. In a conference addressing scientific and education work, Deng said: "We should uphold the policy of letting a hundred schools of thought contend and allow debate. Different intellectual approaches should respect one another and complement one another."[22] The "democracy" of an "active and lively scenario" that Deng advocated was realized in the form of, inter alia, reduced control over mass media, accommodation of public opinions, and people's increased autonomy in forming public and private organizations. Despite sanctioned limits and intermittent conservative backlashes such as the "anti-bourgeois liberalization" and "anti-spiritual pollution" campaigns, China in the 1980s enjoyed a broader latitude of social, political, and cultural, not to mention economic, pluralization compared to the Maoist days.

The Three Gorges Dam controversy arose out of this scenario, in which dissenting intellectuals rode on the state's promotion of "democratic and scientific decision-making" and effectively launched an opposition campaign through publications, open debate in public forums, and coalition-building among intellectuals, journalists, and scientists. Like other political actors in the emerging civil society, they exploited the newly opened channels of articulation, practically testing and pushing the limit of official permissibility.

A focal point of debate in the Three Gorges polemics between the dam technocrats and intellectual opponents was centered upon the composition of the feasibility study group and the procedures by which the experts derived their findings and conclusions. Building the dam had always been favored by the post-Mao leaders ever since they gained power at the end of the Cultural Revolution. From the beginning of the 1980s, well before the National People's Congress endorsed the dam proposal in 1992, Deng had expressed his support for the project on the grounds of flood control and hydroelectricity production, emphasizing that "I am behind the low-dam proposal. Do not sway once we set our mind on it."[23] Preparatory work ranging from ship-gate building to the formation of the Three Gorges Project Development Company was carried out in the first half of the 1980s, with the aim of starting the construction work in 1986 on a 175-meter dam with a 150-meter water level, which was considered a low dam.

By 1985, however, opposition emerged: Chongqing, a city located in the upper reaches of the Yangtze close to the western end of the proposed reservoir, suggested that the dam height be raised to 180 meters so that the city would benefit from the economic prospect of inland navigation. Pluralization in 1980s China enabled bureaucrats to express dissent to the leadership's decision. Moreover, "scientific and democratic decision-making," warranting expert consultation allowed members of the "democratic parties" to voice their opposition. These are not political parties that can run as electoral rivals to the Chinese Communist Party but are groups officially registered in the early days of the People's Republic that comprise veterans who have professional expertise and are able to offer advice to the Party. At the time of the Three Gorges debate, many members of the "democratic parties" were delegates of the Chinese People's Political Consultative Conference (CPPCC), a top advisory body in the formal state structure. These delegates did not hold any bureaucratic position but were specialists in the scientific fields, including geology, economics, and hydraulic engineering. Through the institution of the CPPCC, they conducted inspection tours in 1985 and 1988 in the Yangtze Valley and came back with doubts about the dam proposal. They used the CPPCC meetings as opinion forums to urge the government to perform more detailed research before making a final decision.

These institutional dissidents also formed an alliance with engineers, archeologists, and natural and social scientists outside of the state structure. Together they exploited the official endorsement of consultative deliberation and open debate to question the desirability of the dam project, on the grounds that its unprecedented scale would require technological skills and financial costs that the country was uncertain of bearing. They also queried the environmental impacts and social disruption the dam might bring about. While the "democratic party" members expressed their views through their publication *Voice of the Mass (Qunyan)*, newly founded journals such as the *Journal of Dialectics of Nature* (*Ziran bianzhengfa tongxun*) became a major forum of intellectual dissidents who had no direct access to formal channels of articulation. In 1987, the dissidents further exploited the political space of "socialist democracy" by publishing *On the Macro Decision of the Three Gorges Dam Project* (*Lun sanxia gongcheng de hongguan juece*). The opponents also consisted of journalists. From official mouthpieces such as *Liaowang* (*Outlook Weekly*) and *People's Daily* to intellectual-oriented newspapers *Guangming ribao* (*Guangming Daily*) and *Wenhuibao* (*Wenhui Daily*), reporters published interviews with dissidents and news about the CPPCC meetings and the proposed project in general. Together, these opinions formed what Tian Fang, an author of *On the Macro Decision of the Three Gorges Dam Project* (*Lun sanxia gongcheng di hongguan juece*), called the "second voice."[24]

In 1986, amidst opposition from the CPPCC and Chongqing, the central government made the rare move of withdrawing its proposal and resolving to restart the feasibility study. Under the instruction of the Central Committee, the Ministry of Water Resources and Electric Power (MWREP) invited 412 professionals from 40 fields, ranging from economics to hydraulic technology, to form fourteen expert groups to reexamine the project. Most of the members were initially supporters of the proposed scheme. The composition of the feasibility study group and its findings drew criticism from dissidents over the objectivity of the assessment process by building their argument on the principle of "democratic and scientific decision-making."

The debate over the proposed dam entailed the competition between dam advocates and opponents over the authority or authenticity of knowledge. The dissidents argued that the official technocrats had violated the principle of open inquiry in scientific study in the way the feasibility study group was formed and the bias with which it designed the issues of research. All of the eleven members of the MWREP leading group that appointed the 412 professionals to the reassessment team, they claimed, were former ministers, chief engineers, or top managers who supported the immediate commencement of the project. Out of the fourteen expert groups under this leading body, they added, ten were chaired by personnel from different bureaus and departments under the ministry, while the remaining four had vice-chairs from the ministry.[25] Because of the bias in favor of dam-building, the dissenting intellectuals argued, the feasibility study was centered around the height of a dam predetermined to be constructed at the Three Gorges and how it would be built to maximize the benefits of such a dam and minimize the defects it would bring. "For such an important project," said Zhou Peiyuan, a scientist and the former president of Peking University, "we ought not examine only one proposal, but consider different alternatives to compare the pros and cons of, say, building a Three Gorges dam on the mainstream before developing the tributaries, or harnessing the tributaries before exploiting the mainstream."[26] While some dissidents asserted that such a Three Gorges dam should not be built at all due to unfathomable technical difficulties, others argued that it could be constructed years later when China became better prepared financially. Yet some stated that if a dam had to be built, it should have a lower height in order to reduce the impacts on the ecology and the number of people to be displaced.

Dam proponents formed their counterarguments with knowledge derived from state-funded high-tech research conducted on the Yangtze River or in well-equipped laboratories. Abundant capital was expended by the government to build large-scale modeling on studies ranging from simulated siltation to river water velocity. The contrast between officially appointed experts and dissenting intellectuals in terms of the knowledge they propounded and the way in which it was produced was well illustrated in a statement by Li Boning, the former deputy minister of Water Resources and Electric Power who became the head of the Three Gorges resettlement program:

> The debate has been going on for more than 30 years. Those who favor it, the scientists, technicians, and departments concerned, have been working very hard night and day for the past 30 years – carrying out a large amount of surveying, investigating, planning, designing, research, and experiments – and have achieved considerable scientific results. But up until today, those who oppose the project, as far as I can see, have not been able to present any new or convincing scientific evidence. They simply repeat old slogans of the 1950s, inventing more and more accusatory labels for the achievements made by the [official] scientists and experts, and arbitrarily dismiss them with many irrelevant criticisms. It does not conform with the values we have been promoting, that is, respect for knowledge, respect for science, and respect for intellectuals.[27]

Li's assertion that the opponents used "old slogans of the 1950s" may be an overstatement, but the scientific deductions on which the dissenting intellectuals formed their arguments did not rest on formalistic experiments conducted with advanced technical equipment. Rather, they based their standpoints upon their personal professional experiences combined with, in the case of the CPPCC delegates, field observations and interviews they made in the investigative tours in 1985 and 1988. A professor at Qinghua University, Huang Wanli, for example, was a steadfast opponent of the Three Gorges dam. He did not belong to the CPPCC, nor did he join the inspection tours. But with his experience and professional authority in geomorphology and hydraulic engineering, he articulated opposition to the project in collaboration with fellow dissidents in the newly opened-up channels until the end of his life. Some of his predictions, particularly regarding the potential siltation problems of the dam, turned out to be valid. Huang was born in 1911. His passion for hydraulic engineering brought him in the 1930s to Cornell University and the Engineering Institute of Illinois, where he earned a doctorate degree with the belief that for one to be a good hydraulic engineer, one had to also master astronomy, meteorology, hydrology, and topography. During his stay in the United States, he interned at the Tennessee Valley Authority, visited all the major hydropower works in the country, and sailed down the Mississippi River after its significant floods in 1936 to investigate the region's geological and hydrological conditions. After he returned to China, he surveyed the upstream tributaries of the Yangtze River, covering 3,000 kilometers in area on horseback, by boat, or on foot, and gained first-hand information about the river's topographic formation, hydraulic operations, and movement of sediments. In 1957, he opposed the construction of the

Sanmenxia Dam on the Yellow River under Mao and was labeled as a "rightist." His warning at the time that the dam would silt up and become dysfunctional in fifty years has now proven to be true. From the 1980s up until the end of his life in 2001, he objected to building a dam at the Three Gorges, arguing that the Yangtze's sediment – large amounts of gravel mixed with coarse sand, which is normally flushed down the river during floods and is carried to the estuary – would deposit in the backwater reach and block the Chongqing harbor when the river's flow was slowed by a dam at the Three Gorges.

Huang's contention was indicative of the tension embedded in the discourse of "scientific and democratic decision-making." Reassessing the project, the government conducted the *centralized co-optation* of a wide spectrum of professional personnel, analytical methods, and technical tools in institutions that embraced the officially privileged scientific knowledge. The authorities recognized dissent, with the objective that such an inclusion would bolster the credibility of the dam project and in turn the Party's authority. Yet this form of inclusive, or co-optive, practice contradicted the agenda of the dissenting intellectuals. The latter group insisted that their worldviews, experiences, and professional credentials were worthy of a more important place in the formulation of a Three Gorges scheme. They capitalized on the restoration of the intellectuals' status approved by the reformist regime and exploited the pluralized channels of expression for their articulations as assumed policy advisors. To them, incorporation, albeit in a centralized manner, should accommodate the possibility of supervision, opposition, and critique in the spirit of creative investigation and open inquiry.

In 1988, despite opposition, the feasibility study group released its final report and concluded that the "Three Gorges project is essential for China's Four Modernizations. It is technically feasible and economically reasonable. It is better to be built than not, and the earlier the better." The dissenting intellectuals contested the objectivity of the results and continued with the contestation over knowledge and power. In 1989, *A Second Discussion on the Marco Decision of the Three Gorges Dam Project* (*Zailun sanxia gongcheng de hongguan juece*) was published. Another book, *Yanggtze! Yangtze!* (*Changjiang! Changjiang!*), a collection of interviews conducted by a journalist, Dai Qing, further disseminated the dissenters' views. The opposition culminated in a proposal made by National People's Congress delegates in March, which called for a postponement of the project to the 21st century. In April, the Beijing leadership announced the suspension of the project for five years, which was hailed by the dissidents as a victory.

"Socialist democracy," as practiced in the Three Gorges debate, was part of the liberalization process in the 1980s in China. The regime's promotion of "democratic and scientific decision-making" as a general policy was answered by the public with political effects that spread across segments of society. To the extent that the official endorsement of independent entrepreneurial initiatives encouraged private choice and individual aspirations in the economic sphere, "socialist democracy" in official policy-making sanctioned open articulations and fostered popular expectations of free speech and public participation in government. The pluralization of interests and the emergence of autonomous associations led some scholars to believe that a civil society was in the making.[28] The mushrooming of public opinions and the ineffectual nature of conservative pushbacks in the course of the 1980s emboldened people's confidence that fundamental critiques of the system – not only under Mao but also about the reform policies – could be raised without significant political consequences.

By giving greater latitude for social associations and popular expressions, the authorities allowed views to be articulated and shared beyond the permissible limits. What had been meant as a prescription of political "salvation" from the collapsing socioeconomic order after the Cultural Revolution turned into people's uncontrollable quest for rights and freedoms. Liberalization culminated in the pro-democracy demonstrations in Beijing in the spring of 1989 against the fallout of reform. The protests extended to other parts of China and became across-the-board popular unrest. The military crackdown on June 4 consummated what Stuart Schram called the dialectical cycle of democratization and control characteristic of the politics under Deng.[29] Along with an economic retrenchment, the gunfire shut down all articulations of dissent, including those relating to the Three Gorges Dam proposal, which had been put on hold by the State Council two months earlier. The books were banned; editors of the dissenting journals, including the *Journal of Dialectics of Nature* underwent investigation; and some intellectuals, including Tian Fang and Dai Qing, were accused of "creating public opinions which led up to the bourgeois liberal turmoil and chaos."[30]

The Tiananmen crackdown marked what Foucault calls a "threshold of transformation" in China's development discourse. It shifted from inclusive participation to a muted, depoliticized formulation of progress, heavily tilted toward economic expansion. Such a shift took on its momentum in 1992 when Deng toured the south of China to revive the reforms. It was in this year that the Three Gorges scheme was brought back to the decision table and, with much fanfare, was formally endorsed by the National People's Congress. A discourse of "common prosperity" was re-introduced, with the dam positioned in the center as a perceived driving force for national marketization and material development – void of talks about democracy and inclusivity.

Notes

1 Deng Xiaoping, "Speech at an Enlarged Meeting of the Military Commission of the Central Committee of the Communist Party of China," in *Selected Works of Deng Xiaoping III (1982–1992)* (Beijing: Foreign Languages Press, 1994), 132.
2 Deng Xiaoping, "Zunzhong zhishi, zunzhong rencai" [Value Knowledge, Value Talents], in *Deng Xiaoping wenxuan (1975–1982) [Selected Works of Deng Xiaoping (1975–1982)]* (Renmin chubanshe, 1983), 37.
3 Deng, "Zunzhong zhishi, zunzhong rencai" [Value Knowledge, Value Talents].
4 Tony Saich, "Reform of China's Science and Technology Organizational System," in *Science and Technology in Post-Mao China*, ed. Denis Fred Simon and Merle Goldman (Cambridge, MA: Council on East Asian Studies, Harvard University: Distributed by Harvard University Press, 1989), 69–88.
5 Deng, "Zai quanguo kexue dahui kaimushi shang de jianghua" [Speech for the Opening Ceremony of the National Science Conference], in *Deng Xiaoping wenxuan (1975–1982) [Selected Works of Deng Xiaoping (1975–1982)]* (Renmin chubanshe, 1983), 84.

6 Deng, "Guanyu kexue he jiaoyu gongzuo de jidian yijian" [Remarks on the Work of Science and Education], in *Deng Xiaoping wenxuan (1975–1982) [Selected Works of Deng Xiaoping (1975–1982)]*, 47.
7 Denis Fred Simon, "China's Scientists and Technologists in the Post-Mao Era: A Retrospective and Prospective Glimpse," in *China's Intellectuals and the State: In Search of a New Relationship*, ed. Merle Goldman et al. (Cambridge, MA: Council on East Asian Studies, Harvard University: Distributed by the Harvard University Press, 1987), 141–142; and Richard P. Suttmeier, "Politics, Modernization, and Science in China," *Problems of Communism* (January–February 1980): 22–36.
8 Tang Tsou, "Back From the Brink of Revolutionary – 'Feudal' Totalitarianism," in *State and Society in Contemporary China*, ed. Victor Nee and David Mozingo (Ithaca: Cornell University Press, 1983), 67.
9 Deng, "Guanyu kexue he jiaoyu gongzuo de jidian yijian" [Remarks on the Work of Science and Education], in *Deng Xiaoping wenxuan (1975–1982) [Selected Works of Deng Xiaoping (1975–1982)]*, 51–55.
10 Suttmeier, "Politics, Modernization, and Science," 29.
11 Tsou, "Back From the Brink," 61–62.
12 Tang Tsou, "The Tiananmen Tragedy: The State-Society Relationship, Choices, and Mechanisms in Historical Perspective," in *Contemporary Chinese Politics in Historical Perspective*, ed. Brantly Womack (Cambridge University Press, 1991).
13 H. Lyman Miller, *Science and Dissent in Post-Mao China* (Seattle and London: University of Washington Press, 1996), 19.
14 Lyman Miller, *Science and Dissent in Post-Mao China*, 8–9.
15 Yi Li, "Minzhu, fazhi shi renxing suoxiang dashi suoqu" [Democracy and the Rule of Law is the Desire of the People and the Trend of the Times], *Liaowang* (1988).
16 Tsou, "Back From the Brink," 60.
17 Richard Baum, "The Road to Tiananmen: Chinese Politics in the 1980s," in *The Politics of China*, ed. Roderick MacFarquhar, 3rd ed. (Cambridge University Press, 2011), 408–410.
18 Wan Li, "Juece minzhuhua he kexuehua shi zhengzhitizhi gaige de yige zhongyao keti" [Democratic and Scientific Decision Making is an Important Task of the Political Reform], *Renmin Ribao [People's Daily]*, August 15, 1986.
19 Xiaotong Fei, "Wei juece minzhuhua he kexuehua tigong zhili zhichi" [Providing Intellectual Support for Democratic and Scientific Decision Making], *Qunyan*, January 1987.
20 Quoted in Tsou, "Back From the Brink," 74.
21 Guojie Chen, "Juece minzhuhua yu zhengdun lingdao zuofeng" [Democratic Decision Making and the Rectification of Leadership Style], *Qunyan*, October 1988.
22 Deng, "Guanyu kexue he jiaoyu gongzuo de jidian yijian" [Remarks on the Work of Science and Education], in *Deng Xiaoping wenxuan (1975–1982) [Selected Works of Deng Xiaoping (1975–1982)]*, 54–55.
23 Xiaodong Liu, *Sanxia da yimin [Three Gorges: Displaced Population]* (Beijing: Beijing yachang caise yinshua youxian gongsi, 2003), 26.
24 Fang Tian, Fatang Lin, and Chunxi Ling, eds., *Lun Sanxia gongcheng di hongguan juece [On the Macro Decision of the Three Gorges Dam Project]* (Changsha shi: Hunan kexue jishu chubanshe, 1987).
25 Yueqi Sun et al., "Chapter Five: Views and Suggestions on the Assessment Report of the Three Gorges Project – Written Statement Submitted to the Central Committee of the Chinese Communist Party by Ten Members of the Chinese People's Political Consultative Conference," in *Yangtze! Yangtze!* ed. Patricia Adams and John Thibodeau (English translation), editor-in-chief Dai Qing, Chinese ed. (London: Earthscan Publications Ltd.; Toronto: Earthscan Canada, 1994), 64–65.
26 Peiyuan Zhou, "Guanyu sanxia gongcheng de yixie wenti he jianyi" [Questions and Opinions About the Three Gorges Project], in *Changjiang sanxia gongcheng yingfou xingjian [Should the Yangtze Three Gorges Project Be Built?]*, ed. Dai Qing (Hong Kong: Zhongguo tushu kanxingshe, 1989), 10.

27 Boning Li, "Chapter Nine: Opinions and Recommendations on the Three Gorges Project – A Statement for the Third Session of the Seventh Standing Committee of the Chinese People's Political Consultative Conference," in *Yangtze! Yangtze!* ed. Patricia Adams and John Thibodeau (English translation), editor-in-chief Dai Qing, Chinese ed. (London: Earthscan Publications Ltd.; Toronto: Earthscan Canada), 102–103.
28 Martin K. Whyte, "Urban China: A Civil Society in the Making?" in *State and Society in China: The Consequences of Reform*, ed. Arthur Lewis Rosenbaum (Boulder: Westview Press, 1992), 77–102.
29 Stuart Schram, "Deng Xiaoping's Quest for 'Modernization with Chinese Characteristics' and the Future of Marxism-Leninism," in *China in the Era of Deng Xiaoping – a Decade of Reform*, ed. Michael Ying-Mao Kau and Susan H. Marsh (M.E. Sharpe, 1990), 408–433, and the idea of "three cycles" in Richard Baum, "The Road to Tiananmen: Chinese Politics in the 1980s," in *The Politics of China: Sixty Years of the People's Republic of China*, ed. Roderick MacFarquhar (New York: Cambridge University Press, 2011).
30 Author's interviews, August 1998.

Bibliography

Baum, Richard. 2011. "The Road to Tiananmen: Chinese Politics in the 1980s." In *The Politics of China: Sixty Years of the People's Republic of China*, edited by Roderick MacFarquhar. Cambridge University Press.

Chen, Guojie. 1988. "Juece minzhuhua yu zhengdun lingdao zuofeng" [Democratic Decision Making and the Rectification of Leadership Style]. *Qunyan*, October.

Deng, Xiaoping. 1983. *Deng Xiaoping wenxuan (1975–1982) [Selected Works of Deng Xiaoping (1975–1982)]*. Renmin chubanshe.

Deng, Xiaoping. 1994. *Selected Works of Deng Xiaoping III (1982–1992)*. Beijing: Foreign Languages Press.

Fei, Xiaotong. 1987. "Wei juece minzhuhua he kexuehua tigong zhili zhichi" [Providing Intellectual Support for Democratic and Scientific Decision Making]. *Qunyan*, January.

Li, Boning. 1994. "Opinions and Recommendations on the Three Gorges Project – A Statement for the Third Session of the Seventh Standing Committee of the Chinese People's Political Consultative Conference." In *Yangtze! Yangtze!* edited by Dai Qing (Chinese edition) and Patricia Adams and John Thibodeau (English translation). London: Earthscan Publications Ltd.; Toronto: Earthscan Canada.

Liu, Xiaodong. 2003. *Sanxia da yimin [Three Gorges: Displaced Population]*. Beijing yachang caise yinshua youxian gongsi.

Miller, H. Lyman. 1996. *Science and Dissent in Post-Mao China*. Seattle and London: University of Washington Press.

Saich, Tony. 1989. "Reform of China's Science and Technology Organizational System." In *Science and Technology in Post-Mao China*, edited by Denis Fred Simon and Merle Goldman. Cambridge, MA: Council on East Asian Studies, Harvard University: Distributed by Harvard University Press.

Schram, Stuart. 1993. "Deng Xiaoping's Quest." In *China in the Era of Deng Xiaoping – a Decade of Reform*, edited by Michael Ying-Mao Kau and Susan H. Marsh. Armonk, NY: M.E. Sharpe.

Simon, Denis Fred. 1987. "China's Scientists and Technologists in the Post-Mao Era: A Retrospective and Prospective Glimpse." In *China's Intellectuals and the State: In Search of a New Relationship*, edited by Merle Goldman et al. Cambridge, MA: Council on East Asian Studies, Harvard University: Distributed by the Harvard University Press.

Sun, Yueqi et al. 1994. "Views and Suggestions on the Assessment Report of the Three Gorges Project – Written Statement Submitted to the Central Committee of the Chinese Communist Party by Ten Members of the CPPCC." In *Yangtze! Yangtze!* edited by Dai Qing (Chinese edition) and Patricia Adams and John Thibodeau (English translation). London: Earthscan Publications Ltd.; Toronto: Earthscan Canada.

Suttmeier, Richard P. 1980. "Politics, Modernization, and Science in China." *Problems of Communism* (January–February): 22–36.

Tian, Fang, Lin, Fatang, and Ling, Chunxi, ed. 1987. *Lun Sanxia gongcheng di hongguan juece [On the Macro Decision of the Three Gorges Dam Project]*. Changsha: Hunan kexue jishu chubanshe.

Tsou, Tang. 1983. "Back From the Brink of Revolutionary – 'Feudal' Totalitarianism." In *State and Society in Contemporary China*, edited by Victor Nee and David Mozingo. Ithaca: Cornell University Press.

Tsou, Tang. 1991. "The Tiananmen Tragedy: The State-Society Relationship, Choices, and Mechanisms in Historical Perspective." In *Contemporary Chinese Politics in Historical Perspective*, edited by Brantly Womack. Cambridge University Press.

Wan, Li. 1986. "Juece minzhuhua he kexuehua shi zhengzhitizhi gaige de yige zhongyao keti" [Democratic and Scientific Decision Making is an Important Task of the Political Reform]. *Renmin Ribao [People's Daily]*, August 15.

Whyte, Martin K. 1992. "Urban China: A Civil Society in the Making?" In *State and Society in China: The Consequences of Reform*, edited by Arthur Lewis Rosenbaum. Boulder: Westview Press.

Yi, Li. 1988. "Minzhu, fazhi shi renxing suoxiang dashi suoqu" [Democracy and the Rule of Law Is the Desire of the People and the Trend of the Times]. *Liaowang.*

Zhou, Peiyuan. 1989. "Guanyu sanxia gongcheng de yixie wenti he jianyi" [Questions and Opinions about the Three Gorges Project]. In *Changjiang sanxia gongcheng yingfou xingjian [Should the Yangtze Three Gorges Project Be Built?]*, edited by Dai Qing. Hong Kong: Zhongguo tushu kanxingshe.

4 "Common Prosperity"

Spatial Production and Subject Transformation at the Three Gorges

After the military repression of June 4, 1989, China entered a period of political and economic retrenchment. Discussions on the meaning of "democracy" were silenced. Political dissent, including that regarding the Three Gorges proposal, was suppressed under the premise of combating "bourgeois liberalization," which Beijing considered a main cause of the pro-democracy protests. Economic reforms lost their momentum and gave way to "economic readjustment and rectification," emphasizing stability along the conservative line.

For at least three years after the crackdown, China struggled to redefine its development path. Deng adopted a clear profile of endorsing the military action, but he was adamant that economic reforms had to be pushed forward, although now without sanctioned liberalization. But the hardliners within the Party, upon the quelling of the student protests, gained power and rolled back the reforms, with the "planned economy as primary, [and] the market economy supplementary." It was not until the spring of 1992 that Deng consolidated his political clout to stage a comeback, this time with a revised, and more aggressive, developmental scheme.[1]

His famous southern tour signaled the beginning of China's move toward a more vigorous phase of economic reconfiguration. The "socialist market economy," introduced in June 1992 by the new Party General Secretary Jiang Zemin, went steps further than the "socialist planned commodity economy" Deng and the ousted party chief Zhao Ziyang had sponsored in 1984.[2] It was an economic system unprecedented in any communist society.[3] It formally recognized the role of the market despite the upholding of planning, which would nevertheless gradually diminish and arrive at the limiting of the state's function to macroeconomic management. Reform and opening up in Deng's vision once again held sway in China's political discourse, this time being "aimed at *fundamentally* changing the economic structure rather than patching it up," which was stated as the formal party line in the Fourteenth Party Congress report in that year.[4]

From that moment onward, China entered a new phase of socioeconomic transformation in the direction of marketization. Chinese society underwent significant change not only in the economic setup but also in the political institutions, intellectual orientations, and social activities. The paradigmatic shift in the late 1970s from Maoist utopian radicalism to *liberalizing developmentalism* in the form of

DOI: 10.4324/9781003531494-5

experimental economic opening now turned into *comprehensive marketism* implicating all segments of society in all geographical sites within China.

Discursively, with the all-out marketization, China experienced what Foucault calls a "threshold of transformation" in its development discourse.[5] "Democracy" totally dropped out of the picture of official utterances. "Science" shed the connotation of an impartial decision-making practice and assumed a more prominent meaning of technical knowhow imported from developed countries, which was integral to the formation of markets. The concept of "common prosperity" (*gongfu*), a guiding rationale of the reforms that emerged in the early 1980s, was emphasized in the 1990s in connection with the new notion of "socialist market economy." These two ideas, together with the institutions and practices projected to be established, formed the context in which the "Yangtze development strategy" was introduced and trumpeted. Altogether, they provided the developmental milieu in which the Three Gorges Dam received a redefined position in China's new socioeconomic formulation. It was in 1992, the year when Deng conducted his southern tour and Jiang propounded the concept of "socialist markets," that the dam project was formally tabled at the National People's Congress and given approval. The construction scheme was thereafter incorporated into the exercise of China's market formation, in that a regional center of resource circulation was conceived to be constituted, a developed space to be produced, and modern, rich subjects to be formed – all at the Three Gorges as an embedded part of the overall development schema.

To understand the reproduction of the development ideology through people's lived experiences, we need to explore how gorge displacees would conduct their life in the newly built environment with the kind of subjectivity the Chinese state has worked to produce. However, before we look into the material practices of the resettlers, we will first examine the concept of "common prosperity" as a state strategy to reconcile the contradictions, as mentioned in Chapter 2, of wealth disparity, social polarization, and distributive injustice that intensified as the Chinese economy grew rapidly. After that, the analysis will move on to the Three Gorges project as a key instantiation of the development idea through spatial production and the attempted engendering of modern subjects by means of the everyday practices of dam relocatees. In the end, we will examine the effectiveness of the ideological reproduction of development through an exploration of the resettlers' actual experiences in the process of subject transformation.

"Common Prosperity"

As economic restructuring proceeded, the social polarization that Deng tried so hard to guard against – in his rhetoric – was emerging as a social reality. "Common prosperity" or "shared wealth" (*gongfu*) was invoked in his speeches in the 1980s as a personal vision and the Party's policy objective. From the late 1980s onward and especially in the 1990s, this notion became increasingly prominent in the face of widening income disparity. Serving a political function as an ideology that glossed over the rift between the rich and the poor by putting the haves and have-nots on the leveled plane of shared desire, "common prosperity" was represented as society's collective ideal. It was discussed in public discourse in conjunction with a new development concept – the "Yangtze economic zone" (*Changjiang jingjidai*) or "Yangtze development strategy" (*Changjiang fazhan zhanlue*).

The dual concepts of "common prosperity" and "Yangtze development strategy" were given numerous intellectual explications in official narratives. Wen Qiangzhou, an economist who was awarded by the Central Propaganda Bureau for his article on Deng's development idea, explained that "common prosperity" consisted of two primary propositions: the "priority rich" (*xianfu*) thesis and the "fellow assistance" (*zhaogu zuolin youshe*) notion.[6] The former allowed a certain group of people in certain regions of China to get rich under the reforms before the others. Using international competition as a premise, Wen argued that China would have difficulty catching up with the developed countries if the selective priority policy was not adopted. Given the historical discrepancy between the eastern and western parts of China in material terms, he wrote, the overall progress of China would be dragged down if both the coastal and inland areas were developed at the same pace. China would proceed faster on the modernization trajectory if the eastern seaboard were given priority to accumulate wealth. The rich group, in both demographic and geographical terms, would then provide a basis for the development of the backward inland areas. "Fellow assistance" would enable capital and technical know-how to be shared in the form of aid, economic cooperation zones, or coastal/riverfront opening-up, thereby expanding the rich area from east to west and from south to north.

Key to the fellow assistance thesis, or the overall common prosperity conception, was the identification of the Yangtze River as a "strategic carrying-pole region" (*zhanlue biandan diqu*). After initial success with the special economic zones in the south, in the Seventh Five Year Plan (1986–1990) the government defined the developmental relationship between the eastern, central and western parts of China. It was decided that the eastern coast would be opened up not only to overseas investment but also to central and western China in terms of market share and resource allocation. The Yangtze River, with its geographical position cutting through the east-west axis and its tributary coverage extending through the north-south network, would act as a focal development zone where all the riverfront settlements would be opened up for industrialization and marketization. Wen wrote:

> Deng Xiaoping is concerned that . . . a total dependence on the eastern priority rich zone will not provide an adequate condition [for common prosperity]. It is only by mobilizing the potentials of both the east and west, making use of the geographical advantages of both parts, and highlighting a horizontal zone as a development focal point which combines the favorable circumstances of both regions, that we can convert the east-west ladder-like vertical transfer to a horizontal harmonious synthesis and change the simplistic one-to-one blood-transmission-styled aid to blood-generating open cooperation.[7]

The Yangtze was identified as this "horizontal focal development zone" in that it acted as a "carrying pole" that strategically bore Shanghai on the east end and

Chongqing on the west. It linked up fourteen major cities in the Yangtze River Delta along the coast with another fourteen cities in the river's upper and middle reaches in the inland, supporting 15 percent of China's population and 20 percent of the country's GNP. The Yangtze, considered to have sufficient potential, was trumpeted as crucial in realizing China's "common prosperity" and playing a strategic role in the country's modernization.

Wen's exposition constituted a small part of the broader "Yangtze development strategy." Also involved were top leaders' speeches, bureaucrats' meetings, the establishment of new institutions, and large-scale construction work. Deng, believing that Shanghai was key to his reform blueprints, expressed regret during his southern tours in 1991 and 1992 that he had not included Shanghai in the earliest special economic zones. "If Shanghai had been included," he said, "the situation with regard to reform and opening in the Yangtze Delta, the entire Yangtze River valley and, indeed, the whole country would be quite different."[8] At the end of 1992, developing the Yangtze became a formal party line as the Fourteenth Party Congress endorsed the pursuit of a "Yangtze economic zone." The party endorsement came at a time when meetings were also held by the State Council to decide that hi-tech, high-value-added, export-oriented industries would be built up in accordance with market principles in the Yangtze River Delta; the Pudong District was thereafter open to foreign investment to be produced as the new industrial and commercial core of Shanghai, and the whole of Shanghai would be given priority to develop into an international financial and trading center, thereby leading other cities on the Yangtze riverfront to an economic takeoff. The Three Gorges Dam and its reservoir, located in the middle and upper reaches of the river, were conceived to form a regional market that would facilitate the circulation of labor, capital, and information. Considered an important component of the "Yangtze development strategy," the dam project would engender a new set of social relations. This will be the subject of detailed examination in the next section.

It is noteworthy that conceptions of the "Yangtze economic zone" were numerous and variegated. Among the geometric and figurative theorizations – for example, H-shape tactics, three-ring stratification, 1.5 focal point thesis, and ox-belly theory – the T-shape development strategy was the most prominent and widely discussed.[9] It conceived the coastal region as the horizontal stroke of the letter and the Yangtze as the vertical line, taking both as the axes of China's open-policy structure with the river acting as a "motor" and a "radiator" of economic growth. Involved would be a "Yangtze commercial corridor," where material resources, labor, and commodities would circulate along with a to-be-established network of transportation and telecommunication. This "corridor" would coincide with a zone that embraced a base of energy supply, agribusiness, industrial manufacturing, and tertiary services. These would constitute a part of the market-building process of riverfront cities, where development banks, trusts, and listed companies were to be formed in a new financial and investment structure. The projection was that all these would become fully grown within twenty to thirty years, recreating the Yangtze as one of the most significant inland river economic zones in the world and the largest in the Asia-Pacific region. Such an idea was based on the deduction that the world's economic focus had experienced westward shifts – from Europe to the Atlantic seaboard of North America onto its Pacific coast and then to Japan. In the late 20th and the first half of the 21st centuries, Chinese intellectuals argued, China would be the center of global growth and the mediating point of east-west economic synthesis. "In order to seize this opportunity," wrote Sun Shangqing, "and ensure rapid growth, it is essential to seek out, nurture, and develop a new and sustainable economic region."[10] The Yangtze, given its central geographical position and perceived material potentials, was considered the primary candidate for the role.

Fascinating or dizzying as they are, the variegated conceptualizations of the new Yangtze space are abstracted propositions imbued with development ideology and scientific knowledge – what Henri Lefebvre calls "representations of space."

> "[They are] conceptualized space, the space of scientists, planners, urbanists, technocratic subdividers and social engineers, as of a certain type of artists with a scientific bent – all of whom identify what is lived and what is perceived with what is conceived."[11]

In the case of the Yangtze strategy, the postulated models were formulated with perspectives encompassing statistical, geometric, and politico-economic configurations. Contributing to this discourse were intellectuals ranging from physicists to economists and a former mayor, who, with their institutional affiliations (including universities and research academies) and socially recognized titles (such as state awards for published theses), put forward imaginary representations under the ideological premises of "common prosperity," generalizable wealth expansion, and global material advancement. These intellectual formulations were conceived and might not have had a material existence (except that they were manifested in the form of paper and signs, verbal and nonverbal). But they gained material import by virtue of their being bound up with the actual production of the space they envisioned by indicating, informing, and directing that production process. The contemporary intellectuals' conceptions had a direct impact on social practice in that they were made "real" in part by the development of the Pudong District in Shanghai and the building of the Three Gorges Dam involving, inter alia, the relocation of villagers and the construction of new urban settlements. Moreover, the space to be created would be reproduced by people's activities in their everyday lives. They would inhabit that space, work in it, reproduce offspring and other social relationships, and die in it.

Although people would experience the modernized space as its users, their subjectivities were excluded from the idealized representations. The exclusion of people's agency was congruent with the abstracting effects of the "common prosperity" ideology, which entailed an imposed meaning of human experiences in temporal terms. Under the perceived collective ideal of "common prosperity," represented by the Party as obtainable, every form of human suffering caused by the reforms was rendered ephemeral: unemployment was a momentary byproduct of corrective adjustments of the economy; social communities broke up only to re-cohere as modern settlements; and inequality was a necessary but temporary transition to the envisioned eventual egalitarian distribution. These future visions of the economy, social organization, and wealth possession turned the existing harsh reality into a dream of plenty and imminent pain into prospective happiness (note the oft-used watchword "stepping out of poverty and getting rich" in official narratives). The ephemerality of people's current sacrifices and the obtainability of the prosperity dream – the *hope* – served as the presumed, and therefore justifiably unsaid, basis of the intellectual conceptualizations. Simultaneously, those sacrifices and dreams were made subservient to the conceived configurations which pushed everything, including people and their lives, into a secondary position in order for the economic work to take place.

Production of the "Yangtze Economic Zone"

For the Yangtze development strategy to be realized, the Three Gorges Dam project was considered a crucial component that would help catalyze the construction of inland transportation and telecommunication networks, draw financial capital to build up corporatized industries, and circulate resources for the establishment of commodity and financial markets in the region. Be it the "carrying pole" thesis, "ox-belly" theory, or "T-shape" strategy, the dam scheme was given a central position, along with Shanghai's Pudong District, in the developmental vision of China's modernization.

If the conceptual expositions were what Lefebvre calls *representations of space*, the building of the dam and all the construction work in relation to it – financial, industrial, and urban development – involved what he refers to as the *production of social space* in the inland Yangtze area.[12] *Space* in this sense is not simply a geographical site where people inhabit and conduct their productive activities, although it is the location where social events take place. It subsumes objects – including humans – and things; most of all, it embodies social relations of production and reproduction, embedding networks and circuits of exchange. The emphasis on social relations as a major constituent of *space* is reminiscent of the "disposition of things" under Foucault's governmentality. Both "space" and "things" embody not only physical objects but also the *relations* that connect the objects and the dynamic changes that may occur in their relationships. If we take into consideration that *space* is simultaneously the product and medium of social activities ("Itself the outcome of past actions, social space is what permits fresh actions to occur"[13]), what enables the dynamic change in social relations is *space* itself. That is to say, when "fresh actions" are introduced into *space*, the things, their arrangement, and thereby their relations may be altered and thence a new (or transformed) social space is produced. Insomuch as *space* is at once the medium and product of social activities, the production, reproduction, and differential modifications of existing and new spaces imply a process. *Space* encompasses that process – being enabled by the process, space also makes it possible.[14]

Although the main agent of the generation of social space is day-to-day users – the people – space is indelibly imbued with state power through "a multiplicity of rational institutions ranging from the bureaucracy, . . . to units of economic development, . . . and cultural production."[15] Before the dam project, people's daily activities had engendered a certain social space with the administrative support of the state apparatus. When it came to the construction of a mega-dam and production of an urban space at the Three Gorges – a "high-modernist" project, in the words of James Scott, of massive environmental and social engineering – the level of state intervention was very high. From the designation of the site at Sandouping to the planning of object distribution (such as the dam, the humans, familial settlements, and industrial patterning) to the construction of the built environment (roads, bridges, telecommunication networks, and further, the circuits of exchange of raw materials, manufactured commodities, capital, and information), it was a systematic *creation* of modern space. The governmentality of (re)ordering "things" for a rational state agenda was fully played out here. Take Yichang – the city where the dam is located – for example. It was originally a rural river port; with the Party's developmentalistic arrangements around the dam, Yichang grew into the second largest city within Hubei Province with over 4.1 million people, two universities, and the hub of an inter-provincial infrastructure network, including an airport. Yichang was singled out in the 13th Five Year Plan as the key regional city of central China. In 2017, the city was made into a Pilot Free Trade Zone in the Yangtze Economic Area, specializing in productive activities including biomedicine, digital information, and cross-border e-commerce.[16] (Figures 4.1 and 4.2)

Figure 4.1 Yichang city center (Taken by author, 2015)

Figure 4.2 Yichang railway station (Taken by author, 2015)

The story of Yichang was not an isolated case in the reconfigured river valley. At the Three Gorges, old towns underwent various forms of transformation, ranging from partial rebuilding upslope to total destruction through inundation, all to make way for modern settlements to be constructed in the new social space. (See Figures 4.3, 4.4, and 4.5.) Table 4.1 illustrates the resettlement work, industrial repatterning, and infrastructural constructions up until June 2008, all orchestrated by the state to make way for the new Three Gorges space.

The agents, or "mediators," who carried out the (re)arrangement of material objects (including humans) and reorganization of social relations comprised the Chinese state (such as technocrats, planners, and engineers) who designed, rebuilt, and coordinated the development work. A second group of "mediators" who participated in the daily role of reproducing the space were the people who live, work, and die there – with the (reformed) consciousness of modern subjects. Arguing that the state actors and local residents applied their "social labor" and reconfigured the Three Gorges area does not mean that such "mediation" took place in a purely natural site without prior human intervention. Through the centuries, people had worked on the land and created various forms of institutions, productive activities, and familial organizations, which had accumulated and transformed up to the point where the contemporary Chinese state intervened with the scientific knowledge and developmentalist ideology it prioritized. Space, itself a product of social activities, served as the medium in which "fresh actions" were applied to transform the area into a new social space. (Figures 4.6 and 4.7)

Figure 4.3 Demolition of old settlements (Getty Images)

Figure 4.4 Replaced with a new urban space upslope (Taken by author, 2015)

Figure 4.5 With a new network of roads, bridges, and river ports (Taken by author, 2015)

Table 4.1 Three Gorges Project Resettlement as of June 2008

Items	*Planned*	*Completed*
Number of rural resettlers to be displaced	550,600	518,300
Number of rural resettlers with production resettlement	568,600	546,600
Rural housing reconstruction (thousand m2)	14,157.80	12,137.60
Number of urban resettlers to be displaced	694,900	662,800
Urban housing reconstruction (thousand m2)	22,057	20,715.90
Number of factories to be relocated, bankrupted or closed	1599	1629
Building reconstruction for inundated factories (thousand m2)	7440.30	7385.50
Graded roads (km)	819.97	1265.50
Large bridges (m)	29,160	18,137.35
Wharfs and ports	188	314
Power transmission lines (km)	3832.60	3832.60
Telecommunication lines (km)	3465.36	3465.36
Broadcasting and television lines (km)	4191.03	4191.03
Cultural relics protection projects	364	364

Source: "The Assessment Report on the Feasibility Study of the Three Gorges Project Resettlement" by China Academy of Engineering (CAE), published in Yuefang Duan & Brooke Wilmsen, "Addressing the Resettlement Challenges at the Three Gorges Project," *International Journal of Environmental Studies*, 69:3 (2012): 464. Reprinted by permission of Taylor & Francis Ltd.

Figure 4.6 Fengjie before inundation (Author's collection)

Figure 4.7 The new city of Fengjie (Taken by author, 2015)

The space produced at the Three Gorges, moreover, was not to be a localized space: it was not simply a practice of development in a confined site; its significance was conceived to extend beyond the Three Gorges and the Yangtze to encompass the whole of China's industrialized space, as the intellectual explications of "common prosperity" indicated. Besides new bridges and tunnels that connected local places across the river and through the gorges, a network of highways and railroads was built to link up cities in the reservoir area, such as Chongqing and Yichang, to urban centers in the east (for example, Shanghai) and the west (such as Chengdu)[17] (Figure 4.8).

The pathways of circulation in and beyond the Three Gorges also co-extended to the circuits of power supply. Upon completion in 2010, the Three Gorges' hydropower generation capacity was 84.7 billion kW/h, enough to supply electricity to energy-deficient central and eastern China as well as Sichuan Province in the west. Given its location, the Three Gorges also served as the confluence point of existing separate regional power grids. From 2010, the electricity transmission systems of central, eastern, and western China, for which the dam was designed to provide energy, have linked up with that of the southern region and further with the northeast, north, and northwest to form an integrated nationwide power network (Figure 4.9). This scheme precipitated the development of more hydroelectric production in the western inland, entailing the construction of a series of new dams there, some of which will be taller than the Three Gorges, on the upper tributaries of the Yangtze. The overall electricity scheme was not only designed to power China's growing industries and the modern lifestyle of residential consumers in the urban centers, but it was also planned to enable the economic reform of the

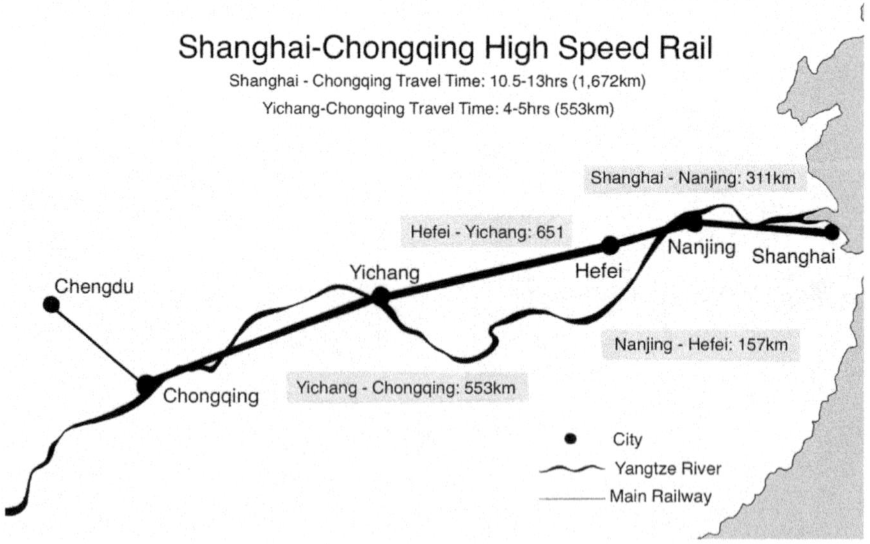

Figure 4.8 Shanghai – Chongqing high-speed train map (Provided by Nicholas Sharifi)

hinterland as part of the Great Western Development drive (*xibu dakaifa*). Tapping the area's hydropower, which was considered uneconomically under capacity, the West would bring in new investment for new industries. Qinghai, for example, the province adjacent to Tibet, which was among the least exploited, has become a new focal point of multinational corporations in gold mining, hydroelectricity generation, and natural gas production.[18]

The "objects" that were reordered as a result of the Three Gorges megaproject encompassed not only material things (the people, infrastructure, houses, and farmland, among others) but also the "networks and pathways" that facilitate the circulation and exchange of things. This process involved transformation, but it also entailed the production of new circuits of exchange, and new relations, among social actors in the space. From a predominantly agricultural economy to an urban-industrial society, the Three Gorges area witnessed the engendering of more capitalist and corporatized relations of production and less tightly knitted, kinship-oriented social fabrics.

One of the factors that enabled the production of such social relations was the flow of capital for the restructuring of existing economic units and the establishment of new ones. In 1998, the then premier Zhu Rongji revoked the State Council's original decision of preserving gorge enterprises and relocating them within the reservoir area.[19] According to his policy of "adjusting the economic structure" applied nationwide, state enterprises that were in debt, had irreversible deficit, or caused serious pollution would be subject to closure or bankruptcy. These also

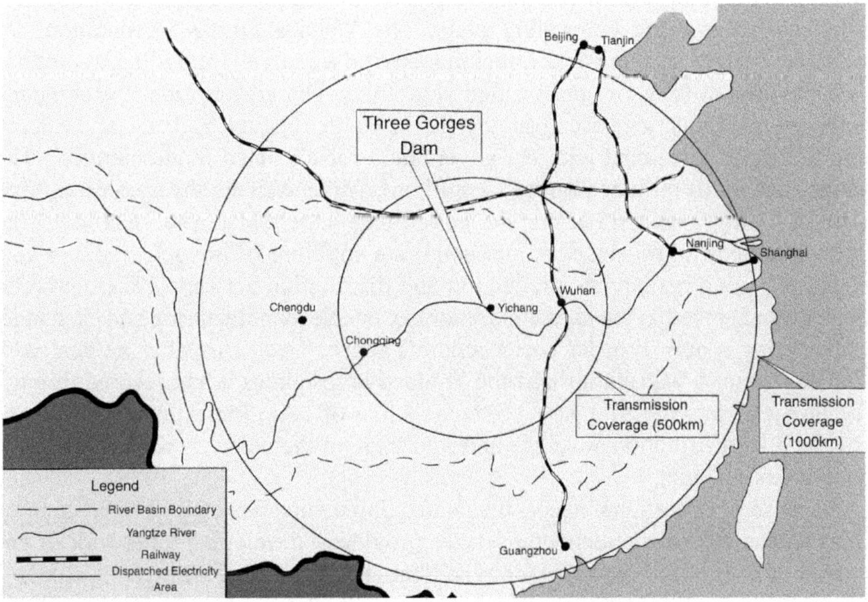

Figure 4.9 Zones of electricity transmission from the Three Gorges power plant (Provided by Nicholas Sharifi)

included factories whose equipment was too old to catch up with the modern scale of production and whose products were of too low quality to compete in the market. Besides bankruptcy and liquidation, the enterprises would also undergo mergers, auctions, or shareholding reforms. The principles of evaluation were productivity and profitability. Because the Three Gorges industries were of small scale and used low-tech machinery producing commodities of low demand – features that in every respect did not measure up to the requirements of market competition – most of the enterprises were considered economically inefficacious. In the county of Fengjie, for example, 94 of the 114 enterprises with a total staff size of 20,214 that were originally scheduled to relocate within the river valley were either liquidated or restructured to become parts of larger companies.[20] In the whole of Hubei Province and Chongqing Municipality, which accommodated most of the resettled population, 1,013 out of the 1,559 enterprises planned to be relocated were either declared bankrupt or closed down.[21]

A majority of the industrial units in the Three Gorges area had been state-owned, collective, or township enterprises. With the economic restructuring, the ownership pattern of these businesses became different. Many surviving enterprises were joined under merger with big corporations, which were headquartered in the more developed urban centers and had established a substantial market share. Their collaborations in the form of shareholding were made under the state arrangement of the Partnership Support Program (*dui kou zhi yuan*), a policy aimed at transferring capital, production techniques, and management methods from the modern industrial establishments on the coast to the economic backwaters at the Three Gorges. Upon merger, the private companies assumed a bigger share in ownership and became the controlling party. The Wahaha Drinks Corporation, for example, bought up three deficit-making enterprises in 1994 in Fuling to produce fruit-flavored milk, wine, and pickled vegetables. Three years later, the company extended its production base to another Three Gorges county, Yichang, and entered into a merger agreement with the government for a canned food enterprise. The county put in 40 million yuan ($6.2 million), while Wahaha invested 60 million yuan ($9.3 million) and became the controlling shareholder. The local industrial units thus became subsumed in the corporate structure of a much larger private business having nationwide production and distribution networks. The new relations further served as the medium of more extensive manufacturing and exchange, engendering a new, broader socioeconomic space. Two years after its deal with Yichang county, Wahaha utilized the productive resources it had secured through the mergers, introduced a new production line of cola drinks, and further consolidated its distribution coverage and sale share in the newly exploited market in southwestern China.[22]

Because of operational needs, the controlling companies often formed connections with material suppliers and service providers, developing a network of circulation that radiated far and wide. The Shanghai White Cat Detergent Company, for instance, merged with the sluggish May First Chemical Company in Sichuan Province to form the White Cat Chongqing Limited Company. Besides its own growth, White Cat brought sales and profits to the connected businesses in Sichuan,

Chongqing, and Hubei through its purchases of sulfuric acid, color printing, and packing boxes.[23] The network, which encompassed circuits of production, consumption, and the exchange of raw materials, finished products, and information, was not confined to industrial manufacturing. Yunyang county, a major agricultural producer in the Three Gorges area, underwent the formation of a cluster of produce suppliers (the farmers), local distribution and sales agents, and a national-scale corporation. This was intended to be, according to official reports, a strategy to transform the county's mode of economy into agribusiness able to strike a position in the Chinese market. In 1996, Weisang Corporation, one of the ten largest food-processing companies in China, agreed to build its factory of soy drink mix in Yunyang's new industrial park. To cater to Weisang's demand, the county had to produce 1,200 tons of soybeans, which was a difficult task with regard to its original pattern of production. The farming, distribution, and marketing of beans in the county had never been systematically organized. The size of the beans had been small, and productivity had been low. Besides using the produce for domestically consumed tofu, individual growers had sold their surplus production in local markets at low prices. To meet the purchase demand of Weisang, the county commissioned 4,800 households on a contract basis to grow a new strain of big soybeans. These farming units were linked up with a network of supply and marketing cooperatives in twenty townships. The chain of production, distribution, and sale was hence established. With satisfactory returns, Weisang decided not only to expand the processing line of soybeans (which eventually involved 21,000 farming households) but also to build its own Three Gorges industrial park to produce over sixty types of commodities, including wine, herbal medicine, and processed meat. The presence of the corporation consequently became significant, almost dominant: the estimated taxes Weisang paid were more than four times that of Yunyang's original countywide revenue in 1997, and job opportunities the company offered made up one-eighth of the county's relocated population.[24]

In official narratives, the companies from the cities were celebrated for their contribution to transforming the gorge economy through the Partnership Support Program, but it is clear to the reader that a hierarchical relationship was formed between the corporate newcomers and local productive units. Yichang, among other counties, was promoted as a showcase of development in the Three Gorges area. Following Wahaha Drinks, a series of corporations specializing in merchandise ranging from cigarettes to fruit juice and range hoods established manufacturing bases in the county. The resources these companies had – capital, production techniques, organizational know-how, and established market share – were considered what the Three Gorges enterprises needed to become modern. These resources, however, enabled the big companies to have a superior position in their relationship with the gorge economic units – a relationship based more upon patronage and dependency than the "mutual benefits and complimentary advantage" (*huhui huli, youshi hubu*) that the central policy of Partnership Support Program promised. The uneven and skewed character of the social relations produced in this respect was well illustrated in the case of Weisang's soy drink mix in Yunyang county. To persuade Weisang to install its production line in Yunyang, the county's Party secretary visited its headquarters "several times" in Xuzhou. When the county head heard that Weisang's president had come to a neighboring county to attend a conference, he went there and "waited for three days," finally convincing him to come to Yunyang and promising all the possible investment incentives the county could offer. "With [the county's expression of] utmost sincerity," it was reported, Weisang decided to build its soy drink mix factory in Yunyang.[25]

Changing the organizational mode of the productive units, economic restructuring also severed the original enterprise-worker relations and exposed the workers to the emerging market as free-floating agents. As previously mentioned, many of the enterprises in the river valley had been state-owned before the dam project, providing an "iron rice bowl" for the employees. The closures, bankruptcies, and mergers of the state enterprises devastated the jobs as well as welfare prospects for the workers. Their relations with the work units as employees or "danwei" members were thus discontinued. During the critical moment of the state's "economic structure adjustment," laid-off workers situated in the Three Gorges were given three options after receiving a lump-sum compensation. First, they would select a private company and, upon its agreement, become its workers as well as shareholders using the compensation; second, they would team up or individually initiate their own business in the form of a shareholding or limited company; and third, they would join the labor market as free agents to seek employment.[26] All of the options required the workers to find their own positions in the market setup, a new and revolutionary (coining the words of Deng) experience China and its people underwent in the process of development.

Changes in the social relations between the gorge residents and their communities were twofold. Whether they were farmers living with close family ties or workers serving as "unit" members of their state enterprises, they were subjected to relocation and being uprooted from the land or "danwei" they were working in. As premier Zhu announced the plan of economic restructuring he also decided that the original scheme of resettling all the gorge villagers within the reservoir area would be revoked because of the shortage of good land. Some people would be displaced uphill after the inundation, while others would move to faraway provinces up to hundreds of miles away. Communities that were organized around kinships would be broken up; farmers would have to either start a new farm on infertile slopes uphill or give up farming to seek jobs in factories or construction sites; and workers would quit their "danwei" and get employment in a new corporatized environment or compete in the market as small entrepreneurs. Being placed in a new set of social relations in the economic sphere because of the structural change, the gorge residents were simultaneously transposed to a new set of social relations in the new communities they were relocated to, in or outside the Yangtze Valley.

The Three Gorges experience was exemplary of what transpired in the whole of China as the "satanic mill"[27] of the market advanced. As marketization unfolded, all aspects of societal organization were drawn in and changed in accordance with the capitalist form of production, organization, and living in general. What the gorge residents went through demonstrated in a magnified and perhaps dramatic way the destruction of old social relations and reconstruction of new ones through the introduction of corporate capital, new modes of production, the breakup of knitted communities, and the human-land or human-human relationships.

Complicating the picture was the transmutation of people's values and self-understanding in connection with the new social structure. As the dam project developed, a new subjectivity on the part of Three Gorges resettlers was engendered through their everyday practice. The daily activities of living, working, and organizing life in general transformed and at the same time reproduced the space. These activities intersected with the countless circuits and pathways of production, consumption, and exchange in the newly built environment, enabling people to make sense of their position in the new space and regenerating their subjectivity as the modern workers, urban dwellers, and citizens of an industrialized nation. These daily practices, carrying the meaning of *progress*, ideologically brought people and their lives one step closer to the imagined scenario of "common prosperity" and further the "Chinese Dream" on the path of modernization.

Interpellation of the Modern Subject

What characterizes the development process of China is not simply industrialization, urbanization, and capitalist formations. At the center and overarching the development practice is the idea of "salvation," which underpins the logic of *political theodicy*. In the Three Gorges resettlement discourse, the phrase "step out of poverty and get rich" (*tuopin zhifu*) was ubiquitous. Purportedly, poverty was a state of misery that one would want to break away from at the expense of present sacrifices such as unemployment and involuntary displacement. Motivating the break – and hence justifying the sacrifice – would be the hope for future riches that the Party promised to deliver.

Poverty in the official narratives was not defined in merely quantitative terms such as one's income; it comprised, among others, the kind of house one lived in, the way one cooked, the type of work one did, and the means by which one commuted. "Poverty," in other words, denoted a way of life that was experienced by the villagers before the inundation – a mode of living that was diametrically opposed to what was considered "rich," "developed," and "modern." The manifested way of life was not confined to one's condition of living in their private space; it also involved the built environment in which individual habitations were situated. "Poverty" in the river valley, therefore, purportedly involved the whole of social space before the dam project, encompassing the conditions of buildings and streets, the things people used to conduct their everyday lives, and the infrastructure they utilized to move around.

In the official discourse of the Three Gorges project, images of a reformed – that is, modern – lifestyle were well publicized: children playing in front of new tile-walled townhouses, people walking in brightly decorated shopping avenues, and cars running among glass-planed high-rises in newly built towns with neat landscaping. From the dwelling of earthen-walled huts to the inhabitation of multistory houses, from cooking with coal-fueled stoves to the use of gas ranges, and from walking on the hillside with back-borne baskets as a primary means of transportation to riding in motor vehicles on highways – in addition to the operating of sophisticated machines in factories like Wahaha's and the attending of classes in the language laboratory of schools updated with advanced equipment – people in the Three Gorges area act out the idea of being "modern" (Figures 4.10 – 4.17). Their actions of cooking, commuting, working, attending school, and enjoying leisure are instantiations of the development ideology realized as people's lived experiences. Inscribed with signs of progress, these are "semiotic practices"[28] that carry the meaning of "eliminating poverty and getting rich." In and from their stations of factory workers, private entrepreneurs, agribusiness farmers, old housewives or teenage students, the gorge resettlers experience development as real and conduct their daily activities in an ensemble of minute acts out of their ideas of a new life – actions that feed back to their beliefs in progressive change and thereby reproduce the state ideology of material advancement.

Key to the reproduction of the development ideology through material practices is the subjection of individuals in the process of what Louis Althusser calls "hailing" or "interpellation." Characteristic of interpellation is its apparent *naturalness*,

Figure 4.10 A building in Yunyang before inundation. The circled Chinese word at the bottom means "demolish" (Photo taken by Linda Butler)

in that the subject acts within their consciousness in a manner that the act is conducted according to their belief:

> [I]deology "acts" or "functions" in such a way that it "recruits" subjects among the individuals (it recruits them all), or "transforms" the individuals into subjects (it transforms them all) by that very precise operation which I have called *interpellation* or hailing, and which can be imagined along the lines of the most commonplace everyday police (or other) hailing: "Hey, you there!"[29]

In the case of the Three Gorges, the subjection of individuals through hailing did not simply involve an "obvious" identity of "[i]t is (really) I! . . . '*So be it*.'"[30] Insofar as development involves a process of change, the positions the gorge people were interpellated into were not merely those of a modern subject; hailing here implied a *transposition* from one identity to another, always in a purportedly positive teleological direction. Whereas in Althusser's theory ideology is essentially used to reproduce already existing subjectivity, in the Chinese case, the state attempted to fundamentally transform people's existing subjectivity. I call this act of transpositional hailing "*double interpellation*." In the process, people in China's hinterland like the Three Gorges underwent the conceived transformation from a "poor," "backward," and "agrarian" individual to a materially "enriched," "progressive," and "modern" subject. The enabling medium through which this process took place was the dam: reconfiguring the social space, the project also changed

Figure 4.11 A building in the new town of Wushan (Taken by author, 2015)

Figure 4.12 Interior of a farmhouse before the dam project (Photo taken by Linda Butler)

people's way of life and reconstituted their everyday practices, transforming people's subjectivity from one to the other.

The process of change not only entailed a transfiguration of real experiences; it was also a reformation of one's consciousness. Explorations of realizing this change were not uncommon in the Yangtze development discourse. A scientist contributor to the *China Three Gorges Project News,* for instance, addressed the issue from a cultural and intellectual perspective. The form of poverty prevailing in the Yangtze Valley before the dam, he argued, was what he called "relative poverty." It was differentiated from the "absolute poverty" existing prior to the reforms, when people had not secured the means to satisfy their basic needs for food and clothing.

Figure 4.13 Kitchen of a resettled family in Guangdong (Taken by author, 2016)

The existing poverty in the Yangtze Valley, he said, was rather a form of impoverishment in the educational, technological, social, and cultural realms, as well as in people's "natural endowment." "Poverty," he wrote,

> is not simply an economic and social phenomenon, it is also a cultural phenomenon. . . . [Traditional] cultural values such as respecting the Way of Heaven and deriving happiness from frugality, prioritizing agriculture over commerce, and being easily content with one's status quo without striving for improvement are ignorant, conservative, and backward attitudes. They distort people's understanding of their self-value as well as their objective living environment, and constrain people's will and creative thoughts in changing their conditions of poverty.[31]

This assertion was echoed by another author who promoted a "technological culture and knowledge" in thoroughly reforming the villagers' traditional consciousness and establishing a "scientific outlook of development and human existence." The aim, this author added, was to get the people to "resolve to eliminate poverty and get rich."[32]

Figure 4.14 Street market in Wanxian, present-day Wanzhou, before the dam project. (Author's collection)

Figure 4.15 A grocery store in new Fengjie (Taken by author, 2015)

Figure 4.16 Before the dam's construction, back-borne baskets were an important transportation method for items. (Author's collection)

Along with the reversal of cultural values also came suggestions for the formation of the consciousnesses of an urban dweller and modern worker. The settlement pattern of Three Gorges residents, which had been largely organized along the lines of kinship through generations, was criticized as enclosed and homogeneous in terms of a village member's lifestyle, values, customs, and beliefs. "People identify themselves only with their respective community culture," wrote an economist. "When this kind of community culture is internalized and becomes people's ideas and mentality which impinge on their behaviors, there is no possibility for other cultures to intervene."[33] The key to reform, he noted, was to break open this geographical, social, and emotional lock and incorporate new cultural values characteristic of modern society and market economy. These would include a mindset of accepting social change, aggressively pursuing new experiences, and actively embracing competition and efficiency. In the context of a factory shop

Figure 4.17 In the new town of Wanzhou, private cars, minivans, and buses have become common means of transportation. (Taken by author, 2015)

floor, the transformation of consciousness entailed a routinization of people's behaviors that served the operation of a modern organization. In Wanxian county, between 1994 and 1998, more than 9,800 people who had been farmers were resettled and became workers in relocated factories.[34] Despite initial training, these villagers could not adapt to the noise of machines and the style of co-inhabitation in dormitories. Resistance ensued to night shifts and morning calls. Instead of following the schedules of mealtime, they ate whenever they were hungry. The same happened to their arrival and departure times: they came to work early and left before the end of the factory hours. In any sense, their behaviors defied the organizational pattern of a modern institution. "Facing such a sheet of loose sand," the report went, "managers helped the resettlers change their mindset and establish a *consciousness of modern worker*, while offering them technical training."[35]

First interpellated as agrarian subjects – backward, traditional, and conservative – the people of the Three Gorges were put on a continuum of reconstitution into urban dwellers, factory workers, market players, and technical knowledge holders – roles that were used in the second hailing and that lived up to the definition of modern social beings. Through this reconstitution, people would decipher the ubiquitous signs in the new living environment and form intelligible actions that would result in the reproduction of the modern space. The transformation of people's "natural endowment" and cultural values, accordingly, would develop to the point where the residents would conduct their activities and organize their life in the new space in a pre-reflexive and non-cognitive manner, thereby reproducing the progressivist ideology in a manner that one lived the new social relations as if they had chosen them "in all consciousness" as a free subject.

Unevenness in the Ideological Practice of Development

Among various findings, one of the most striking things that the author encountered during the fieldwork inside and outside the Three Gorges area after dam completion was the spontaneity with which relocatees lived their new life in the resettled space. An informant in Wushan, forty-five-year-old Tang, recounted his story and expressed how he had not "even dared to dream"[36] of the change in the material environment and means of living as a result of the dam project. He came from a family of three generations, including himself, who had worked in a coal mine away from home. When his father was twenty-one years old, he became ill and traveled back home with the intention to be cured there. Yet on the way home, his health deteriorated, and he died. To this day his family does not know where he was buried. At the time of his father's death, Tang's mother was two months pregnant with him and his older brother was only two years old. After Tang finished the eighth grade, he also took up a job at the same coal mine. On the day of our interview, we strolled up and down the slopes of the new town, visiting a park nested in the center of a valley that opens up to the river and the surrounding gorges. The expansive park, flanked by newly planted maple trees, was lined with white-stone sculptures of traditional Chinese motifs. In the valley, many high-rise buildings had been built overlooking the river, and more were under construction. I asked if he had anticipated such a change in Wushan. He replied, "I didn't even *dare* to imagine it."[37] He said Wushan had been a very small and poor town, with only one single-lane road, which was "so short that you could run the whole course of it within less than the time you take to smoke a cigarette." Now the road had been extended more than four times (under the aid of the Guangdong Province), and people's apartments had doubled in size. Tang and his mother lived on the third floor of an apartment block overlooking the Yangtze River. On the day of my visit, his mother was cooking in a tile-lined kitchen with a gas range. Tang had long since quit his coal-mining job and was making a handsome living out of the new tourist industry including the Autumn Leaf Festival and the sale of his Three Gorges rare rocks collection. This life that Tang "did not dare to imagine," he remarked, was made possible "by the state (*guojia*) and the dam."[38]

Tang's story testifies to the political theodicy: he had been poor at the bottom of society, but under the Party's directives on the dam project, he became much better off with a much more comfortable life – a life that he had never dared to dream of.

Another interviewee from Fengjie, Wu, established a local museum that displayed antiquities excavated in the gorge area and historical artifacts as well as furniture collected during the time of massive displacement. In 2000, the former teacher in a rural school put together 3 million yuan (US$500,000) from donations, his own savings, a government grant, and bank loans to set up the museum. The intention, he said, was to "leave a mark in the Three Gorges memory."[39] According to Wu, there was a great deal of sadness during the resettlement, especially among the elders. The bright side of the dam project, however, was the increase in government funding for the river valley. "The Three Gorges area," he noted, "used to be very poor, very backward." To get to Chongqing, which is about 248 miles away, he had needed to travel three to four days by boat, which was the only means of transport before the dam. Now, he said, it would take about four hours because of the freeways and high-speed train. "With the dam project," he said, "our houses have become bigger in size, and I can travel much faster."

Like Wu, his friend Zhu changed the course of life amid the disruption brought about by the dam. Zhu had been a factory worker before the inundation. As the state enterprise he worked in went bankrupt, he got laid off and he had scraped a living out of different low-income jobs ever since then. As the resettlement process set in, demand for architectural consultants and interior designers in the new towns increased. Zhu made use of his skills and started a business in the new Fengjie and achieved certain success. Now he could purchase a house from a farmer "to spend some leisure time in the rural setting" and send his daughter to the United States for college. His new life also enabled him to take up photography, which led him to rather frequent travels between China and the United States for contests and exhibitions. "Actually if you turn your brain (*dong dong naojin*), you can find many opportunities under this change," Zhu said.[40]

The people I talked to in the river valley invariably pointed at how "poor and backward" the Three Gorges had been and how it transformed with the dam. For this group of relocatees, despite drawbacks (such as temporary unemployment, the loss of scenic landscape, shorter autumns and less breezy summers), the project had brought improvements to their lives in terms of more efficient infrastructural connections, bigger living spaces, and better material conditions.

Outside the Three Gorges, resettlers told of more sacrifices, but they acknowledged a higher income in the new industrial structure and most of all, a different future for their children. According to my informants, more than 10,000 people from Wushan had been relocated to the southern province of Guangdong.[41] In two of the villages I visited (Village A and Village B), residents took advantage of the proximity to nearby factories and took up jobs there. Fang was in her late sixties. She had moved with her son and two grandchildren to the Resettlement Village A of twenty-seven households, all of whom were from the same Three Gorges clan. Her family had been orange farmers in Wushan. After the move, her son picked up a job in a light fixture factory near their village with a monthly salary of 3,000 yuan (US$500). Now he owned a car, which he drove to work every day. According to Fang, 3,000 yuan was the average income of a shop floor worker. For those who could operate the computer, the salary would be over 4,500 yuan (US$750), and those in the managerial position would receive up to 6,000 yuan (US$1,000).[42]

In both of the villages which were neighboring each other and were apparently well-to-do, the residents described themselves as "having got used to" life in Guangdong. They told of difficulties in the early stage of resettlement because of differences in diet and dialect between Guangdong and Wushan. While the linguistic discrepancy was a social barrier for them to find their position in the workplace and school, adjusting their habits from those of farmers to those of townspeople was a challenge. "But we don't have much problem with our life here now," Chen of Village B said. "We have jobs in the factories; our children go to the school at the end of the road outside the village, and they all speak Cantonese."[43] From where we talked, children were playing on bikes and roller skates amidst cars parked by the houses. (Figures 4.18 and 4.19) Notwithstanding the initial disruptions, the resettlers adjusted (or transformed) themselves into the daily users of the state-created social space and were living the life of modern townspeople in a pre-reflexive manner.

Yet the reproduction of the development ideology was not always neat. While some resettlers readily transitioned to their new social position and lived their life with great spontaneity, others were unable or unwilling to fit into the new interpellated roles. The picture the author gathered from fieldwork and the research findings of scholars following the dam project is remarkably uneven. Despite the official narrative of progress and despite the repetitive activities people conduct in the newly developed space, what they think, feel, and experience may not be commensurate with the Party's orientations. The state's "homogenization of space" at the Three Gorges and in distant resettlement sites is hardly impeccable and fissure-free.

By 2005, the unemployment rate in the resettlement areas reached 12.8 percent.[44] The lack of education and skills on the part of gorge residents put them in an unfavorable position in the competitive recruitment process of new private enterprises. Many business owners preferred to hire people from outside the Three

Figure 4.18 Children playing in a new resettlement town (Taken by author, 2016)

Figure 4.19 Mothers caring for their children in public spaces in the new resettlement town (Taken by author, 2016)

Gorges area because of their higher educational levels.[45] Worse still, on top of factory closures during the economic restructuring from the end of the 1990s, over two-thirds of the new enterprises that the government succeeded in bringing to the Three Gorges during the early days of the project had left or claimed bankruptcy by 2009, undercutting the availability of job opportunities for the relocatees.[46]

In a study conducted by Brooke Wilmsen on the livelihoods of Three Gorges migrants, farmers who were resettled in new urban areas were found to have a declined livelihood after displacement compared to their peers who underwent rural-to-rural or urban-to-urban resettlement.[47] In part due to higher costs of living in cities, 49 percent of the surveyed households from rural land reported that they did not have sufficient income to cover their expenditures. Moreover, about 30 percent of the same group went without enough food in the urban sites when surveyed in 2011, whereas only 3 percent of them had lived in such a plight before the resettlement as they could grow their own food.

The points of unemployment and deteriorating urban livelihoods experienced by rural migrants call into question the uninterrupted transformation of subjectivities represented in official rhetoric. From "conservative" farmer to "modern" factory worker, from "agrarian" rural inhabitant to "urban" dweller, the process of progressivist transformation was punctuated by factors such as the unavailability of jobs and inadequate skills and education – circumstances that had been unexpected or underestimated by the state. Wilmsen quoted in detail a description given by Hohai University in 2016 on the "New-Type Urbanization Approach to Reservoir Resettlement," a policy promoted by the central government as part of the latest urbanization drive: "Reservoir resettlers finally undergo a lifestyle transformation from a rural one to an urban one, and an *identity transformation from villagers to citizens*, and their living standard is improved and subject to sustainable growth."[48] If we understand the concept of "citizen" as the social member of a nation-state – a modern subject, in this case, able to decipher the meaningful signs of an urban space and conduct their life accordingly – the "identity transformation from villagers to citizens" falls in line with my analysis of subject (re)formation in a newly produced (urbanized) space. The supposition of uninterruptedness on this teleology precludes situations where the "villagers" cannot reach the conceived destination of rich, modern "citizens."

If we look further at the new life of some relocatees in distant provinces outside the Three Gorges, the failure of the double interpellation comes more sharply into focus. During field research in Villages C and D in Guangdong in 2001, the author met a family that had just moved from Wushan.[49] The family of three generations was split up into two groups, and they were resettled in separate sites miles apart. The eldest son's family of four (Mr. Wang Junior) was assigned to Village C, which consisted of five households displaced from the Three Gorges, while the parents (Mr. and Mrs. Wang Senior) lived with their second eldest son's couple and their twenty-six-year-old daughter who had a baby in Village D of seven households. Adjusting to the new life was no easy task, and their complaints at the time were typical of those who went through distant resettlement,[50] including the difficulty of integrating into the local community – particularly because of the dialect – failed promises of official compensation, and loss of social networks and inadequate technical support to reestablish their livelihood. Mr. Wang Junior made a living by selling food and drinks to migrant workers who were being employed by the bricks and electroplating factories nearby. His sister, who was living with the parents, had worked in a factory near their village for three months but the employer deferred her salary payment and she quit the job. The Wangs went to the local township head for help, but they were told to "be patient" and were given a bag of rice or a bottle of cooking oil every once in a while.

In 2014, the author went back to the villages to visit the Wang families.[51] Mr. Wang Senior's house had gone into a state of dilapidation. His daughter had died of cancer at the age of thirty-nine, and Mrs. Wang Senior had developed heart disease, high blood pressure, and diabetes; she was also blind in one eye. Mr. Wang Senior had developed problems with his legs; he had had surgery on the right leg but did not have money to do the other one. The couple were receiving 180 yuan (US$29.2)[52] every month from the government as old-age allowance and had no other help.

In Mr. Wang Junior's village, all the neighboring families had long since moved out to seek a living in other towns. The bricks and electroplating factories had closed down because they were classified as polluting industries. No migrant workers stayed in the area, and the Wangs lost their friends as well as patrons for their little neighborhood store. Mr. Wang had gone to Shenzhen, which is adjacent to Hong Kong, a few times to look for factory jobs, but he was turned away as soon as the managers saw his Three Gorges identity papers. Ever since then, he had taken up different kinds of work, including fishing, construction, and scavenging. The township head who had given them rice and cooking oil had now moved on, and the new cadre told them that he was not in office when the Three Gorges resettlement took place, so he held no responsibility for their livelihoods.

In 2001, when the families were complaining about their distressed situation, they expressed hope for the younger generation. "Now we are in great difficulty, but we hope our granddaughter will have a better life," said Mrs. Wang Senior.[53] She was referring to the eight-year-old daughter of Mr. Wang Junior. Every day, she walked on country trails for about an hour each way to and from school. In winter, she left home before dawn and walked in the company of an adult. Wang had the hope that his daughter would grow up to be a school teacher, with the education that she was receiving in the new place. In 2014 when I went back, his daughter had entered college. He was uncertain whether their dream would come true. At the time, he seemed to be more preoccupied with the precarious job market situation and the mounting school fees he had to pay for his two daughters.

The case of the Wangs is illustrative of what many project displacees experienced in distant resettlement. Having had their social networks disrupted, the relocatees could not easily reestablish their lives on a distant land particularly where people speak an unfamiliar dialect. The represented vision of "common prosperity" and "eliminating poverty and getting rich" cannot be reproduced in a natural manner by simply moving people to a more well-to-do province through the "developmental mode of resettlement." The purported equal proximity to envisaged prosperity and wealth becomes uneven and, in some cases inaccessible, when individual resources, including education, skills, and social capital, come into play in their everyday practices.

The misrecognized representation of progress has caused some relocatees to fall into depression. In a study on the mental well-being of displacees in Wanxian, Juan Xi and Sean-Shong Hwang found that gorge residents, having had suffered a very high level of distress even before the displacement, had a 20 percent increase in the number who showed post-resettlement depressive symptoms.[54] Causes of such mental depression included unmet expectations, adverse life changes such as income loss and worsening of housing conditions, and adjustment difficulties in terms of integration problems because of unfamiliar customs, and unfriendly treatment by host communities, among others.

Because of the various hardships faced by the relocatees, protests and resistance, which were well documented in foreign media and scholarly writings, further fractured the process of double hailing. Official embezzlement, inadequate compensation, and substandard farmland and housing replacements were among the appeals made by gorge residents in the course of project construction. The tale of equal proximity to the fruits of prosperity was contradicted, particularly by rampant bureaucratic corruption. In 2000, the National Audit Office acknowledged that officials had embezzled $600 million of resettlement funds in the central Hubei province. It was also reported that about 12 percent of the entire budget to relocate the million-odd people had disappeared.[55] Because of the embezzlement, many gorge residents were left uncompensated or only partially compensated. Public discontent mounted. Some villagers organized themselves to lodge complaints not only to the local bureaus but also to the central government in Beijing. But their articulations were always repressed, usually at the local level. In some cases, the demonstrating leaders were arrested and detained.

If unemployment and declined livelihoods are inhibitions for the migrants to arrive at the imagined destination of prosperity as enriched subjects, the petitions, conflicts, and protests against the authority represent punctures in the trajectory of progressivist development. While the Party tried every possible way to displace the old site with a modern built environment to ensure that people used it for the production of a developed space, news about faulty constructions and collapsed bridges in the process of dam building, landslides, environmental pollution, and deteriorating water quality undermined the robustness of the official rhetoric. The social reality was far too complex for the state ideology to totalize and the engineered scheme to design. Cast in the light of critical examination, the ideological reproduction of "common prosperity" as a political strategy to reconcile the contradictions of social polarization and distributive injustice was hardly complete and seamless.

Putting together all the stories mentioned earlier, one comes up with a picture of profound unevenness in the reproduction of the ideology of political theodicy. While some gorge migrants reestablished a new livelihood in the resettled sites acquiring skills of modern industries and living through the life of an urbanized space, some struggled with depression, unemployment, and declined living standards – experiences that fracture the imagined scenario of "common prosperity" and "stepping out of poverty." The official representation of modernization and the intended transposition of subjectivities, far from being natural and flawless as the state would have people believe, is full of fissures, deflections, and untidiness. The promise of redemption in the face of present suffering may be deliverable for some, yet for others, it may remain as elusive as the imaginary of material plentitude.

Notes

1 Joseph Fewsmith, *China Since Tiananmen: The Politics of Transition* (New York: Cambridge University Press, 2001), 21–82; Tony Saich, *Governance and Politics of China*, 4th ed. (Palgrave, 2015), 54–58.
2 "Jiang Zemin zai zhongyangdangxiao fabiao zhongyau jianghua" [An Important Speech Made by Jiang Zemin at the Central Party School], *Renmin ribao [People's Daily]*, June 15, 1992.
3 Dali Yang, *Remaking the Chinese Leviathan: Market Transition and the Politics of Governance in China* (Stanford, CA: Stanford University Press, 2004), 6–10.

4 Fewsmith, *China since Tiananmen*, 64.
5 Michel Foucault, "Politics and the Study of Discourse," in *The Foucault Effect: Studies in Governmentality*, ed. Graham Burchell, Colin Gordon, and Peter Miller (Chicago: The University of Chicago Press, 1991), 53–72.
6 Qiangzhou Wen, "Deng Xiaoping dongxibu gongfu gouxiang yu Changjiang kaifa zhanlue" [Deng Xiaoping's Vision of the Common Prosperity of Eastern and Western China and the Yangtze Development Strategy], *Renmin ribao*, January 24, 1995.
7 Wen, "Deng Xiaoping dongxibu gongfu gouxiang yu Changjiang kaifa zhanlue" [Deng Xiaoping's Vision of the Common Prosperity of Eastern and Western China and the Yangtze Development Strategy].
8 Deng Xiaoping, "Excerpts From Talks Given in Wuchang, Shenzhen, Zhuhai and Shanghai," in *Selected Works of Deng Xiaoping III (1982–1992)* (Beijing: Foreign Languages Press, 1994), 364.
9 Peigang Zhang, "Niuduzi lilun yu Zhongguo jingji fazhan zhanlue" [The Ox-Belly Theory and China's Economic Development Strategy], *Sanxia gongcheng bao [China Three Gorges Project News]*, January 8, 1998; Guodi Xu, "Shiwu shiqi yingzhang Changjiang jingjidai de zonghe kaifa fangzai gengjia zhongyao de zhanlue diwei" [The Comprehensive Development of the Yangtze Economic Zone Should Be Placed in a More Important Strategic Position], *Sanxia gongcheng bao [China Three Gorges Project News]*, January 13, 1998; Guobang Leng, "Changjiang jingjidai zai ershiyi shiji Zhongguo jingji fazhanzhong de zhanlue diwei yu zuoyong" [The Strategic Position and Function of the Yangtze Economic Zone in China's Economic Development in the 21st Century], *Sanxia gongcheng bao [China Three Gorges Project News]*, February 10, 1998; Chuanxun Gu, "Fazhan yu fanrong: zouxiang ershiyi shiji de Changjiang jingjidai" [Development and Prosperity: Toward a Yangtze Economic Zone in the 21st Century], *Sanxia gongcheng bao [China Three Gorges Project News]*, February 17, 1998; Hengshun Lei, "Jianshe Changjiang jingjidai zhanlue yiyi zhongda" [The Great Strategic Significance of Constructing a Yangtze Economic Zone], *Sanxia gongcheng bao [China Three Gorges Project News]*, April 23, 1998; and *Changjiang kaifa kaifang [Development and Opening of the Yangtse River]*, ed. Sun Shangqing (Beijing: Zhongguo fazhan chubanshe, 1996).
10 Sun, *Changjiang kaifa kaifang [Development and Opening of the Yangtse River]*, 3.
11 Henri Lefebvre, *The Production of Space*, trans. Donald Nicholson-Smith (Oxford, UK; Cambridge, USA: Blackwell, 2001), 38.
12 For an explication of Lefebvre's space, see Neil Brenner, "Global, Fragmented and Hierarchical: Henri Lefebvre's Geographies of Globalization," *Public Culture* 10, no. 1 (1997): 137–169; Manu Goswami, *Producing India: from Colonial Economy to National Space* (Chicago: University of Chicago Press, 2004), esp. 31–72; and Mark Gottdiener, *The Social Production of Urban Space* (Austin: University of Texas Press, 1994), 110–156, and 195–228.
13 Lefebvre, *Production of Space*, 73.
14 This idea resonates with the theory of "social structure." To explore space as a social possibility for structuration, see analyses in relation to structure and agency, Anthony Giddens, *The Constitution of Society: Outline of the Theory of Structuration* (Berkeley: University of California Press, 1984); and William Sewell, "A Theory of Structure," in *Logics of History: Social Theory and Social Transformation* (Chicago and London: The University of Chicago Press, 2005), 124–151.
15 Lefebvre, *Production of Space*, 278–282.
16 "Yichang jiasu maixiang quanguo quyuxing zhongxin chengshi" [Yichang Accelerates Toward the National Status of Regional Center City], *Jingchuwang*, June 13, 2017, http://www.cnhubei.com/xw/2017zt.hbddh/201706/t3845357.shtml.
17 Zongwei Peng, "Tianxian bian tongtu" [Creating a Thoroughfare], *Sanxia gongcheng bao [China Three Gorges Project News]*, January 19, 1996; Ronggang Sun, "Sanxia kaixing quanlu shoulie hunbian lieche" [The First Train Running in the Three Gorges],

Sanxia gongcheng bao [China Three Gorges Project News], April 11, 1997; and Guang Li, "Changjiang yanan jiaotong fazhan fangxingweiai" [The Rapid Development of Transportation in the Yangtze Valley], *Sanxia gongcheng bao [China Three Gorges Project News]*, January 28, 1999.

18 Liancun Li, "Zaori shixian quanguo dianli lianwang" [A Wish for the Realization of an Integrated Nationwide Power Network], *Sanxia gongcheng bao [China Three Gorges Project News]*, September 15, 1998; "Xiashiji shi woguo dianli fazhan gaochao shidai" [The Next Century Will Be the Peak Period of China's Electricity Generation], *Sanxia gongcheng bao [China Three Gorges Project News]*, December 22, 1998; "Xibu dakaifa yinqi guangfan guanzhu" [The Great Western Development Drive Has Drawn Extensive Attention], *Sanxia gongcheng bao [China Three Gorges Project News]*, December 28, 1999; Rushu Wang, "Sanxia gongcheng jianshe cujin xibu dakaifa" [The Three Gorges Project Precipitates the Great Western Development Drive], *Sanxia gongcheng bao [China Three Gorges Project News]*, April 18, 2000; and Yuan Pan, "Sida gongcheng: zhongguo jingji xin zengzhangdian [The Three Gorges Dam as the New Focus of Economic Growth in China] and "Xidian dongsong fengfan zhengqi" [The Take-Off of the West-East Electricity Transmission Scheme], *Sanxia gongcheng bao [China Three Gorges Project News]*, April 11, 2001.

19 Lin Chen et al., Series reports on the bankruptcy and closure study of Fengjie County's relocated enterprises: *Sanxia gongcheng bao [China Three Gorges Project News]*, August 17, August 19, August 24, and August 26, 1999.

20 Lin Chen et al., Series reports on Fengjie County, *Sanxia gongcheng bao [China Three Gorges Project News]*.

21 Bing Bai, "Baiwan yimin de shiji banqian rechao" [The Unprecedented Relocation of Million-Odd Resettlers], *Sanxia gongcheng bao [China Three Gorges Project News]*, February 9, 2001.

22 "Duikou zhiyuan, qiaodong jingji gongzuo de zhidian" [Partnership Assistance Provides an Impetus for Economic Work], *Sanxia gongcheng bao [China Three Gorges Project News]*, May 27, 1997; Bo Wang ed., "Sanxia kuqu duikou zhiyuan gongzuo zongshu" [An Overview of the Partnership Assistance Scheme in the Three Gorges Reservoir Area], *Sanxia gongcheng bao [China Three Gorges Project News]*, October 13, 1997; Shuangchao Zhou and Xuejun Yu, "Furu yiye chunfeng lai" [Just Like a Spring Breeze Blowing in Over the Night], *Sanxia gongcheng bao [China Three Gorges Project News]*, May 7, 1998; Guangde Wang and Shujun Wu, "Kuangda duikou zhiyuan zhanguo, jiahuai kuqu jingji fazhan" [Enhance the Achievement of Partnership Assistance and Speed up the Economic Development of the Reservoir Area], *Sanxia gongcheng bao [China Three Gorges Project News]*, September 17, 1999; and Aihua Qi and Dalan Sun, "Yichang yuan duiyuan xiangmu yueguenyueda" [Partnership Assistance in Yichang is Gaining Momentum], *Sanxia gongcheng bao [China Three Gorges Project News]*, April 30, 2000.

23 Shuangchao Zhou and Xuejun Yu, "Furu yiye chunfeng lai," *Sanxia gongcheng bao [China Three Gorges Project News]*, May 7, 1998.

24 Xiaoyun Liu, "Xiaodoudou jing dashichang" [A Little Bean Enters a Big Market], *Sanxia gongcheng bao [China Three Gorges Project News]*, June 2, 1998.

25 Liu, "Xiaodoudou jing dashichang" [A Little Bean Enters a Big Market], *Sanxia gongcheng bao [China Three Gorges Project News]*.

26 Lin Chen et al., Series reports on the bankruptcy and closure study of Fengjie County's relocated enterprises, in particular "Zhigong 'duannai' yihou . . ." [Ever Since the Milk Stops . . .], *Sanxia gongcheng bao [China Three Gorges Project News]*, August 26, 1999.

27 Karl Polanyi, *The Great Transformation* (Beacon Hill, Boston: Beacon Press, 1944).

28 Lisa Wedeen, "Conceptualizing Culture: Possibilities for Political Science," *American Political Science Review* 96, no. 4 (2002, December): 713–728.

29 Louis Althusser, "Ideology and Ideological State Apparatus," in *Lenin and Philosophy and Other Essays*, trans. Ben Brewster (New York: Monthly Review Press, 2001), 118 (original italics).

30 Althusser, "Ideology and Ideological State Apparatus," 123.
31 Guang Li, "Changjiang liuyu kechixu fazhan yu tuopin zhifu" [The Sustainable Development of Yangtze Valley and the Elimination Of poverty], *Sanxia gongcheng bao [China Three Gorges Project News]*, February 22, 2000.
32 Hengshun Lei, "Jiakuai Changjiang liuyu pinkun diqu tuopin zhifu de duice" [Speed up the Elimination of Poverty in the Impoverished Area of Yangtze Valley and Let People Get Rich], *Sanxia gongcheng bao [China Three Gorges Project News]*, March 2, 2000.
33 Dening Cheng, "Sanxia yimin yu kuqu wenhua de bianqian" [The Three Gorges Resettlement and Change in the Culture of the Reservoir Area], *Sanxia gongcheng bao [China Three Gorges Project News]*, May 21, 1998.
34 Hui Wang, "Ni zai gongchang hai hao ma?" [How Are You Doing in the Factory?], *Sanxia gongcheng bao [China Three Gorges Project News]*, May 19, 1998 (emphasis added).
35 Wang, "Ni zai gongchang hai hao ma?" [How Are You Doing in the Factory?], *Sanxia gongcheng bao [China Three Gorges Project News].*
36 Author's interviews, May 2015.
37 Author's interviews, May 2015.
38 Author's interviews, May 2015.
39 Author's interviews, May 2015.
40 Author's interviews, May 2015.
41 Author's interviews, April 2016.
42 Author's interviews, April 2016. US$1 = approximately 6 yuan at the time.
43 Author's interviews, April 2016.
44 "Aid Plan for Resettled Residents," *China Daily,* February 28, 2007.
45 Yuefang Duan and Brooke Wilmsen, "Addressing the Resettlement Challenges at the Three Gorges Project," *International Journal of Environmental Studies* 69, no. 3 (2012): 461–474.
46 Juan Xi and Sean-Shong Hwang, "Unmet Expectations and Symptoms of Depression Among the Three Gorges Project Resettlers," *Social Science Research* 40 (2011): 245–256.
47 Brooke Wilmsen, "Damming China's Rivers to Expand Its Cities: The Urban Livelihoods of Rural People Displaced by the Three Gorges Dam," *Urban Geography* 39, no. 3 (2018): 345–366.
48 Wilmsen, "Damming China's Rivers to Expand Its Cities: The Urban Livelihoods of Rural People Displaced by the Three Gorges Dam," 350. (Italics added).
49 Author's interviews, August 4, 2001.
50 Yan Tan, Graeme Hugo, and Lesley Potter, "Government-organized Distant Resettlement and the Three Gorges Project, China," *Asia-Pacific Population Journal* 18, no. 3 (September 2003): 5–26.
51 Author's interviews, July 3, 2014.
52 Exchange rate: US$1= 6.16 yuan.
53 Author's interviews, August 2001.
54 Xi and Hwang, "Unmet Expectations and Symptoms of Depression."
55 "China Uncovers Corruption Rackets," *BBC News*, January 21, 2000.

Bibliography

Althusser, Louis. 2001. "Ideology and Ideological State Apparatus." In *Lenin and Philosophy and Other Essays*, translated by Ben Brewster. New York: Monthly Review Press.

Bai, Bing. 2001. "Baiwan yimin de shiji banqian rechao" [The Unprecedented Relocation of Million-odd Resettlers]. *Sanxia gongcheng bao [China Three Gorges Project News],* February 9.

BBC News. 2000. "China Uncovers Corruption Rackets." January 21.

Brenner, Neil. 1997. "Global, Fragmented and Hierarchical: Henri Lefebvre's Geographies of Globalization." *Public Culture* 10 (1): 137–69.
China Daily. 2007. "Aid Plan for Resettled Residents." February 28.
Chen, Lin et al. 1999. "Series Reports on the Bankruptcy and Closure Study of Fengjie County's Relocated Enterprises." *Sanxia gongcheng bao [China Three Gorges Project News],* August 17–26.
Cheng, Dening. 1998. "Sanxia yimin yu kuqu wenhua de bianqian" [The Three Gorges Resettlement and Change in the Culture of the Reservoir Area]. *Sanxia gongcheng bao [China Three Gorges Project News],* May 21.
Deng, Xiaoping. 1994. *Selected Works of Deng Xiaoping III (1982–1992).* Beijing: Foreign Languages Press.
Duan, Yuefang, and Brooke Wilmsen. 2012. "Addressing the Resettlement Challenges at the Three Gorges Project." *International Journal of Environmental Studies* 69 (3): 461–74.
Fewsmith, Joseph. 2001. *China since Tiananmen: The Politics of Transition.* New York: Cambridge University Press.
Foucault, Michel. 1991. "Politics and the Study of Discourse." In *The Foucault Effect: Studies in Governmentality*, edited by Graham Burchell et al. The University of Chicago Press.
Giddens, Anthony. 1984. *The Constitution of Society: Outline of the Theory of Structuration.* University of California Press.
Goswami, Manu. 2004. *Producing India: From Colonial Economy to National Space.* University of Chicago Press.
Gottdiener, Mark. 1994. *The Social Production of Urban Space.* Austin: University of Texas Press.
Gu, Chuanxun. 1998. "Fazhan yu fanrong: zouxiang ershiyi shiji de Changjiang jingjidai" [Development and Prosperity: Toward a Yangtze Economic Zone in the 21st Century]. *Sanxia gongcheng bao [China Three Gorges Project News],* February 17.
Jingchuwang. 2017. "Yichang jiasu maixiang quanguo quyuxing zhongxin chengshi" [Yichang Accelerates Toward the National Status of Regional Center City]. June 13. http://www.cnhubei.com/xw/2017zt/hbddh/201706/t3845357.shtml
Lefebvre, Henri. 2001. *The Production of Space.* Translated by Donald Nicholson-Smith. Oxford, UK and Cambridge,USA: Blackwell.
Lei, Hengshun. 1998. "Jianshe Changjiang jingjidai zhanlue yiyi zhongda" [The Great Strategic Significance of Constructing a Yangtze Economic Zone]. *Sanxia gongcheng bao [China Three Gorges Project News],* April 23.
Lei, Hengshun. 2000. "Jiakuai Changjiang liuyu pinkun diqu tuopin zhifu de duice" [Speed Up the Elimination of Poverty in the Impoverished Area of Yangtze Valley and Let People Get Rich]. *Sanxia gongcheng bao [China Three Gorges Project News],* March 2.
Leng, Guobang. 1998. "Changjiang jingjidai zai ershiyi shiji Zhongguo jingji fazhanzhong de zhanlue diwei yu zuoyong" [The Strategic Position and Function of the Yangtze Economic Zone in China's Economic Development in the 21st Century]. *Sanxia gongcheng bao [China Three Gorges Project News],* February 10.
Li, Guang. 1999. "Changjiang yanan jiaotong fazhan fangxingweiai" [The Rapid Development of Transportation in the Yangtze Valley]. *Sanxia gongcheng bao [China Three Gorges Project News],* January 28.
Li, Guang. 2000. "Changjiang liuyu kechixu fazhan yu tuopin zhifu" [The Sustainable Development of Yangtze Valley and the Elimination of Poverty]. *Sanxia gongcheng bao [China Three Gorges Project News],* February 22.
Li, Liancun. 1998. "Zaori shixian quanguo dianli lianwang" [A Wish for the Realization of an Integrated Nationwide Power Network]. *Sanxia gongcheng bao [China Three Gorges Project News],* September 15.
Liu, Xiaoyun. 1998. "Xiaodoudou jing dashichang" [A Little Bean Enters a Big Market]. *Sanxia gongcheng bao [China Three Gorges Project News],* June 2.
Pan, Yuan. 2001. "Sida gongcheng: zhongguo jingji xin zengzhangdian" [The Three Gorges Dam as the New Focus of Economic Growth in China]. *Sanxia gongcheng bao [China Three Gorges Project News],* April 11.

Peng, Zongwei. 1996. "Tianxian bian tongtu" [Creating a Thoroughfare]. *Sanxia gongcheng bao [China Three Gorges Project News],* January 19.

Polanyi, Karl. 1944. *The Great Transformation.* Beacon Hill, Boston: Beacon Press.

Qi, Aihua, and Sun, Dalan. 2000. "Yichang yuan duiyuan xiangmu yueguenyueda" [Partnership Assistance in Yichang Is Gaining Momentum]. *Sanxia gongcheng bao [China Three Gorges Project News],* April 30.

Renmin ribao [People's Daily]. 1992. "Jiang Zemin zai zhongyangdangxiao fabiao zhongyau jianghua" [An Important Speech Made by Jiang Zemin at the Central Party School]. June 15.

Saich, Tony. 2015. *Governance and Politics of China.* 4th ed. Palgrave.

Sanxia gongcheng bao [China Three Gorges Project News]. 1997. "Duikou zhiyuan, qiaodong jingji gongzuo de zhidian" [Partnership Assistance Provides an Impetus for Economic Work]. May 27.

Sun, Ronggang. 1997. "Sanxia kaixing quanlu shoulie hunbian lieche" [The First Train Running in the Three Gorges]. *Sanxia gongcheng bao [China Three Gorges Project News],* April 11.

Sanxia gongcheng bao [China Three Gorges Project News]. 1998. "Xiashiji shi woguo dianli fazhan gaochao shidai" [The Next Century Will Be the Peak Period of China's Electricity Generation]. December 22.

Sanxia gongcheng bao [China Three Gorges Project News]. 1999. "Xibu dakaifa yinqi guangfan guanzhu" [The Great Western Development Drive Has Drawn Extensive Attention]. December 28.

Sanxia gongcheng bao [China Three Gorges Project News]. 2001. "Xidian dongsong fengfan zhengqi" [The Take-off of the West-east Electricity Transmission Scheme]. April 11.

Sewell, William. 2005. "A Theory of Structure." In *Logics of History: Social Theory and Social Transformation.* The University of Chicago Press.

Sun, Shangqing, ed. 1996. *Changjiang kaifa kaifang [Development and Opening of the Yangtse River].* Beijing: Zhongguo fazhan chubanshe.

Tan, Yan, Graeme Hugo, and Lesley Potter. September 2003. "Government-organized Distant Resettlement and the Three Gorges Project, China." *Asia-Pacific Population Journal* 18 (3): 5–26.

Wang, Bo, ed. 1997. "Sanxia kuqu duikou zhiyuan gongzuo zongshu" [An Overview of the Partnership Assistance Scheme in the Three Gorges Reservoir Area]. *Sanxia gongcheng bao [China Three Gorges Project News],* October 13.

Wang, Guangde, and Wu, Shujun. 1999. "Kuangda duikou zhiyuan zhanguo, jiahuai kuqu jingji fazhan" [Enhance the Achievement of Partnership Assistance and Speed up the Economic Development of The Reservoir Area]. *Sanxia gongcheng bao [China Three Gorges Project News],* September 17.

Wang, Hui. 1998. "Ni zai gongchang hai hao ma?" [How Are You Doing in the Factory?]. *Sanxia gongcheng bao [China Three Gorges Project News],* May 19.

Wang, Rushu. 2000. "Sanxia gongcheng jianshe cujin xibu dakaifa" [The Three Gorges Project Precipitates the Great Western Development Drive]. *Sanxia gongcheng bao [China Three Gorges Project News],* April 18.

Wedeen, Lisa. 2002. "Conceptualizing Culture: Possibilities for Political Science." *American Political Science Review* 96 (4): 713–28.

Wen, Qiangzhou. 1995. "Deng Xiaoping dongxibu gongfu gouxiang yu Changjiang kaifa zhanlue [Deng Xiaoping's Vision of the Common Prosperity of Eastern and Western China and the Yangtze Development Strategy." *Renmin ribao [People's Daily],* January 24.

Wilmsen, Brooke. 2018. "Damming China's Rivers to Expand its Cities: the Urban Livelihoods of Rural People Displaced by the Three Gorges Dam." *Urban Geography* 39 (3): 345–66.

Xi, Juan, and Sean-Shong Hwang. 2011. "Unmet Expectations and Symptoms of Depression Among the Three Gorges Project Resettlers." *Social Science Research* 40: 245–56.

Xu, Guodi. 1998. "Shiwu shiqi yingzhang Changjiang jingjidai de zonghe kaifa fangzai gengjia zhongyao de zhanlue diwei" [The Comprehensive Development of the Yangtze Economic Zone Should Be Placed in a More Important Strategic Position]. *Sanxia gongcheng bao [China Three Gorges Project News],* January 13.

Yang, Dali. 2004. *Remaking the Chinese Leviathan: Market Transition and the Politics of Governance in China.* Stanford University Press.

Zhang, Peigang. 1998. "Niuduzi lilun yu Zhongguo jingji fazhan zhanlue" [The Ox-belly Theory and China's Economic Development Strategy]. *Sanxia gongcheng bao [China Three Gorges Project News],* January 8.

Zhou, Shuangchao, and Yu, Xuejun. 1998. "Furu yiye chunfeng lai" [Just Like a Spring Breeze Blowing in over the Night]. *Sanxia gongcheng bao [China Three Gorges Project News],* May 7.

5 "Mother River" and "Second Cradle of Chinese Civilization"

The Cultural Re-encoding of the Yangtze as a Futurist Nation

Aside from the production of an urban space and the engendering of modern subjects at the Three Gorges area through quotidian activities, the state's ideological practices of development extended to the non-social world in the form of cultural encoding in nonhuman objects – the river, the gorges, and historical artifacts. Along with the concept of "common prosperity" discussed in the previous chapter, there arose in the dam discourse of the 1990s a new vision of the *nation* through the reinscription of meaning in the Yangtze River. This was made possible by the dam symbol, which worked together with another symbol drawn from the semiotic code particular to China: the Yangtze. The river has been represented in official media, textbooks, and writings as the "second cradle of Chinese civilization" (with the Yellow River being the "first") and a "mother river" raising her Chinese children of various generations with her "milk." With the dam imposed upon and harnessing it, the river was given a new value and became a sign of a *forward-looking* nation progressing on the trajectory of modernization. This is not simply a *futurist* nation, but also one that is able to build the biggest dam in the world, commanding the highest technology of hydropower production. The size of the dam, the physical scale of the five-tier ship-gates, and the sheer power of water passing through the turbines *speak* for themselves on the reconstituted nation's strength, regardless of linguistic representation.

If we combine the material practice of Three Gorges resettlers with the cultural re-encoding of the Yangtze in favor of techno-nationalism, we see the dissemination of the ideology of political theodicy in full swing: transforming individual subjects of rural poverty into ones with modern riches, the promise of redemption is also carried to a collective level of the Chinese community as a whole. "Poverty elimination" and "common prosperity" are indelibly connected with "national rejuvenation" and the "ascendancy of a powerful China." Besides its conceived material function as an engine of capital and knowledge circulation to the inland as part of the Great Western Development Drive for nationwide prosperity, the dam is an embodiment of a futurist nation that severs the understanding of a civilizational past in favor of an outlook based on technological supremacy.

The Yangtze is in itself an immense mass of water with rocks and vegetation, starting from a certain point with some living creatures inhabiting the region. But through the semiotic encoding of social agents, this natural landscape is turned into

DOI: 10.4324/9781003531494-6

a terrain of signs that carry meanings particular to people with specific interests and power. The Dengist state's vision of the futurist nation is an illustration of Roland Barthes' "second-order semiological system."[1] It builds upon the first layer of linguistic signification – the stream of water and its surrounding mass of rocks and vegetation, together called the "river valley." In the exercise of meaning assignation by the Chinese state, the "second-order semiological system" subsumes the history of the Yangtze, including its physical characteristics, the geographical formation, and the evolution of human communities, all of which are embraced by the linguistic concept of "Yangtze River" with its extensive historical and cultural connotations.

Insofar as the natural landscape is used as a medium of representation, "it is a material 'means'," in the words of W. J. T. Mitchell, "like language or paint, embedded in a tradition of cultural signification and communication, a body of symbolic forms capable of being *invoked* and *reshaped* to express meanings and values."[2] The variability and plasticity of "meanings and values" invested in an object of the natural landscape, as indicated in Mitchell's idea, add to the instability and uncertainty of Barthes' "semiological system." In the contestation over the Yangtze's development and more broadly China's development, as will be shown in this chapter, dam proponents assigned a materialist value and a new nationalist meaning to the river. This reconceived idea of the natural landscape was instantiated through the act of dam building and the concomitant inundation of the gorges and their cultural artifacts. The new signification of the river and its surrounding land and relics "reshaped" the meaning of the Yangtze by superscribing its time-honored representation as China's "mother river." The malleability of the "symbolic forms" was also manifested in the claims of dissenting intellectuals who invoked the cause of ancient civilization to argue for the protection of historical relics at the Three Gorges as the preserved continuity of national culture. Developing China, they asserted, did not have to exclude the nation's past.

In what follows, we will explore the politics of historic preservation at the Three Gorges by first explaining how the dissidents mobilized the concept of Chinese civilization to resist the coming waters. Then we will examine how this ideological proposition was disputed by the state, which, through the reinscription of a new meaning in the river, sought to reconstitute the *nation* semiotically with the modern principle of development. The process illuminated the political strategy of the state, which incorporated non-human objects in its reproduction of the progressivist ideology through the deployment of the Yangtze symbol. The analysis will also show how the dissidents' preservationist discourse became integrated into developmentalism in the late 1990s via the trope of tourism and purportedly wealth-generating touristic activities.

Three Gorges as the Embodiment of Chinese History and Culture

Among the various issues of protecting the environment at the Three Gorges in the face of inundation, the preservation of cultural artifacts was a focus of debate. Historical temples, fortresses, remains of battles, rock inscriptions of poets' compositions, ancient plank walkways built along the gorges, and suspended coffins on the face of the cliffs which dated back thousands of years were among the most widely known relics, which have been consumed for decades by tourists who cruised along the mainstream and occasionally went onshore to sightsee. As the construction work proceeded, excavations yielded findings that ranged from Stone Age artifacts to relics of relatively recent dynastic eras. All these were submerged underwater when the dam was completed if they were not saved.

As dam construction and resettlement proceeded, concerns became audible from archeologists who put increased emphasis on the value of the Three Gorges region as a crystalized showcase of Chinese history which, according to them, dated from the Paleolithic period through to modern times. The plea for preservation was part of the campaign launched by dissenting intellectuals who contested the project. Flooding the Three Gorges area, they argued, was tantamount to erasing the part of Chinese history that bore witness to the nation's civilization. Their contestation in this period no longer concerned whether the dam should be built, as this had become a lost cause with the approval of the National People's Congress in 1992. It was rather about remedial measures that might minimize the environmental and social impacts on the people and natural environment of the reservoir area.

In August 1996, one year before the first phase of inundation took place, fifty-six intellectuals, including writers, archeologists, and academics, submitted a petition letter to the Politburo and the then party head, Jiang Zemin, pleading for a prompt allocation of funds for the rescue of historical artifacts in the reservoir area. The dissenters portrayed the Three Gorges as a "*focused* embodiment of the Chinese nation's (*zhonghua minzu*) history as well as culture," on the grounds that "historically the Three Gorges is among the earliest developed areas in the Yangtze Valley, and contains a rich collection of cultural relics both underground and on the surface."[3] They wrote:

> Especially, the various historical relics in the area have already merged with the sublime natural scenery into one, which becomes the rich heritage that nature and our ancestors give to their existing Chinese descendants (*huaxia ernü*). It is also the pride of the posterity of the Yellow Emperor (*yanhuang zisun*). This immense value of the Three Gorges relics has been a consensus widely shared among people, both within and without China, who admire the Chinese civilization (*zhonghua wenming*).

Embedded here is a notion of an unbroken continuity in which currently living people, the Chinese, are connected with the dead (the ancestors, the Yellow Emperor) and the yet unborn (posterity). Their connectedness and concomitant comradeship as members of a solidary community are imagined in the context of a finite, delineated space – the territory of China, epitomized by the Three Gorges. The intellectuals believed that they, and the Chinese people at large across both space and time, shared a continuous genealogy, common historical memories, and a public culture, all borne out and manifested by the Three Gorges.

If the intellectuals conceived of the Three Gorges area as a landscape encoded with a nationalist meaning, the medium through which this naturalization was made was cultural relics. The archaic artifacts, the historic temples, the ancient tombs and monuments are embodiments of the myths, the history, in short, the "memory" of the Chinese past. In their concrete form, they objectify the fatality of individuals who lived the ephemerality of events that occurred in Chinese history. Some of the artifacts the dissidents referred to belong to prehistoric times (the Paleolithic period and the Neolithic age) and to tribes (such as the Ba people) who lived before a unified concept of "China" came into place.[4] But these objects were put together with the dynastic artifacts and classified under the overarching category of "Chinese" cultural relics, thereby incorporated into the nationalist conception. With what the intellectuals called the "merging (of these relics) with the sublime scenery into one," the land and water of the Yangtze were made to embrace a specific meaning – one that was particular to the Chinese lineage. This imagining of the "merging" co-extended with the discourse of "mother river" and "cradle of Chinese civilization" and consummated the appropriation of the physical geography as a "heritage" left by the Chinese ancestors. It was through this "merging" that the Three Gorges took on a second-order signification as the "focused embodiment of the Chinese nation's history as well as culture."

However, the intellectuals were not initiators of the nationalization project, which partook of the historical objects, be they "Chinese" and non-"Chinese" or pre-"Chinese." The intellectuals' co-optation was part of a broader venture of naturalizing the Three Gorges that appropriated the array of artifacts and turned them into ethnic symbols. The fact that the intellectuals leaned on this line of argument with the presumption that it would be an effective appeal indicated that their nationalistic conception was shared to a significant extent by some Chinese, possibly including the Beijing leaders. The historic preservation and reproduction of the relics were mostly carried out in the Tang, Ming and Qing dynasties (around 700–1911 AD) succeeded by both the Nationalists and the Communists who reinforced or extended the sites. The symbols themselves also underwent numerous transformations at different points in time as a result of the interaction between official images and folk interpretations.[5] The history revolving around these symbols, in other words, was constructed layer upon layer, each embedded within the others, forming the "end products" of the existing preservations. A full examination would be too ambitious for a chapter of this length. Instead, we select a few relics that were among the foci of the cultural preservation debate and that played an important role in giving the Three Gorges its symbolic meaning.

Heroes of the Three Kingdoms (220–280 AD)

The lore of the Three Kingdoms is among the richest in the Three Gorges folk history: the battles and defeats, the loyalty and betrayals of state leaders and officials, their myths and legends, the relics and commemorations, as well as later novels and poems, were all situated and played out in the Three Gorges area and on the waters of the Yangtze.

It was a time when the unified Han dynasty disintegrated into three kingdoms – Wei in north China, Shu in the southwest on the upper reaches of the Yangtze, and Wu in the east downstream on the lower reaches of the Yangtze. Much revered in the folklore are the heroes of Shu: the king Liu Bei said to be of average caliber but able to rally capable people and command their loyalty. Among them was Zhuge Liang, a gifted political advisor and a strategist with extraordinary talents, and the others were the king's two sworn brothers, Zhang Fei and Guan Yu, both of whom became demigods to the Chinese people. Shu, starting as a weak state, stabilized its position through an alliance with Wu, which reaped success in the decisive Battle of Red Cliff fought against the third state Wei in the Three Gorges area. However, out of distrust the alliance broke down and Shu was eventually annexed by Wei. Relics that sustained the memory of the Three Kingdoms included a rock pillar that was said to have been used by the Shu troops during the battle to create a blockade against the enemy ships. It stood in the middle of the river and could be seen above the water before the inundation. Since the rise of the water level, it has been submerged in the reservoir.

The Three Kingdoms is a story of individuals in the historical play of political interests, their vicissitudes and sacrifices for the state's survival or the country's reunification. The memory of the Three Kingdoms as part of China's history was transmitted and perpetuated by the novel *Sanguozhi yanyi* [The Romance of the Three Kingdoms] written by Luo Guanzhong in around 1500 AD, which remains a widely read classic. Poets living several centuries after the Three Kingdoms visited the historic sites and wrote poems which invoked imaginations of the events and expressed yearnings for the building of a unified state. A scene conjured up by the Tang dynasty poet, Du Fu (712–770 AD), and some others was visualized in one of the historic sites, the White Emperor Fort, where the king of Shu, Liu Bei, was said to have died after his defeat in a major battle. It is about his entrusting of his son to Zhuge Liang with a plea for assisting the new king to fulfill his ideal of state unification (Figure 5.1). The episode, well known among people through written and oral narratives, was reproduced through sculptures.[6] The existing visual representation open for display to visitors at the fort was made under the communist regime (Figure 5.2). The theme as represented is predominantly the shattered dreams of state survival and hopes for the formation of a unified and rejuvenated nation. To the observer, these representations in a physical form are the visualization of an epistemological constellation – a combination of knowledge and sensual images creating visual objects that function to anchor the memory and help *construct* the history of a nation.

Through centuries the Three Kingdoms lore has been interwoven with folk culture. The lore was sustained by adaptations of its episodes in operas and by storytellers passing down the story to later generations.[7] Some key figures have been apotheosized as demigods and their statutes were put inside temples devoted to them. These temples were constantly visited by the common people. The general Zhang Fei, for example, was memorialized in the Zhang Fei Temple at the Three Gorges, a site that has been removed and rebuilt upstream, upon local villagers' demand.[8]

Figure 5.1 Sculptures of Liu Bei entrusting his son to Zhuge Liang at the present-day White Emperor Fort. (Taken by author, 2015)

Figure 5.2 White Emperor Fort enclosed by the newly formed Three Gorges Dam reservoir (Taken by author, 2015)

Through time, images of the Three Kingdoms heroes and the myths surrounding them were given numerous redefinitions to serve a nationalist purpose. Symbols in the Lord Guan myth which originated from the general Guan Yu, for example, experienced what Prasenjit Duara calls "superscriptions."[9] Starting from the Song dynasty the state has patronized the cult. In 1614, Guan Yu was given the title *di*, a rank tantamount to the emperor's, as a protector of the empire. In the Qing period, the lore underwent systematic co-optation and took up the symbolic meaning of Confucian loyalty to state authority. The superscribing symbols connected with the imperial concerns did not erase the preexisting ones prevailing in folk culture, but rather interacted and negotiated with them to evolve into new ones. Through time Guan Yu was conceived to embrace images including the Chinese god of war, a protector of temples, and the military god of wealth worshipped in temples throughout China. Whereas the Three Kingdoms protagonists remain preeminent in local history and are the Three Gorges area's major cultural symbols, nationalist attributes have been imposed upon their myth and lore.

In the 20th century, the Three Kingdoms icons were incorporated by the Republican state to serve its goals of modernization and the formation of a collective subject. These were further appropriated in the 1990s by the contemporary dissenting intellectuals who constructed their views upon the established meaning of the relics, thereby imposing on the Three Gorges a new nationalist cause. Through the artifacts and their symbolism, the dissenters inscribed the landscape with historicist connotations, and promoted a concept of *nation* that was constituted by a particular collective history and ancient culture. Their strategy was targeted at the technical-minded dam officials and in turn the Dengist regime's sponsored ideology of techno-nationalism. They argued that as China "marches into the twenty-first century, while much success has been achieved in modernization, preserving the motherland's historical heritage and promoting the nation's cultural traditions are particularly important."[10] They highlighted the idea of "socialist spiritual civilization" frequently employed in state propaganda and injected into it a culturalist content to challenge the state's propensity to look to the future while forgetting the past.

Historic preservation was not an issue in the Three Gorges debate during the 1980s and the beginning of the 1990s when most of the attention focused on the economic and technical viability of the proposed dam. However, as the project entered its implementation phase and construction work was underway from 1994 onward, increasingly audible pleas for the rescue of relics could be heard. Contestation in this period concentrated on problems in the resettlement process including corruption, environmental dangers in the reservoir area, and the lack of official commitment to relic protection. According to Yu Weichao, the director of the National Museum of Chinese History, who oversaw the overall planning of the rescue program and was one of the petitioners, the government authorities delayed the funding of preservation work. Up to July 1994, he said, the program was assigned RMB 2 million (US$230,000), which had to be used to cover the work of more than 200 archeologists in an estimated number of 1,270 sites in the Three Gorges area. These included the survey and excavation of various burial grounds, tombs, and ancient resettlement areas of the Bronze Age. Many of the researchers could not get prior funding and had to pay out of their own pockets, lodging at inns that cost RMB 6 (US$0.69) a night. According to international conventions, Yu argued, the budget of historic preservation should constitute 3–5 percent of a project's total investment. This would entail about RMB 5 billion (US$578.7 million) at the time. But the government agreed to offer up to a tenth of that amount and instead allocated money to the construction and resettlement work. Archeologists including Yu called for not only international collaboration on finances but also personnel involvement in the excavation because of the shortage of time. But their request was rebuked by officials of the State Council's Three Gorges Project Construction Committee, who asserted that the Three Gorges project, including historic preservation, should be and could be borne by the Chinese and that contribution from "foreigners" was not necessary.[11] Yu and his colleagues insisted on taking their case outside China and made appeals to sympathizers in Taiwan and Hong Kong. Their action did not result in a transnational movement of Three Gorges historic preservation like the one that will be analyzed in Chapter 6 on environmental protection and human rights, but the persistent calls of the dissenters and their alliance with journalists, who wrote articles and broadcast features in the media, gradually built up momentum on the issue and drew public attention.

The disagreement between the dissidents and the government authorities manifested a difference in ideology despite the point that both groups shared the common ground of nationalism. While the civilizational claim of the intellectuals won over certain well-wishers among local and overseas Chinese, the official reformists asserted their progressivist worldviews through the semiotic appropriation of cultural symbols at the Three Gorges and practically reproduced that ideology with the dam's construction and the productive activity of tourism.

The Landscape as a Nation of Development

A reading of the official discourse on relic protection revealed nuanced changes as the project proceeded. Up until the mid-1990s, historic preservation had received little attention if not outright resistance from dam bureaucrats. It was not that they did not discern any cultural attributes in the landscape, but more that their developmentalist aspirations to conquer the river and harness it in pursuit of material gain overwhelmed all other considerations. Around the end of the 1990s, however, the discrepancy between the dam proponents' views and those of the dissenting intellectuals became subtler. Official recognition was given to the importance of relic protection as a means to preserve Chinese "civilization," but this cultural value of the Three Gorges was simultaneously subsumed into the prevailing discourse of regional economic development and was made a constitutive component of the nation's marketization drive.

The Value of the Yangtze

In the preface of a book published in time to lobby the National People's Congress deputies for the project's endorsement in 1992, the river was narrated as follows:

> [The Yangtze's] never-ending stream rolls on the land of China, and has reared more than one-third of the Chinese population. It is also the birthplace of the ancient Chu culture. Throughout history numerous literati portrayed this majestic landscape with colors and passions, and passed down lots of cultural heritage as well as fascinating legends. The Yangtze is a product of nature. She has an unrestrained character. Whenever there is unusual weather, [she] causes disastrous floods and brings tragedies to the people. . . . Water conservancy is a fundamental property of the national economy; it has been the basis of our country's security and prosperity. . . . The Three Gorges project is a water conservancy project with comprehensive functions. Its major benefits are flood control, electricity generation, navigational improvement, marine agriculture, and water supply, etc.[12]

Noteworthy is the sequence of the presentation about the river. The three characteristics of the Yangtze – its cultural attributes, natural features, and economic potentials – were juxtaposed. But the weight of perceived significance in fact increases as one moves down the order. Such an observation is made in the context of the wider official discourse on the dam project. Read with other published materials, speeches, and pictures, the preface was but one example indicating the official propensity to downplay the river's cultural significance as an embodiment of Chinese civilization and to exalt its economic values to be exploited by means of the project. From the 1980s to the mid-1990s, the official discourse basically concentrated on the feasibility of the project; that is, its economic effectiveness, technicalities and financial viability, and the implementation details of the scheme. In this period of time, official expressions about the cultural relics were either brief references acknowledging the irreversibility of inundating the sites without suggesting possible remedies or arguments that the loss of tourist spots the relics provided could be easily compensated by new scenery to be made by the dam. Besides objections to the archeologists' efforts to appeal to the international community on relic protection and the withholding of funds as mentioned earlier, the officials claimed that the preservationists' estimate of 1,270 historic sites was ten times the actual number. Meeting the demand, they said, did not "conform to the interests of the state," for "the Chinese people are not that interested in cultural preservation."[13]

The bureaucrats' words and deeds manifested a suppression of the river's historicist signification and more precisely that of the Three Gorges. In contrast with the intellectual petitioners' views, the technocrats' interpretations of the Yangtze and its relics were devoid of civilizational content. For the latter, the cultural signifiers could be easily displaced by a new symbol, the dam, and the economic attributes this sign represented. The landscape they conceived in the Three Gorges was essentially developmentalist, defined by the utilization value it was perceived to carry for economic exploitation and human consumption. An examination of school textbooks and other published materials in this period indicates that the Yangtze was almost invariably ascribed by official writers and dam technocrats alike with three characteristics.[14]

1. The Yangtze as a "disease in the vital organs of the nation China" (*zhonghua minzu de xinfu zhi huan*): The Yangtze was considered a cradle of the nation's civilization, but its flood menace had also caused tremendous loss. The river was the largest in China with more than 400 tributaries covering the southwestern, central, and eastern parts of the country. In the rainy season, the immense body of water presented a threat of flooding to the middle and lower reaches. The capacity of the two existing major flood control devices, the Jingjiang flood diversion area and the Dongting Lake, was diminished due to siltation. The threat of floods exerted destabilizing effects on the agricultural, industrial, mining, and commercial activities in both the Yangtze Valley and various cities along its banks. The government's aspirations were to keep this river under control and thereby secure a stable environment for economic development in the region. The Three Gorges Dam, it was believed, would hold back floods as big as those occurring in a hundred-year cycle.
2. "Eastward the Yangtze water goes, flowing is all oil and coal" (*gungun jiangshui xiang dongliu, liu de doushi mei he you*): The river was said to contain half of the country's exploitable hydropower, yet so far less than 10 percent of that capacity had been developed. Technocrats saw it as a valuable source of energy, as an inexhaustible and non-polluting alternative to coal and oil. The hydropower station to be built at the Three Gorges, they estimated, would produce more than 18,000 megawatts of electricity, which was equivalent to a coalmine with a production capacity of 40 to 50 million tons per year. The electricity the river generated, it was hoped, would alleviate the power shortage in central and eastern China and thereby accelerate industrialization there. In turn, it would contribute to the country's modernization.
3. The Yangtze as a "golden waterway" (*huangjin shuidao*): The river was a major shipping channel linking the hinterland in the west and the coast in the east. Together with its tributaries, the Yangtze formed China's largest navigational network connecting the economic activities of the southwest with those of the central and eastern regions. Dam proponents believed that the "golden waterway" would be further developed with the Three Gorges project which would submerge torrents and facilitate more efficient navigation for up to 10,000-ton ocean-going ships. Moreover, the reservoir behind the dam would create new harbors for some inland cities and help the economy there to prosper.

All in all, the Three Gorges project was intended to serve the purposes of "taming" the river and harnessing it for economic gain. Promoted as having comprehensive functions, it was designed to control floods, generate electricity, improve inland navigation, and provide irrigation and water supply for the parched northern China. Moreover, it was projected to play an important role in the development of the southwestern inland region which was perceived as impoverished.

The dam, considered a "historical monument," would displace the cultural relics and supersede the sites as a dominant sign on the river. (It was anticipated to be a major attraction for domestic and foreign travelers who toured the Yangtze.) Like the dissenting intellectuals who conceived a cultural landscape through their perception of the merging between the relics and the land, dam supporters imputed a materialist value to the water by means of the dam. The construction, with the progressivist meaning it embodied, would merge with the soil and water and become part of the landscape there. In this way the Three Gorges and the Yangtze area would turn into a land of "prosperity" and "development" – even more so given the official projection that the resettled population would yield higher income from the restructured economy, cargo transportation would increase fivefold every year, and factories would raise their productivity with modernized machinery powered by hydroelectricity.

Moreover, the re-encoding of meaning in the landscape was closely connected to a modern form of aesthetics that is produced out of a mechanical civilization. In a state-supported publication, the dam was represented as follows:

> The project will create *a harmonious unity between the magnificence of nature and that of a social engineering scheme*. . . . The dam's height, its electricity generation capacity, the size of the reservoir to be formed, the task of "a million's resettlement," and the finances committed are all unprecedented in China's thousands of years of engineering history and that of the world. As a social engineering project, it also manifests scenery of majestic glamor, an aura of extraordinary grandeur, and the power of human conquest of nature. In the Three Gorges, one can appreciate *not only the beauty of the landscape, but also the sublimity of a social engineering project*.[15]

What the dissidents perceived as "sublime" and "elegant" was to be displaced by a product of modern technology, the dam, which proponents considered a "gigantic sculpture" to be harmoniously coordinating with the Three Gorges' natural scenery. "The gorge area after the project's completion," noted one writer, "will build its style upon green mountains, blue water, and the white-gray dam."[16]

The erasure of the old landscape along with its historicist and culturalist meaning represented a redefinition of the *nation* the landscape was conceived to signify and a reconfiguration of the nationalist ideology it expressed. Such an erasure was tantamount to a truncation of time displacing the past along with the ancient civilization and antiquated culture considered as associated with that past. The truncation of time as indicated in the discourse of this period manifested a temporal break that negated the age-old nation honored by the intellectuals in favor of the initiation of a *futurist* forward-looking nation. Flooding the relics was not only a physical displacement of the old symbols with a new unitary symbol, but it was more importantly a redefinition of the nationalist ideology they expressed. The Three Kingdoms heroes were originally local figures who lived and died in the Three Gorges area. But with the nationalization of their myths and lore, their signification and symbolic content transcended the local level to attain a national meaning. By the same token, the Three Gorges dam was intended not only as a dam on and for the Yangtze but also as a project of and for the nation. This "new" nation, suppressing its historicist imperative, was constituted by the high culture of development actualized in everyday practices such as those analyzed in Chapter 4.

Yet the dam, carrying the semiotic functions of encoding the river and in turn redefining the *nation*, is itself a representation of that nation's power. Built to be the largest in the world, it was compared with other large dams including the Hoover in the United States and the Itaipu in Brazil, and was said to be "unrivaled" (*jushi wushuang*) in terms of its scale, its comprehensive benefits, and the component structures such as the ship-gate and turbines. The dam would be an embodiment of the forefront of scientific knowledge and technical skills, even more so because China built it without the support of the World Bank. Moreover, the blocking of the Yangtze took place at the time when China resumed sovereignty over Hong Kong in 1997. The conquest of nature and the mastery of technological know-how were at once attributes of the newly expanded territorial boundary of an emerging world power. Constructing a "nationalist dam" (*dazao minzu daba*), as it was commonly called in official narratives, and the concomitant generation of a new urban space was a simultaneous act of ideological representation and the reproduction of that ideology in practice.

Reconstituting the Nation's Culture

What appeared as a clear demarcation of temporality and re-signification of the landscape in the mid-1990s underwent a change around the end of the decade as we discern nuances in the dam discourse. The official stance started to recognize the importance of historic preservation: longer and more prominent coverage in printed media was given to the issue; more discussion was initiated and public attention drawn to the imminence of excavation; and more financial resources were committed to the activity.[17] From the late 1990s onward, there was an overlapping discourse between the dissenting intellectuals' and that of the dam supporters. In an introduction to a newspaper series on the Three Gorges historic preservation, for example, it was noted:

> China is an ancient civilization, and the Yangtze is the cradle of Chinese civilization. In the developmental chain of Chinese civilization, the Three Gorges constitutes an essential component. The rescuing and preserving of historical relics at the Three Gorges is another grand project comparable to the Dam that marks the century.[18]

Parallelism between the dissenting and official articulations acknowledging the Three Gorges relics as epitomizing the Chinese civilizational process was not uncommon in the late 1990s and early 2000s. It was a time when the first phase of inundation was being implemented and pleas for imminent preservation were more earnestly made by intellectuals. Persistent calls from the dissidents, despite their lack of institutional support to make binding resolutions on the government, had drawn public attention to the issue. More news reports and feature stories were dedicated to the cultural relics at the Three Gorges and the urgency of saving them. There were also reports of rampant thefts of artifacts in the gorge area. A bronze candelabra around 2,000 years old, for example, which had been excavated from an ancient Han tomb and categorized as a "national treasure," was smuggled out of the country and sold for US$250 million in New York,[19] stirring up public outrage both within and outside China over the problem of looting in the reservoir area. The apparent change of heart on the part of the government culminated in remarks from Beijing leaders, including the then president Jiang Zemin and premier Zhu Rongji, who referred to the protection of Three Gorges relics as a means to preserve the Chinese "national heritage."[20]

In June 2000, three years before the water level would be raised to 135 meters, the State Council's Three Gorges Project Construction Committee approved RMB 1 billion (US$120.7 million) to the relic rescue program. This would make provision for the preservation of 829 historical relics and sites by sixty-four archeological teams drawn from more than twenty provinces and cities in China.[21] Although only a portion of cultural artifacts could be saved and the amount fell short of the international convention's 3–5 percent of the project's total budget as Yu estimated, it was much higher than the original pledge the government had made in the mid-1990s.

However, the emerging civilizational enunciations were quickly subsumed into the dominant discourse of economic development and material progression. Arguments in support of the Three Gorges landscape's cultural significance were prominent in printed media, but they were juxtaposed with or made part of arguments that the preserved relics and their surrounding geographical features could be utilized as resources for an expanding tourist industry at the Three Gorges. This future economic sector, it was projected, would create employment opportunities for the relocated population, thereby eliminating poverty and making the goal of "common prosperity" more attainable. "Fengjie county," it was written in one article, "uses its rich touristic resources as a promotion point, bringing more than 1,000 relocated villagers onto the road of economic resettlement by means of tourism." Those touristic resources, according to the article, included the Qutang Gorge, one of the Three Gorges, and the White Emperor Fort where the Three Kingdoms stories unfolded.[22] The latter, being part of the relics rescue program, was preserved with massive concrete dikes. But the new reservoir turned the fortress into an island, and its ancient architecture submerged underwater.

The incorporation of the civilization discourse into the modern development discourse indicated a new conception of the *nation* and a new definition of *culture*. Instead of a temporal truncation delineating the past from the present/future and a relinquishing of "antiquated" culture, the landscape and its artifacts now underwent a process of re-signification that embraced *both* the ancient culture and a futurist nation in a conceived temporal continuity. The "focused embodiment of the Chinese nation's history as well as culture" took on a different meaning: while the previous conceptions of the Yangtze as a "mother river" and "cradle of Chinese civilization" were not superseded, they were reconceived to register a *new*

Chinese civilization constituted by scientific knowledge, technological advancement, and calculated economic gains. In other words, with the dam as a medium of re-signification, the "second-order semiological system" of the landscape underwent a reworking of "mother river" and "cradle of civilization" to embrace a new meaning of modern development and became a new signification of a reformist nation. This "nation" was essentially forward-looking, but it did not negate the past: it reconciled the past with a developing present and a progressive future, encompassing the ancient culture through to the futurist development scenario in a conceived unbroken continuum of time. It would undergird a civilization that was to be born out of what Lewis Mumford calls a "long development of technics,"[23] one that would prioritize scientific knowledge over unsystematized practice, and an alienated subject-object relationship over an empathetic human-environment connection.

Approaching the end of the 1990s, the term "culture," which appeared more and more often in official writings, acquired new meanings as it was combined with other words to become "transportation culture," "engineering culture," and "tourism culture."

1. Culture as a Process of the Nation's Evolution

A book titled *An Introduction to the Culture of the Three Gorges in China* endorsed by a top official who masterminded the "developmental mode of resettlement" expounded two kinds of culture or cultural implications for the dam project. The first was the idea that the dam was a manifestation of the Chinese nation's struggle for modernity.

> Building the Three Gorges Dam is a process starting from dream to reality. This process is also the process of the Chinese people's incessant pursuits of science and democracy; it also represents the process by which Chinese people overcome all the adversaries and attain the Four Modernizations. It illustrates the following profound cultural content.[24]

The authors, putting forward the project's objective as "strengthening national power, increasing the country's wealth, and rejuvenating the Chinese nation," traced the experience of China since 1840 when the Qing court lost a series of battles to the Western powers and Japan, which resulted in unequal treaties, indemnities, and territorial annexations. "Over more than 100 years," the authors wrote, "the Chinese people ceaselessly struggled and explored, and eventually realized a truth: one will be stepped upon if one is backward, and one is bound to be bullied as long as one remains a weakling." "Over more than 100 years, the main theme of Chinese history has been the striving for an independent position in the world community of nations, for wealth, power, and prosperity."[25] Building upon this argument, the writers asserted that the Three Gorges project was an expression of those yearnings, a product of the pursuits of the Four Modernizations, and most of all, a "historical inevitability."

Here the voice of political theodicy cannot be clearer. The resonance between the authors' words and the advocacies of both Sun Yat-sen and Deng Xiaoping was loud and distinct: From a military weakling to an international strongman, from an impoverished and backward people to a state of wealth and power, the idealized trajectory is projected toward national redemption. The Three Gorges Dam, for the contemporary authors, was not only a representation of the aspirations for a nation's modernizing evolution. It was also an attainable, "historically inevitable" realization of such aspirations in practice.

The relevance of Sun and his ideas was explicitly illustrated as the dam-supporting writers proceeded with their argument on China's evolving socioeconomic conditions from the dynastic period to the 20th century. For them, despite the long tradition of water conservancy in China, a project like the Three Gorges Dam could not possibly be conceived under an agrarian economy in pre-modern times. "It was not until the 20th century," they wrote, "when the development of scientific techniques empowered people to conquer rivers like the Yangtze that a conception of building a modernized project at the Three Gorges was produced." It was not a coincidence, according to them, that Sun's proposal to build a Three Gorges Dam emerged in the same year, 1919, as the May Fourth Movement when the latter advocated "science" and "democracy." "The twenties of the 20th century," they argued, "was the time when modern scientific and technical ideas rapidly disseminated within China. The conception of constructing a dam at the Three Gorges was the result of such a dissemination."[26]

The projected historical trajectory was further extended from the early 20th century to the second half of the century as China was argued to be establishing an "advanced" social system that enabled the Three Gorges "dream" to be realized. Contrasting the politico-economic situation under the Nationalist government with that of the Communists', the writers extolled the post-1949 set-up as a progressive structure that was exemplary of a modern system:

> Although the scheme of building a Three Gorges dam was conceived more than 70 years ago by Sun Yat-sen, it remained a mere idea [under the Nationalist leadership]. . . . This was because the economic condition at that time was backward, the national power weak, and most of all, the Nationalist government corrupt. No serious work was done to practically construct a dam at the Three Gorges to harness the river. After New China was established, not only a Yangtze Valley Planning Office was organized. Numerous large-scale surveys and research projects were conducted, and special conferences were initiated by the top-level leadership. Contrasting the two (the Nationalists and the Communists), it is clear that a grand project bringing benefits to people can only be realized under an advanced social system.[27]

The authors' conceived teleological path of China's modernization experience was consummated at the point of the so-called scientific, democratic mode of decision-making in the first decade of the reform. From the competing proposals of "low dam" and "high dam" to the experts-fielded feasibility study to the final approval of the National People's Congress, the writers traced the process of the project in the 1980s and 1990s up to its endorsement. This decision-making process, they argued, was the ultimate manifestation of an exemplary sociopolitical structure.

The concepts of science and democracy have always been a concern in the 20th-century politics of China. From the "science" and "democracy" promoted by the May Fourth activists in 1919 to the "science" and "democracy" contemporary dam supporters advocated, the two ideas traveled a full circle. For the dam proponents, however, "science" and "democracy" had progressed along a linear track and attained an "advanced" form compared to that of the 1910s. Moreover, the process of change – essentially "advancement" – between the two temporal ends was embodied by the Three Gorges Dam. But the dam's temporal significance extended far beyond the nation's pursuits of "science" and "democracy" in the 20th century: it also embraced the dynasty's decline in the 19th century, the defeats and vicissitudes the country experienced, and the dawning possibility of redemption the incipient nation glimpsed. This conceived process of decline, demise, resuscitation, and eventual revitalization was also the process of the Chinese nation's progressive evolution – one that constituted what the authors called the Three Gorges project's "profound cultural content," all epitomized by the dam. Culture, in this context, was considered a bounded entity that seamlessly contained the nation's otherwise multifarious twists and turns of historical experience. It was devoid of the multiplicity of cultural practices and of networks of polyvalent meanings subject to renegotiation and recomposition that make up cultures in actuality.[28] This "culture," moreover, placed overwhelming emphasis on the modern and contemporary experience of the *nation* centered upon "democratic" pursuits and "scientific" achievement (with different meanings in different times), and disregarded its temporal and sociohistorical connection with what the dissenting intellectuals valued as China's ancient civilizational heritage.

2. Culture as Practices of Material Accumulation

Since the late 1990s, the term "tourism culture" (*lüyou wenhua*) has been frequently invoked in dam proponents' discourse. Along with this notion there also emerged the concept of "resettlement culture" (*yimin wenhua*), and the two were often used in an interconnected manner. In a newspaper article "A New Landscape: the Three Gorges Resettlement Culture," it was suggested that a "resettlement culture" created by the 1.3-million-people relocation project could be "developed to be directly utilized in the tourist industry."[29] Components of this "culture" were to include the dam, which was said to have been nominated in the United States to an honor roll of the "20th Century's Ten Greatest Construction Achievements in the World" and was thereby expected to generate "unprecedented cultural effects." Elements of the "culture" also included the new resettlement towns along with the new factories, schools, and commercial buildings, various Paleolithic fossils, Neolithic settlements, and ancient artifacts excavated in the process of relocation, and the Three Gorges resettlement museum, monument and memorial hall. The dam, the relics, the cities, and the newly built environment – in short, the new space to be produced at the Three Gorges – were all implicated in the productive activities of tourism. For the dam, the resettlement towns, and the infrastructural network, this amounted to a doubling of their perceived material value: on top of being means of industrial and agricultural production, they were also utilized as objects of consumption in touristic activities.

In this "tourism culture," or "resettlement culture," historical relics at the Three Gorges are stripped of their "pure" meaning of embodying the nation's ancient civilization. The reconceived national essence which consists of a continuum from the past through to the modern, futurist time, as discussed earlier, is thereby packaged in a new form of "Chinese culture and civilization." It is promoted on the market as a commodity to be consumed by touring spectators. The relics, in this way, serve as an antiquated or more precisely *nostalgic* counterpart of the modern/contemporary cultural products that are also on offer in the Three Gorges tourist industry, such as the new infrastructural landscape, the resettlers' towns, and the dam.

In the Three Gorges Relics Rescue Program, the government designated four sites as "state treasures." One of them was Zhang Fei Temple, constructed 1,700 years ago to commemorate the Three Kingdoms general. It was dismantled and rebuilt in the west of the reservoir area, including the sculptures, stelae, tiles, stone steps, wood carvings, and calligraphic inscriptions. Another one was Baiheliang (White Crane Ridge), a 1600-meter-long rock formation that was recognized by the United Nations Educational, Scientific and Cultural Organization (UNESCO) as "the world's only well-preserved ancient hydrological station." It emerged only in the dry season, exposing carvings of Bodhisattva, fish, and a crane. It also carries the inscriptions of 30,000 characters of poems and comments that record 1,200 years of the Yangtze's water-level changes and harvests. Under the preservation program, the ridge was protected by a pressure-free glass container filled with purified water and is now housed in an underwater museum. The "state treasures" were also joined by about 6,000 "precious" relics and 50,000 "more commonplace" artifacts, which ranged from pottery and lacquer work to bronze-ware and silverware excavated from the submerged area. These are collected in museums in Hubei Province and Chongqing Municipality, some of which were newly established, for tourists who visit for a glimpse of the Three Gorges and, more generally, Chinese history (Figures 5.3 and 5.4).

It was not only objects that were incorporated into the economic activities of touristic production and consumption. Also involved were an appropriation of people's customs valued for their tribal heritage and an erasure of other people's accumulated practices, particularly in the old towns. The ancient Dachang Town and Guilin Village were settlements built in the Ming and Qing dynasties. For hundreds of years, these had been inhabited by people who carried out their daily activities. Flooding them entailed an eradication of the practices that had sustained the community's dynamic organization but that were seen by the state as "poor" and "backward." Dachang Town, for example, was built about five hundred years ago and was listed as one of the four state-level relics. It was known for the picturesque cobbled streets, wooden carvings, and ancient temples. In the preservation operation, the town was reconstituted uphill with new stones and an imitation of

Figure 5.3 Historical relics collected in the Three Gorges Museum in Chongqing (Taken by author, 2015)

the architectural structure as a tourist park (Figure 5.5). It is no longer inhabited and is separated from the houses of the resettled Dachang residents who live outside the park.

Another case that illustrated the appropriation of local people's customs for the generation of wealth was the commodification of the Tu clan's "culture." This clan

Figure 5.4 Renderings of the Yangtze River and Three Gorges at the Three Gorges Museum. Note the tragically acclaimed barge haulers on the top right. (Taken by author, 2015)

is believed to be the descendants of the legendary Ba tribe which inhabited the Three Gorges about 4,000 years ago and whose traces of existence vanished in the first few centuries AD. According to archeological findings, the Ba tribe had a penchant for singing and dancing. They lived through fishing and hunting, and

Figure 5.5 The old town reproduced in the new site of Dachang as a tourist park. The government had promised a relocation brick by brick. However, except for some wooden shopfronts, all other structures were made anew. (Taken by author, 2015)

worshipped the white tiger as their god. Known for their valiant character, they were deployed to fight in major battles from the Zhou to Han dynasties. There is as yet no precise answer as to when and how this tribe went into decline and possible extinction. But from certain customs maintained by the Tu clan, such as the use of a tiger motif as their entrance god, anthropologists and archeologists believe that the clan was descended from the Ba tribe.

As discussion of "tourism culture" was underway, the government was planning to build a "Tu village of folk customs and culture" reproducing the songs, dance, and customary practices of the clan. "With meticulous packaging and nurturing," it was proposed, "the original character of the Tu cultural features can be preserved and made into a Tu cultural commodity series to attract domestic and foreign tourists."[30] Note that the first "culture," the "Tu cultural features," was distinct from the second one, the "Tu cultural commodity series," in that the former indicated a coherent system of signs and practices meaningful to a specific group of people, the Tu clan. It was itself a product of appropriation, modification, and reinvention of the Ba tribe's semiotic structure, given that the two communities' kin relationship was established. Adapting it to become a tourist commodity was a recomposition of the clan into a new cultural system dominated by the logic of capitalist exchange and instantiated by practices of material accumulation.

For decades, touring the Yangtze Three Gorges has meant cruising along the mainstream, occasionally going ashore to do some sightseeing of the historical relics. Under the proposed scheme of tourism after the dam's completion, the exploited area would extend to some previously unspoilt natural landscape. This included the tributaries, minor gorges, and mountains which would become accessible with the rise of the water level as a result of inundation. Not only would the natural environment be exploited, but commercial constructions would also be erected on the sites to turn the land into a money-generating locale. A new infrastructural and communication network was proposed to connect the different spots; people's daily productive activities such as agriculture would be made a component of the tourist route; and even the work of environmental protection, including conserved marine species threatened with extinction because of the dam project, would turn into a resource of the industry through exhibition.

From 1998 onward, there has been a wide range of discussions about how different geographical, social, and cultural features could be utilized, how individual provinces might "develop" their potentials for the building up of a corporate-oriented tourist sector, and how many travelers would be brought in and thereby how much revenue generated. In a "development strategy," the Badong county, located in the eastern part of the Three Gorges, announced its plan for a series of construction works ranging from a tourist pier to a highway to exploit a tributary that had been known for its remoteness and the possibility of having primordial "barbaric" humans inhabiting there. Under the development plan, spa resorts, hotels, river parks, and cave sites would be built. These were to be combined with an extensive recreational spot using local people's activities of sheep rearing, tea cultivating, and vegetable farming as a pastoral attraction. Estimating the economic effectiveness of such a scheme, it was said:

> The tourist industry under formation in Badong is gradually revealing its power as a driving force for the development of the region's primary, secondary, and tertiary industries. . . . Up until the end of 1997, out of the 21 counties, municipalities, and districts within the Three Gorges, which accommodate more than 16 million people, there were 17, involving 12 million people, considered national- and provincial-level poor localities. The ratio of the primary, secondary, and tertiary industries has been estimated at 42:36:22. The agricultural sector concentrates on crop, vegetable, and fruit cultivation, producing mainly unprocessed, primary products. The industrial sector, given the region's geographical limitations, has suffered from slow development and small scale. Its manufactured products are of low quality, able to take up only a minimal share of the market. . . . The tourist industry, in contrast, shows a great potential in leading the tertiary sector to push forward the region's economic development. With the Three Gorges as a famous tourist route . . . the exploitation of tourist resources will rapidly transform the resource advantage into an economic advantage.[31]

What was suggested in the various "strategies," with Badong's being but one, was the formation of an integrated system of development at the Three Gorges area through commodification in the form of tourism. In this system, all objects – from grass and rocks to animals and water, all aspects of people's life including that of resettlers, tribal customs, and local productive activities, not to mention historical relics that had already been exploited for tourist consumption – were incorporated. This system was considered the key to the people's material prospects and to the economic progress of that part of China, which had been seen as "poor." It tapped into a resource, tourism, that was thought of as "rich" and "renewable" on a par with the Yangtze water and was thereby expected to make the area's development "sustainable." More importantly, what makes this system so significant in our analysis is the culture it seeks to promote through an apparently normal and common state of affairs. Through the relations of production, circulation, and exchange, people's actions are defined in terms of the capacity they can produce, the value of the relics measured in the form of the potential income the sites will bring, and the water and land are translated into how much they generate in monetary units – the megawatts of hydroelectricity from the water and the volume of farm produce from the land – all of which are convertible into money (Figure 5.6).

Re-encoding the meaning of the Yangtze landscape and its cultural relics, the reformist state has incorporated non-human objects into its ideological practices of development and, further, subsumed the dissidents' civilizational understanding of

Figure 5.6 World Tourism Day held in Yichang on May 18, 2021. Note the bamboo basket, which was a traditional mode of transport in the Three Gorges area before the dam project. Here, the basket is refashioned into an outsized 2.1 meters × 1.5 meters stage prop for touristic promotion. (Getty Images)

the *nation* into its progressivist discourse. The conceived continuum of temporality, which encompasses an ancient past, a developing present, and a forward-looking future, undergirds the ideational representation of the objects, which is reproduced daily through the economic activity of tourism.

The revamped tourist industry sells a combination of commercialized displays of historical relics and technological showcases of China's modernization (such as the dam, the reservoir, and agribusiness). The semiotic representation of "national redemption" through the achievement of the world's largest dam has merged with the material practice of money-making through tourism. The reformed tourist industry promises new jobs and increased income, which the Party claims will contribute to the "elimination of poverty and getting rich." National rejuvenation thus acquires a double meaning of not only technological supremacy but also the redemption of prior individual suffering by means of a promised improvement in livelihood through touristic activities.

The dissidents' contestation contributed to the increased commitment of the state to historic preservation, but their campaign was largely confined within the territorial boundary of China. Toward the end of the 1990s, as the scandals of "tofu projects" including collapsed bridges and the cracked structure of the dam discovered during construction broke out, central leaders showed increased interest in bringing in international help to ensure the scheme's technical soundness. Introducing the dam to the international engineering arena, the technocrats also took the project onto the stage of global politics through the solicitation of transnational capital. This move was representative of the reformists' policy orientation and the development of the Chinese economy in the direction of globalization. The opening up, however, made possible the intervention of transnational environmental activists to campaign against the project.

Notes

1 Roland Barthes, *Mythologies* (New York: Hill and Wang, 1972). Selected and translated from the French by Annette Lavers.
2 W. J. T. Mitchell, ed., *Landscape and Power* (Chicago: University of Chicago Press, 1994), 14 (italics added).
3 For the letter, see "Shangshu: Baohu zhonghua minzu lishi yichan" [Petition: Preserving the Historical Heritage of the Chinese Nation," *Yazhou Zhoukan (Asiaweek)*, September 1, 1996, 20–21 (italics added).
4 Qin is considered to be the first kingdom that united the fragmented warring states into the integrated territory of "China" in 221 BC. But the concept of a sovereign polity with a delineated boundary vis-à-vis the others did not come into being until 1689 when the Qing court signed its first treaty with Russia. See Tang Deyang, *Zhongguo wenhua de yuanliu [The Origin and Development of Chinese Culture]* (Shandong renmin chubanshe), 2–5.
5 For the case of Guan Yu, one of the Three Kingdoms heroes, see Prasenjit Duara, "Superscribing Symbols: the Myth of Guandi, Chinese God of War," *Journal of Asian Studies* 47, no. 4 (November 1988): 778–795; and *Culture, Power, and the State* (Stanford, CA: Stanford University Press, 1988), 118–157.
6 The sculptures can be seen in Youyi Shi, ed., *Changjiang sanxia [The Three Gorges on the Yangtze River]* (Haifeng chubanshe, 2001), 15.

7 Lyman Van Slyke, *Yangtze: Nature, History and the River* (Reading, MA: Addison-Wesley, 1989), 139.
8 Qing Dai and Weijia Xue, eds., *Shui de Changjiang [To Whom Does the Yangtze Belong?]* (Hong Kong: Oxford University Press, 1996), 120–136.
9 Duara, "Superscribing Symbols;" and *Culture, Power, and the State*, 118–157.
10 "Shangshu [Petition]," *Yazhou Zhoukan*, 21.
11 "Sanxia wenwu guji gaoji: fang Yu Weichao" [An Urgent Plea From the Three Gorges Historical Relics – an Interview With Director of the National Museum of Chinese History, Yu Weichao], in *Shui de Changjiang [To Whom Does the Yangtze Belong?]*, ed. Dai Qing and Xue Weijia (Hong Kong: Oxford University Press, 1996), 120–136.
12 Qingyu Hong, "Bianzhe de hua" [From the Publisher], in *Hongwei de gongcheng [The Magnificent Project]* (Shuili dianli chubanshe, 1992).
13 Patrick E. Tyler, "Dam's Inexorable Future Spells Doom for Yangtze Valley's Rich Past," *New York Times*, October 6, 1996.
14 See, for example, *Dili [Geography]*, Book 3 for Junior High School (Renmin jiaoyu chubanshe, 1996), 70–76; "Bianzhe de hua" [From the Editor], in *Hongwei de gongcheng*; "An Exposition of the Three Gorges Proposal – a Speech Given by Vice-Premier Zhou Jiahua in the National People's Congress," *Jiefangjun bao [People's Liberation Army Daily]*, March 22, 1992; and Kexiong Chen, "The Ins and Outs of the Three Gorges Project – an Interview with Qian Zhengying," in *Sanxia de tiaozhan [The Challenge of the Three Gorges]*, ed. Shu Ye (Jingji ribao chubanshe, 1992), 56–70.
15 Jingdong Zheng, ed., *Zhongguo sanxia wenhua gailun [An Introduction to the Culture of the Three Gorges in China]* (Zhongguo sanxia chubanshe, 1996), 82 (italics added).
16 Yuan Pan, "Sanxia baqu: fajuezhong de lüyou fukuang" [The Three Gorges Reservoir Area: A Rich Mine of Tourism Under Excavation], *Zhongguo Sanxia gongcheng bao [China Three Gorges Project News]*, January 27, 2000.
17 Xiaoyun Zeng, "Guojia bokuan yiyiyuan, qiangjiu sanxia wenwu" [The Government Allocates a Hundred Million Yuan to Rescue the Three Gorges Relics], *Zhongguo Sanxia gongcheng bao [China Three Gorges Project News]*, May 25, 2000.
18 Gang Liu et al., "Sanxia wenwu lianjie zhonghua wenming" [The Three Gorges Historical Relics Link Up the Chain of the Chinese Civilization], *Zhongguo Sanxia gongcheng bao [China Three Gorges Project News]*, January 17, 2001.
19 Shilong Zhao, "Yu daojuezhe he gongqi saipao" [Racing Against the Looters and Construction Schedule], *Nanfang zhoumo [Southern Weekly]*, November 7, 1997; and Zhao Shilong, "Jiujiu yaoqianshu, jiujiu sanxia wenwu" [Save the Treasure, Save the Three Gorges Relics], *Zhongguo Sanxia gongcheng bao [China Three Gorges Project News]*, June 19, 1998.
20 Shilong Zhao, "Jiujiu yaoqianshu," *Zhongguo Sanxia gongcheng bao [China Three Gorges Project News]*, June 19, 1998; and Liu Gang et al., "Yixiang shijie hanjian de wenwu baohu gongcheng" [A Rare Historic Preservation Project in the World], *Zhongguo Sanxia gongcheng bao [China Three Gorges Project News]*, January 19, 2001.
21 "Saving the Cultural Relics of the Three Gorges," *Zhongguo wang (china.org.cn)*, April 9, 2003, http://www.china.org.cn/english/features/Archeology/96925.htm; and Hongyi Wang, "Work to Save Three Gorges Relics," *China Daily*, September 3, 2008, http://www.chinadaily.com.cn/china/2008/09/03/content_6992751.htm.
22 Rongguo Hu, "Fengjiexian kaifa lüyou ziyuan anzhi yimin" [Fengjie County Develops Its Tourism Resources for the Resettlement of Relocated Villagers], *Zhongguo Sanxia gongcheng bao [China Three Gorges Project News]*, January 15, 1998.
23 Lewis Mumford, *Technics and Civilization* (New York: Harcourt, Brace & World, 1963).
24 Jingdong Zheng, ed., *Zhongguo sanxia wenhua gailun [An Introduction to the Culture of the Three Gorges in China]* (Zhongguo sanxia chubanshe, 1996), 77.
25 Zheng, ed., *Zhongguo sanxia wenhua gailun [An Introduction to the Culture of the Three Gorges in China]*, 77–78.

26 Zheng, ed., *Zhongguo sanxia wenhua gailun [An Introduction to the Culture of the Three Gorges in China]*, 78.
27 Zheng, ed., *Zhongguo sanxia wenhua gailun [An Introduction to the Culture of the Three Gorges in China]*, 79.
28 Lisa Wedeen, *Ambiguities of Domination: Politics, Rhetoric, and Symbols in Contemporary Syria* (The University of Chicago Press, 1999), especially 1–31; and William Sewell, "The Concept(s) of Culture," in *Logics of History: Social Theory and Social Transformation* (Chicago and London: The University of Chicago Press, 2005).
29 Xiucai Yao, "Xin jingguan: sanxia yimin wenhua" [A New Landscape: The Three Gorges Resettlement Culture], *Zhongguo Sanxia gongcheng bao [China Three Gorges Project News]*, September 24, 1999.
30 Aimin Xu, "Badong lüyou: gaizao shenlongxi" [Tourism in Badong: Transforming the Shenlong River], *Zhongguo Sanxia gongcheng bao [China Three Gorges Project News]*, November 28, 2000.
31 Lin Chen, "Badong weihe yaochi lüyoufan" [Why Does Badong Live on Tourism?], *Zhongguo Sanxia gongcheng bao [China Three Gorges Project News]*, January 18, 2000.

Bibliography

Barthes, Roland. 1972. *Mythologies*. Translated by Annette Lavers. New York: Hill and Wang.

Chen, Lin. 2000. "Badong weihe yaochi lüyoufan" [Why Does Badong Live on Tourism?]. *Zhongguo Sanxia gongcheng bao [China Three Gorges Project News],* January 18.

Dai, Qing, and Xue Weijia, eds. 1996. *Shui de Changjiang [To Whom Does the Yangtze Belong?]*. Hong Kong: Oxford University Press.

Dili [Geography]. 1996. Book 3 for Junior High School. Renmin jiaoyu chubanshe.

Duara, Prasenjit. 1988a. *Culture, Power, and the State*. Stanford University Press.

Duara, Prasenjit. 1988b. "Superscribing Symbols: The Myth of Guandi, Chinese God of War." *Journal of Asian Studies* 47 (4) (November): 778–95.

Hong, Qingyu. 1992. *Hongwei de gongcheng [The Magnificent Project]*. Shuili dianli chubanshe.

Hu, Rongguo. 1998. "Fengjiexian kaifa lüyou ziyuan anzhi yimin" [Fengjie County Develops Its Tourism Resources for the Resettlement of Relocated Villagers]. *Zhongguo Sanxia gongcheng bao [China Three Gorges Project News],* January 15.

Jiefangjun bao [People's Liberation Army Daily]. 1992. "An Exposition of the Three Gorges Proposal – a Speech Given by Vice-premier Zhou Jiahua in the National People's Congress." March 22.

Liu, Gang et al. 2001a. "Sanxia wenwu lianjie zhonghua wenming" [The Three Gorges Historical Relics Link Up the Chain of the Chinese Civilization]. *Zhongguo Sanxia gongcheng bao [China Three Gorges Project News]*, January 17.

Liu, Gang et al. 2001b. "Yixiang shijie hanjian de wenwu baohu gongcheng" [A Rare Historic Preservation Project in the World]. *Zhongguo Sanxia gongcheng bao [China Three Gorges Project News]*, January 19.

Mitchell, W. J. T., ed. 1994. *Landscape and Power*. University of Chicago Press.

Mumford, Lewis. 1963. *Technics and Civilization*. New York: Harcourt, Brace & World.

Pan, Yuan. 2000. "Sanxia baqu: fajuezhong de lüyou fukuang" [The Three Gorges Reservoir Area: A Rich Mine of Tourism under Excavation]. *Zhongguo Sanxia gongcheng bao [China Three Gorges Project News]*, January 27.

Sewell, William. 2005. "The Concept(s) of Culture." In *Logics of History: Social Theory and Social Transformation*. Chicago and London: The University of Chicago Press.

"Shangshu: Baohu zhonghua minzu lishi yichan" [Petition: Preserving the Historical Heritage of the Chinese Nation," *Yazhou Zhoukan (Asiaweek)*. September 1, 1996, 20–21.

Shi, Youyi et al., eds. 2001. *Changjiang sanxia [The Three Gorges on the Yangtze River]*. Haifeng chubanshe.

Shu, Ye, ed. 1992. *Sanxia de tiaozhan [The Challenge of the Three Gorges]*. Jingji ribao chubanshe.

Tang, Deyang. 1993. *Zhongguo wenhua de yuanliu [The Origin and Development of Chinese Culture]*. Shandong renmin chubanshe.

Tyler, Patrick E. 1996. "Dam's Inexorable Future Spells Doom for Yangtze Valley's Rich Past." *New York Times*, October 6.

Van Slyke, Lyman. 1989. *Yangtze: Nature, History and the River*. Reading, MA: Addison-Wesley.

Wang, Hongyi. 2008. "Work to Save Three Gorges Relics." *China Daily*, September 3. http://www.chinadaily.com.cn/china/2008-09/03/content_6992751.htm.

Wedeen, Lisa. 1999. *Ambiguities of Domination: Politics, Rhetoric, and Symbols in Contemporary Syria*. The University of Chicago Press.

Xu, Aimin. 2000. "Badong lüyou: gaizao shenlongxi" [Tourism in Badong: Transforming the Shenlong River]. *Zhongguo Sanxia gongcheng bao [China Three Gorges Project News]*, November 28.

Yao, Xiucai. 1999. "Xin jingguan: sanxia yimin wenhua" [A New Landscape: The Three Gorges Resettlement Culture]. *Zhongguo Sanxia gongcheng bao [China Three Gorges Project News]*, September 24.

Zeng, Xiaoyun. 2000. "Guojia bokuan yiyiyuan, qiangjiu sanxia wenwu" [The Government Allocates a Hundred Million Yuan to Rescue the Three Gorges Relics]. *Zhongguo Sanxia gongcheng bao [China Three Gorges Project News]*, May 25.

Zhao, Shilong. 1997. "Yu daojuezhe he gongqi saipao" [Racing against the Looters and Construction Schedule]. *Nanfang zhoumo [Southern Weekly]*, November 7.

Zhao, Shilong. 1998. "Jiujiu yaoqianshu, jiujiu sanxia wenwu" [Save the Treasure, Save the Three Gorges Relics]. *Zhongguo Sanxia gongcheng bao [China Three Gorges Project News]*, June 19.

Zheng, Jingdong, ed. 1996. *Zhongguo sanxia wenhua gailun [An Introduction to the Culture of the Three Gorges in China]*. Zhongguo sanxia chubanshe.

Zhongguo wang (china.org.cn). 2003. "Saving the Cultural Relics of the Three Gorges." April 9. http://www.china.org.cn/english/features/Archeology/96925.htm.

6 "March Toward the International"

The Politics of Global Capital and Transnational Resistance[1]

At the turn of the 21st century, the political theodicy of material elevation took a transnational course as the Chinese economy embraced the global market and became a major player in the cross-border milieu. The shift represents another threshold of transformation in China's developmental path. This new tactic of development changed from the high-modernist mode of social engineering in a local setting to a neoliberal form of calculated progress on a global scale. As a result, what had initially appeared as a nationalist project took on a dimension of globalism. As the scheme entered the second half of the 1990s, it was discernible that the dam was increasingly made to express a vision of China as a nation looking beyond its borders to embrace the world.[2] The "globe," the "world," or the "international" was always at the center of discussion on the Three Gorges – "Create a first-rate dam in the world" and "Embark on the international stage" were just two examples.

The idea became more prominent early in the new century, when "common prosperity" gradually retreated into the background and gave way to President Hu Jintao's "scientific outlook of development." His new "human-oriented, all-round, coordinated, and sustainable" idea of development was a major strategy on the part of the Communist Party to reconcile the socioeconomic contradictions that had emerged from more than two decades of reform – the drastically increased disparity between rural and urban residents,[3] the deteriorating environment, and the intervention from the global community as a result of the open economy. According to the official line, this policy direction signaled "a new stage of development" that shifted national priorities from rapid economic growth merely aimed at providing food and clothing for 1.3 billion people to a "coordinated" and "balanced" form of development in both the rural and urban areas through a transfer of rural populations to non-rural ones by means of industrialization and urbanization.[4]

It was in the context of this "new stage of development" that the dam project embarked on a new threshold of global involvement. China's new membership of the WTO was leading the country to the core of the globalized economy, and its interactions with the transnational community became increasingly intense. While some people in China were cautious about the challenges the latest development would pose to their society, others considered it a golden opportunity for the country's material advancement. A State Council economic expert, for example, projected that the surplus capital of developed countries would be made readily

DOI: 10.4324/9781003531494-7

accessible in the global financial market for capital-deficient developing countries.[5] His views echoed the Three Gorges officials' plans at the time to solicit cross-border funds for the dam's construction.

However, the opportunity brought about by China's participation in the global arena also came with a reverse current of possibilities that conflicted with the state's developmental agenda. Transnational activist groups used the environment – a core issue of President Hu's "scientific development concept" – as a focus for lobbying against the dam. In every possible way, the campaign targeted the project's global financing bids and tried to block the stream of funding. Its charges and criticisms exposed the project's contradictions, which led to the undermining of investors' confidence in the scheme's social integrity and financial prospects. Many chose to stay away, while some joined the campaign to oppose the dam.

The conflict illuminated the complex interplay of forces at work in the global arena. In contrast with the view that globalization is a homogenizing, all-encompassing megatrend, the Three Gorges environment-development struggle involved a multiplicity of voices, interpretations, and ideas that interacted, clashed, and negotiated in a heterogeneous scenario. The variegated sociopolitical standpoints, put forward by different people and institutions, might at times overlap, with one appropriating the other, or all confronting one another in interconnected global-national-local processes. The Three Gorges story of globalization was one concerning ideologies, global capital, and transnational civil society. By becoming a protagonist on the stage of the global economy, China gained access to resources such as development rhetoric, technological knowledge, market share, and capital. But at the same time, China brought upon itself constraints by opening up opportunities for transnational groups to connect with Chinese society and intervene in the government's policies.

The tension between transnational environmentalism and national development arises from the interweaving relationship among the global, national, and local structures of social relations. Constituting those structures are not only circulating material objects such as people and construction machinery but also circuits of exchange of information, knowledge, and in an abstract yet real form, capital. The increasing interconnectedness of the various structures, which makes their boundaries ever blurrier, enables a project as local as the Three Gorges to gain worldwide attention and assume global significance. Considered an issue of general concern in the human community, the dam became a part of the global (competing) discourses of development and environmentalism as it was made into a topic of exchange among scientists around the world and the target of a campaign by transnational environmental activists alike. These were in addition to the flow of images and ideas in the Western media, and the transfer of capital for the dam's construction by supranational financial corporations (under the orchestration of Chinese technocrats). The Three Gorges project, loaded with nationalist meanings and import, thus became a global issue that traversed the delineated terrains of the "inside" and "outside,"[6] the domestic and international. In what follows I will use the human rights dispute between the Chinese developmentalists and transnational environmentalists to elucidate the project's global politics.

"The World" at the Three Gorges

Approaching the end of the 1990s, the construction of the dam entered a more critical phase. The phrase "the world" and its semantic variations, which were featured prominently in the discourse on the dam in this period, essentially represented the enabling possibilities in global financial, scientific, and engineering domains. After the initial blockage of the Yangtze in 1997, technological know-how circulated more intensively, and international bidders were brought in to compete for contracts for component parts. In the newspaper article "Belonging to China, [the Dam] also Belongs to the World," the author celebrated the international attention the project had received in terms of, among others, media coverage, visits of political leaders from interested countries, and participation of multinational machinery and hydropower equipment corporations. Exchange and cooperation projects with foreign institutions took place on technical issues ranging from large-scale concrete pouring for the dam wall to wildlife preservation. Delegations were also sent to Japan, the United States, and Hong Kong in preparation for the effort to raise capital for the dam in the global financial market. "The international interchanges," the article stated, "enable the Three Gorges scheme to tackle many challenging issues. Building on the achievements of our contemporary world, the dam will further propel international technological development by adding to it a new experience."[7]

For years the Yangtze River Three Gorges Project Development Corporation (hereafter referred to as Three Gorges Corporation) had envisioned the accomplishment of the project with the support of international capital. The plan was highlighted in March 1999, when a cash flow crisis arising out of the second phase of construction (1998–2003) prompted the dam authorities to seek funding sources for the estimated \$3 billion shortfall.[8] China had raised more than \$12 billion from a tax on domestic household electricity, but it was insufficient for the \$25 billion project. A quarter of that budget, it was estimated, would have to be secured from overseas funders. The Three Gorges Corporation tried to issue bonds in its name on the international market, but the various attempts it had made since 1994 to launch global offerings had been canceled due to a lack of investor interest. In 2003, upon the founding of the China Yangtze Electric Corporation, of which the Three Gorges Corporation was the major shareholder, dam officials sought to raise funds by listing the project on domestic and overseas stock markets. The goal was to gather sufficient capital for the dam's twenty-six electric generators through a series of public offerings to be made in six years, up until the end of the construction in 2009. With a listing on Shanghai's A-share index that was expected to bring about \$500 million, the Three Gorges Corporation initiated negotiations with the American energy firm Mirant and Hong Kong-based CLP Power to take part of a 10 percent block of shares offered to strategic private investors for the domestic offering. Moreover, plans were underway to list the project in Hong Kong and London, in part because of the consideration that some of the project's creditor banks were European. Participating in the endeavor were Merrill Lynch, Morgan Stanley, Nomura, and Goldman Sachs, all of which had drawn up plans to contend for positions as lead underwriters. The state's ambitions to float some of the Three

Gorges' shares in the market, however, proved to be futile. The delegation led by Li Yongan, then vice president of the Three Gorges Corporation, to Hong Kong in 2002 for talks with Mirant and CLP Power did not succeed in attracting private foreign investors' interest. After this, the dam company withdrew all the plans to list the project on the Hong Kong and London stock exchanges.[9]

The Three Gorges Corporation's debacle in the financial market coincided with a noticeable subsiding of the celebration of the dam's world significance in official discourse. The initial excitement about international interest and the assertion of the construction's exemplary role in global technology were no longer discernible. Since the dam first began producing electricity in 2003, the focus has become almost *introverted*, with accounts of, inter alia, what the Partnership Support Program (*duikou zhiyuan*) had achieved, how the reformulated tourist industry would prosper, and how China would be able to produce its own turbines. There were reports about the offering on the Shanghai Stock Exchange, but no mention was made of the planned overseas listings.

Given that the Three Gorges Dam was a state-sponsored project, which implied a low-risk investment, and that the issuing company promised that half of the net profits would go to dividends, it was puzzling that the bond and stock offerings attracted little investor interest. Some blamed the dam's costs for the failure. A large part of these had been the result of the resettlement of 1.2 million people and, most of all, official embezzlement. Bribery, many believed, was associated with substandard workmanship, which led to investors' doubts about the dam's safety and durability. Some were also worried that the environmental impact of the dam would impose tremendous expenses on the company. Besides, part of the capital to be raised was planned to finance other dam projects on the upper reaches of the Yangtze, which offered no specific date of return on the investment. This uncertainty was in addition to the general tendency of hydropower projects to take longer than coal power stations to reap results.[10] But if profits were a major consideration, if costs and risks were investors' main concerns, why did the listing succeed in the domestic market while the attempted overseas floatation failed?

The author argues that a large part of this international reluctance was related to the lobbying of the transnational environmental campaigns, which targeted potential foreign investors in the global capital market. Funding had been the focal point of the anti-Three Gorges opposition. Starting with conventional loan providers such as the World Bank, nongovernmental organizations (NGOs) shifted their intended audience in the course of the campaign to Wall Street financiers and investment bank shareholders as the dam became increasingly involved in global capital. With different means of promotion, some of them quite innovative as far as environmental politics is concerned, these opponents managed to bring attention to the problems and defects of the dam. The sowing of doubts among the investors, about issues from corruption to environmental impacts to resettlement abuses, would not have been possible were it not for the lobby's ardent appeals to the general public (outside China), together with reports in the Western media. Their campaign represented one of the social forces that exploited an authoritarian state's political fissures – forces and fissures whose emergence was made possible in the globalizing context of circulating capital and information. The opposition had the limitation of operating within the confines of a beyond-China terrain. However, its activities and moral claims reached across geographical domains as a transnational sociopolitical activism that influenced the implementation of a local project. The lobby did not succeed in bringing down the dam, but it effectively restrained it by uncovering otherwise covert or faulty operations, thereby placing the scheme under the world's scrutiny and dissuading potential investors from participating while restricting the dam company to costly loans.

Interaction Between Developmentalism and Environmentalism

On November 20, 1997, a full-page advertisement commissioned by the International Rivers Network (IRN) and Friends of the Earth appeared in the *New York Times*: "An Exclusive Bond Offering: Here's your chance to invest in a Grand Monument to China's Authoritarian Regime." "We urge you to call your fund managers," said the advertisement, "and insist that your money does not get funneled into Three Gorges Dam." The argument they used in support of their plea was consistent with what Chinese dissidents had maintained since the 1980s. The dam, they claimed, would be ineffective in controlling the Yangtze floods, and it would not produce sufficient electricity to remedy China's power shortage. The reservoir, moreover, would lose its function within fifty years because of siltation, which made it unreasonable to commit $75 billion – almost seven times the $11 billion official projection made in 1992 and three times the existing government estimation of $25 billion – to build the dam. In short, according to the campaigners, the scheme would be an "economic and ecological catastrophe."

The Three Gorges Dam was in itself a local project. In the 1980s, much of the debate was confined within China to dissenting intellectuals and the government together with its technocrat supporters. After the 1989 Tiananmen crackdown, all the opposing voices were suppressed. Conflict reemerged around 1992 but subsided after the National People's Congress approved the scheme that year and made it an accomplished fact. In 1994, however, a book edited by Dai Qing, one of the Chinese opponents who continued to campaign and eventually brought the case to the international environmentalists, was published in English.[11] The book, which collected essays and interviews with Chinese intellectuals and experts who opposed the project, had originally been published in China but was banned after Tiananmen. The translation was sponsored by Probe International, a Canadian environmental group that became one of the most active opponents in the transnational anti-Three Gorges lobby. A local project thus erupted into a global issue, with a wider audience in the English-speaking world (with added contributions from the media) becoming informed of the pitfalls of a dam that was to be built on a microscopic (from the viewpoint of Planet Earth) river site in a central Chinese province.

A transnational discourse of anti-Three Gorges environmentalism coalesced. This discourse was rooted in a broader globalized discourse that centered on the idea that the natural environment was fundamental to human well-being and on the insistence that environmental goals be considered in the development process.[12] These notions, which were part of international agreements such as the Declaration of the United Nations Conference on the Human Environment (1972) and the Rio Declaration on Environment and Development (1992), were well publicized, giving environmental groups worldwide a strong argument. The goals of environmental protection and sustainable development gave much moral strength to the anti-Three Gorges campaign. Frequently, the lobby used the phrase "environmentally and socially destructive" to describe the Three Gorges Dam project in its press releases and appeals until 2000.

This notion was further amplified when it was connected to a relatively new idea in the environmental discourse – the anti-big-dam concept. The latter was based on an extensive database gathered by the World Commission on Dams (WCD) after more than two years of consultations with stakeholders, reviews of experts, and surveys of dams worldwide. Its report, released in November 2000, concluded that large dams had led to, among other things, the loss of species populations, emissions of greenhouse gases, and disruption of the livelihoods of the displaced, which were rarely restored.[13]

The WCD's argument drew in part on the Impoverishment, Risks and Reconstruction (IRR) model advanced by Michael Cernea, who breaks down the socioeconomic content of the displacement process into the principal risks of landlessness, joblessness, homelessness, marginalization of relocated people, food insecurity, increased morbidity and mortality, loss of access to common property resources, and community disarticulation. "[A]rguably the most influential contribution to contemporary resettlement studies," the IRR approach was used by the WCD to connect the impacts of involuntary dislocation with human rights.[14] In its report, the WCD made an innovative proposal that "an approach based on 'recognition of rights' and 'assessment of risks' (particularly rights at risk) be developed as a tool for guiding future planning and decision making."[15] It called for the inclusion of all stakeholders in the decision on dams. The emphasis on human rights was picked up by transnational environmentalists and became a focal point, as will be shown, of the anti-Three Gorges campaign in the new century.

Individual member groups of the Three Gorges opposition, which principally came from the United States, Canada, Sweden, and Switzerland, carried out separate or joint activities countering the worldviews, practices, and institutions of development – the primary discourse that had been equally globalized and highly entrenched. This discourse is deep rooted. From the Hoover Dam in the United States to the Aswan in Egypt to the Itaipu in Brazil, water engineering megaprojects are embodiments of a modernist worldview that espouses the human potential in exploiting nature for the fulfillment of social progress. This worldview is particularly connected with national development, in that large dams, with their purported benefits of power supply, irrigation, and flood control, were and still are considered important engines of economic growth and modernization in certain developing countries.[16] The WCD report was, however, rejected by China and India, and it never received official acceptance by the World Bank and Asia Development Bank. Worse still, after a decade-long suspension of big dam financing, the

World Bank signaled in a 2003 water strategy paper its plans to resume large dam constructions.[17]

In the case of the Three Gorges, the discourse of development employed by international financial institutions and national governments was countered in the global setting by a discourse of environmental protection espoused by NGO activists. Finance was always the target of the environmentalists. It was their belief that funding would be a crucial target in the plan to stop the Three Gorges project, especially given the scale of the undertaking. Intensive efforts were made toward that end, with the hope that some success could be achieved before 2003, when the dam would start generating electricity, which would be the point of no return. They started with official and semi-official organizations that were considered conventional supporters of development, some of which had expressed interest in the project. The United States, for example, offered a $2 billion loan in 1979 in a five-year technical assistance agreement on China's hydropower construction. In 1980, China and the United States drew up a cooperation pact to develop the Three Gorges' natural resources. The Canadian government also conducted a feasibility study in 1986 and came to the conclusion that a dam at the Three Gorges would be both feasible and beneficial. Its findings were basically the same as those of China's own feasibility study, except that Canada recommended a lower reservoir level of 160 meters (compared to China's 175 meters). Both the US and Canadian governments were prepared to participate in the project. But with intense opposition from the environmental groups, both of them withdrew. In 1993, seven American NGOs filed a lawsuit against the US Bureau of Reclamation and the Army Corps of Engineers, which had offered advice on the project since the 1940s, on the grounds that "such assistance would violate US law because the reservoir will flood the habitats of a dozen endangered species."[18] The action resulted in the Bureau of Reclamation's decision in late 1993 to withdraw from the project, with the explanation that "[r]eclamation's current priorities are water-resource management and environmental restoration, not large dam projects."

Following the government agencies' refusal to support the dam, other potential funders also backed down. In May 1996, the US Export-Import Bank announced that it would not lend to the project, which greatly restricted American companies' ability to bid for contracts related to the dam. The reason given was that "[t]he information received . . . fails to establish the project's consistency with the Bank's environmental guidelines."[19] The bank maintained that it had made this decision according to its congressional charter and after consultation with the National Security Council, exporters, and Chinese officials. However, the timing of its deliberations coincided with a meeting it had with Dai Qing and representatives of the IRN, Probe International, and Friends of the Earth. A similar meeting was also held between dam opponents and the World Bank, which finances many infrastructural projects around the world.[20] In the end, China did not submit any application to the World Bank.

The withdrawal of the agencies and institutions signaled to some extent a retreat of development discourse: the World Bank had become stricter about the environmental standards of borrower countries in the 1990s (which caused India to give up the last installment for the Sardar Sarovar Dam), and some countries including the United States started to decommission dams to restore ecosystem function and native fish populations. The anti-Three Gorges lobby could not completely seal off the funding stream for the dam – the Canadian Export Credit Agency gave support, and Germany and Sweden issued export risk guarantees despite opposition from European groups such as the Swedish Society for Nature Conservation and the Berne Declaration. This said, the campaign significantly restrained major sources of financing and posed clear questions about the project. The Three Gorges scheme turned to an alternative way of funding its construction, but in so doing it encountered another round of struggle that was embroiled in global capital exchange.

Global Capital Versus Transnational Environmental Lobby

Unable to launch bond offerings in its name, as mentioned earlier, the Three Gorges Corporation embarked on an indirect path. The China Development Bank, formed in 1994 under the name State Development Bank of China to finance state-owned enterprises and infrastructural projects, became the largest funder of the dam. Its loan made up 65 percent of the Three Gorges budget, and the project was the bank's biggest creditor. In 1996, the bank introduced its first international bonds, of RMB 30 billion (US$3.6 billion), underwritten by Nomura Securities in Japan.[21] In the following year, it turned to Wall Street financiers and issued US$330 million global bonds. Lehman Brothers and J.P. Morgan were the lead managers. The two companies, together with Credit Suisse First Boston and Morgan Stanley, each contributed $66 million. Smith Barney underwrote $46.2 million, and Bank of America $19.8 million.[22] A similar move took place in 1999, when the China Development Bank launched a $500 million bond issue. Merrill Lynch and Salomon Smith Barney each invested $225 million. In total, 40 percent of the bonds were bought by Asian-based investors, while 30 percent went to European financiers, with the remainder taken up by American buyers.[23] Two years later, in 2001, another $1.75 billion bond offering was made, this time not in the United States, but in Hong Kong and Luxembourg, although sales were intended for the United States. It was said that China's decision to avoid the American market was due to pressure from the environmental activists as well as more stringent disclosure requirements in the United States. The outgoing Securities Exchange commissioner, Laura Unger, had required more reporting of human-rights-related issues. But bond offerings continued. In 2004, the China Development Bank issued another $1.1 billion of global bonds and invited six investment banks to manage the sale. This time about half of the offering was taken up by Goldman Sachs, Merrill Lynch, and Morgan Stanley for US dollar investors, while the remainder was sold by BNP Paribus, HSBC, and UBS to euro financiers.

As proponents of the dam turned from official and semi-official institutions to investment banks, albeit through an indirect route, the locus of conflict shifted. Environmentalists targeted individual funders who had underwritten bonds for the China Development Bank and managed to bring some of them to their side. The Bank of America, which participated in the 1997 bond offering, agreed in

December of that year that it would not undertake any direct lending to the Three Gorges Dam and would carefully examine any deals that might indirectly benefit the project.[24] Playing by different rules of the game, the activists moved away from the traditional meeting table to the corporations' multinational operations and conglomerates of customers. They campaigned against credit cards issued by the banks, such as Discover and CitiCard. More than forty groups, whose combined mailing lists totaled millions of people, joined a boycott of Discover, an affiliate of Morgan Stanley, that was initiated by the IRN. The NGOs also tackled the ownership at its source and challenged the corporations from within, through shareholder actions. Shareholder resolutions were forwarded to Merrill Lynch and Citigroup and at one point managed to bring the two companies to the table to discuss their policies regarding the Three Gorges Dam. Morgan Stanley Dean Witter was a particular target of the environmental lobby. The firm managed and owned 35 percent of a Chinese joint-venture investment bank, China International Capital Corporation (CICC), which provided expert advice to the Three Gorges on overseas capital collecting. In 1999, the CICC co-underwrote a domestic bond of about $250 million that funneled part of the proceeds to the dam.[25] Starting from 1998, Trillium Asset Management, a Boston investment company concentrating on socially and environmentally acceptable projects, led a shareholder campaign to press Morgan Stanley for a review of its underwriting, investing, and lending criteria, "with the view to incorporating and fully disclosing" any transaction's impacts on the environment and human rights.[26] The resolution never received sufficient votes to pass. But for at least three years it marshaled enough support to be reintroduced, enabling the campaigners to question executives at the annual meetings and refreshing shareholders' memory of the Three Gorges dispute with the mailed papers. In 1999, the resolutions drew the attention of Morgan Stanley's top personnel, who agreed to meet the activists. The session did not result in any concrete commitment on the part of Morgan Stanley, whose representatives said they "want[ed] to enter China's emerging markets, with good favor from the government." However, continued pressure from the environmentalists induced the company to avoid the New York venue in 2002 and change the location of its general meeting to London.

The Three Gorges polemics illuminated a new kind of development politics in which conflicts were played out in the global context. Deviating from conventional funding sources, such as the World Bank, China's developmentalists looked to multinational corporations for finances and lined up with global capitalists in their vision to realize a highly centralized national modernization project. Environmental groups, in response, adopted a new strategy aimed at the supranational financiers behind the scheme and for the first time challenged their investment policies as endangering the universal principles of environmental protection and human rights. Making use of the interconnectedness of the contemporary world and its circulating knowledge and information, they launched a full-scale media and Internet campaign to persuade the public to boycott the banks' credit cards and sign petitions demanding that the companies establish environmental and human rights guidelines for their business practices. The campaign was supported by a gradually coalescing network of environmental NGOs, human rights advocates, consumer groups, and investment companies that promoted socially responsible investments in line with the petitioners' cause. The Three Gorges dispute revealed the power, and the limitations, of a transnational civil society that linked up uncountable grassroots individuals in an increasingly interconnected world. Under what David Harvey calls "time-space compression,"[27] the lobby mobilized small actions in local settings, such as cutting up one's credit card, and pulled on the infinite intangible strings that were linked simultaneously to the global circuits of ideological, information, and capital exchange.

But what was at work here was not simply a clash between developmentalism and environmentalism, with global finance as the medium as well as field of conflict. The two sets of discourses were not integrated wholes with clear-cut boundaries that never interacted or overlapped. Trillium Asset Management, the aforementioned Boston investment company behind the shareholder resolution against Morgan Stanley, and Domini Social Investments, which filed another resolution with Merrill Lynch, were participants in the global market that generally adopted the developmentalist line of project financing. Yet they stood by environmental principles and played an important role in challenging the financial giants by mobilizing their knowledge and information about the world of capital. Their examples illustrated the connection between different forces in the global scenario: although in rivalry, developmentalism and environmentalism also communicated and came into negotiation at points where definitions and categories could interpenetrate and amalgamate.

Around the turn of the century, as the dam's construction progressed, the focus of the activists' argument changed from "environmental and social destruction" to "human rights violation." From that point on, the anti-Three Gorges lobby came to lean predominantly on the "human rights" issue in its appeals to investors, with "environment" playing a supportive role. The shift in the opposition argument came with more frequent news about official oppression in the resettlement sites. Long-standing tensions arising out of reported corruption, inadequate compensation, and migrants' protests culminated in March 2001, when news of the first unlawful arrest broke in Yunyang County. Five villagers who planned on travelling to Beijing to lodge a petition were intercepted on their way and detained. They had complained that local officials had inflated the number of residents and amount of land to collect more compensation money from the central government. The funds did not go to the peasants but were pocketed by the officials or spent on new buildings for the government and police or used to build luxury hotels for profit. The arrested villagers were later charged with "disturbing public order," "leaking state secrets," and "maintaining illicit relations with a foreign country," which referred to their liaisons with the international press in Hong Kong.[28] He Kechang, considered the leading organizer, was sentenced to three years of imprisonment. According to an eyewitness report compiled by a Chinese researcher who interviewed people in the reservoir area and released the findings under a pen name to the environmental activists, protesters were beaten, quelled by riot police, or accused of belonging to the outlawed Falun Gong religious sect. As of January 2003, at least seven peasants in Yunyang County had been jailed.[29] The story of Yunyang was one of the numerous accounts in which injustice was done in the resettlement process without legal means of redress. In some other cases, resettlers were not formally arrested and were punished in more covert ways. A farmer in Hubei province contacted German reporters in May 2006 to expose his local county party secretary's alleged embezzlement of resettlement funds. After the interview, according to the villager, he was attacked by hired thugs and struck on the neck with a blunt instrument, which crippled him for life. The police gave him the verdict that he had fallen down and injured himself.[30]

The environmental lobby built its argument upon human rights abuses and appealed to the corporations and various governments providing export credits to withdraw their support for the Three Gorges Dam. Their claim, however, derived moral strength from universal principles that collided with and were challenged by the particularist interests and interpretations of Chinese developmentalists.

National Government Versus Transnational Civil Society

The tensions between global capital and cross-border environmental forces and conflict between the national government and transnational civil society culminated in the polemics over political and civil rights violations in the reservoir area. According to eyewitness reports distributed by the activists, the Chinese government was abusing human rights in three ways. First, the land and jobs promised to migrants were often unavailable. The land that was offered – in the resettlement sites uphill or in distant places outside of the Yangtze Valley – was in most cases infertile, loose, or uncultivable. The claim was in congruence with research findings made by Duan Yuefang and Shawn Steil,[31] who noted that the availability to rural migrants of virgin lands to be exploited in the reservoir area was insufficient. According to the central government's policy, new cultivated land uphill should have a gradient of less than 25 degrees. But given the mountainous nature of the reservoir area, sloping land below 25 degrees with good topsoil and a water source for irrigation was very limited. As a result, displaced villagers cultivated land of more than 25 degrees, even 40–50 degrees, on high ground that was often a mixture of sand and stones. Duan and Steil also pointed out that in the early phase of the resettlement plan, the government tried to transfer rural migrants to secondary industries by offering them jobs in township and village enterprises (TVEs). However, given their poor management, outdated equipment, and, in some of them, production of severe pollution, the TVEs eventually either went bankrupt or were closed down by the government. With the unemployment rate standing at 12 percent in the gorge area, many of the resettlers could not find jobs.

Second, embezzlement of resettlement funds by local officials led to inadequate compensation of villagers.[32] In Hongmiao Village in Yunyang County, out of the officially stipulated RMB 29,000 (US$3,502), villagers who organized their own resettlement received RMB 20,000 ($2,415). Those who went through government-sponsored relocation received only RMB 6,773 ($818).[33] In January 2000, the National Audit Office announced that RMB 500 million ($60.4 million) had been embezzled in 1999 by fourteen officials. Thereafter, despite reports that part of the amount had been retrieved, RMB350 million ($42.3 million) was eventually reported as having been embezzled.[34]

The third point put forward by environmental opponents was the lack of an independent redress system to handle complaints and penalize responsible officials. According to the investigative report, the resettlement program was conducted "in an atmosphere of officially orchestrated secrecy and intimidation:"[35] villagers were asked not to speak to journalists; when they protested to the local government, the riot police suppressed them by force; when they tried to petition Beijing, they were intercepted, beaten up, and/or detained by local officials. Rules and laws were used to punish the victims instead of helping them redress injustice and protect their rights. The petitioners from Yunyang County, for example, were imprisoned under the charge of "disturbing the Three Gorges resettlement." The county's secretary general, moreover, issued a mandate of "resettlement with legal means," which authorized local officials to use police force to relocate people. This rule was made upon his interpretation of Beijing's regulations released in early 2001, which stipulated that no one was allowed to resist moving. In an article addressing the Three Gorges resettlement, Jun Jing argued that intensified policing had begun in the early 1990s. In May 1992, he noted, 179 people were arrested in Kaixian County. The police claimed that these people belonged to a so-called Democratic Youth Party, an "allegedly dissident group accused of 'counter-revolutionary activities aimed at sabotaging the policy of opening and reform and at disrupting the smooth progress of the Three Gorges project'."[36] These arrests, Jing argued, indicated that the police had been put on guard against local resistance to relocation.

It is noteworthy that the environmental activists' argument based upon documented evidence has undermined the official promise of poverty elimination and distress relief premised upon the political theodicy of material improvement. Notwithstanding the element of hope embedded in the ideological workings of political theodicy, the transnational environmental lobby held the "developmental mode of resettlement" under strict scrutiny and questioned the plausibility of such a promised future redemption.

Their argument largely derived its rhetorical force from an understanding of human rights rooted in Euro-American traditions, but it did not rely simply on the universalism of "natural rights." Rather, it was centered upon what Charles Beitz refers to as "a set of *norms* for the regulation of the behavior of states together with a set of modes or strategies of action for which violations of norms may count as reasons."[37] This set of norms, Beitz explains, stems from the Universal Declaration of Human Rights after the Second World War and subsequent covenants that put its provisions into legal force. Instead of appealing to the philosophical conception of rights as a divine gift or an independent moral order, the global politics of human rights emphasizes the "inherent dignity" of human beings as a fundamental value that transcends ethnic, religious, and cultural differences. The "normative practice of human rights," in the words of Beitz, resides in a global discursive community that encompasses a diversity of agents including national governments, international organizations, business corporations, NGOs, and individual domestic and transnational members of social networks. The norms in defense of human dignity, which act as sources of reasons and principles of action in global practice, are employed by a particular group of agents – in the Three Gorges case, the transnational environmental activists – to seek to regulate the behavior of other agents – the Chinese state and supranational investment banks.

In the anti-Three Gorges campaign, environmentalists acted out the idea that the world community is morally entitled to intervene in a state's actions if it is violating its own people's human dignity as defined by globally endorsed norms. In a response to the Chinese authority's particularist interpretation of human rights, the IRN asserted: "International human rights advocates have a right and responsibility to investigate and report the social impacts of decisions made by international governments and their fiscal sponsors."[38] Backing up "right and responsibility" in this argument were the "international norms" to which the IRN and Friends of the Earth International appealed when they reported to the UN Commission on Human Rights in Geneva in April 2003.[39]

The global practice of human rights sought to constrain not only the behavior of the national government of China but also that of the Western governments that indirectly participated in the project through export credits. In January 2003, more than one hundred NGOs from thirty-four countries called on the governments of Germany, Sweden, Switzerland, Brazil, and Canada, which together had provided more than $1.4 billion in export credits, to demand that China suspend the submergence of the Yangtze until human rights disputes in the reservoir area had been resolved. "The export credit agencies," stated the press release, "that finance the dam and the governments that back them share in the responsibility for the impacts of the Three Gorges Dam, including the resettlement problems and human rights violations."[40] Villagers, asserted the NGOs, "must be resettled, compensated and rehabilitated in line with *acknowledged international standards* such as World Bank operational policies and the UN Guiding Principles on Internal Displacement."[41] Normative constraints exercised by transnational civil society were not legally binding, but the moral claim of human rights gave the activists leverage in holding Western governments accountable and eliciting compliant responses from some of them. The Swiss foreign minister, for example, agreed to " 'gathering additional information from a variety of sources' on the problems of the Three Gorges Project."[42]

However, the transnational lobby's argument regarding human dignity was counteracted by the Chinese state with a particularistic interpretation. In a statement responding to the campaigners' charge of human rights violations in the reservoir area, Gan Yu-ping, the vice-chairman of the State Council's Three Gorges Project Committee, which oversaw the scheme's overall implementation, asserted that

> [a]ll countries have their own ways to protect and perceive human rights because of the differences in historical background, social systems, status of economic development and cultural traditions. The human rights problems in their countries are mainly solved by their own governments and people.[43]

Large-scale construction projects and resettlements such as the Three Gorges', Gan argued, were necessary for economic growth and the eventual realization of human rights for all Chinese people. He claimed:

> China combines the universal principles of human rights with the realities and realization of modernization, and thus puts the rights of subsistence and development at the top. Under the circumstances for reform, development and stability, China gears up to promote human rights, which not only realizes the historical transfer from subsistence to sufficiency levels so as to realize the people's rights of subsistence and development as well as economic, social and cultural rights, but also forms a more complete political and legal system to protect the people's democratic rights, and to attain great achievements in human rights under the legal system.

Gan's position was consonant with what the government's White Paper on Human Rights in 1991 put forth: that the provision of food and clothing was the guarantee of the right to subsistence, which is the most basic human right. Gan's statement quoted earlier indicates the logic that modernization, development, and reform were premises of economic progress and prerequisites for all human rights. In this projected process, China's economy would rise from subsistence to sufficiency, which would unfold along with another set of stages involving the country's human rights "advancement" – from the realization of the rights of subsistence and development to economic, social, and cultural rights, and eventually to the fulfillment of political, civil, and judiciary rights under a political and legal system that would protect people's democratic and human rights. China's teleological way of conceiving the progression of human rights, which allowed the establishment of civil and political rights *after* society attained a certain level of economic growth, was in tension with the environmentalists' insistence that such rights had to be respected as an integral part of development.

In the argument for its economic, historical, and cultural particularity, as asserted in Gan's statement, China also linked the relevance of human rights with a country's, especially a developing country's, national condition. According to this line of reasoning, sovereignty, or a nation's independence, is a fundamental condition for a developing state to safeguard the lives of its people and in turn realize their human rights. Han Peide, the chief writer of "Human Rights: Theory and Practice," a 1,158-page report sponsored by the government and co-written by more than fifty researchers, argued that the "Marxist human rights theory" that China adopted was different from the "capitalist human rights theory" of Western Europe and the United States. The former, he said, emphasized the protection of individual as well as collective rights, with the rights to subsistence and development being the most important and most basic human rights.[44] This assertion of particularity, as the author sees it, is not simply a criticism of the universality of rights purportedly applicable to all human beings "as such." It is linked with an implicit critique of the disparity of power in the international hierarchy dominated by Western states, which in this case is manifested, from China's point of view, in the moral discourse of human rights. In the remarks of Gan and Han, we discern a perceived connection between rights and development, which is characteristic of developing countries' assertions of autonomy in determining their specific paths of economic progression vis-à-vis Western models.

The contrast in the understanding of rights between the environmental activists and the Chinese authority betrays a tension in the concept of political theodicy. Inasmuch as present suffering would lead to future redemption, the promise of theodicy is predicated on a diachronic process, which is not unlike the progression from current insufficiencies to subsistence, and further, to the attainment of civil and political rights. However, theodicy also addresses a human condition that is supposed to be generally applicable regardless of space and time. In this sense, it is a synchronic conception that falls in line with the environmentalists' argument that rights should be respected as an integral part of development. The ideology of political theodicy put forward by the Party fails to address this tension, and the conflict between the Chinese national government and transnational civil society remains irreconcilable.

The developmentalist-environmentalist struggle over the generation of hydroelectric power illustrates an open-ended chain of action and reaction, strategy and counter-strategy. In the case of the Three Gorges Dam, when the Chinese bureaucrats in charge of the dam appealed to Western governments and semi-official institutions such as the World Bank for technical and financial support, the transnational activists responded with a campaign of opposition upholding the principles of environmental protection and sustainable development. Chinese technocrats turned to funding sources in the global capital market. Their action, however, was met with a counter-tactic from cross-border environmental groups, which first targeted stock exchanges and then individual supranational investment banks as Chinese dam advocates resorted to indirect funding through the China Development Bank. In the course of the campaign, the focus of the activists' charge shifted from environmental disruption to human rights violations. But the universal notion of rights clashed with the particularist interpretation of human rights by Chinese developmentalists, who insisted on the national autonomy of a developing country in defining its specific path of development. Their views, however, met with the NGOs' assertions of globally endorsed norms in defense of human dignity.

As the chain of events unfolds, we discern conflicts and exchanges not only in the interlacing global-national-local social structures but also between the competing as well as interacting and at points overlapping discourses of developmentalism and environmentalism. Interpenetrating these spatial structures and discourses, moreover, are sub-discourses of development, such as the one on the Three Gorges, and of environmental protection, which is against big dams. In the contestation, agents ranging from local villagers and national governments to multinational corporations and transnational NGOs were involved. Each put forward its worldviews – in word and in practice – from different institutional and ideological positions, expressing multiple forms of assertions and protestations, negotiations and dissension.

The Three Gorges polemics elucidate a new kind of development politics in which conflicts are played out in the global setting. In the struggle between the Chinese authorities, supranational corporations, and transnational environmental campaigners, there were new institutional and ideological alignments, such as those between the Chinese developmentalists and Wall Street investment banks, and those among the transnational NGOs, consumer groups, and financial companies that promoted socially responsible investments in line with the petitioners' cause. Both sides employed resources available in the globalization process to form their methods and strategies in pursuit of their goals but were at times constrained by those resources that enabled their actions in the first place. Capital and knowledge circulating in the global scenario contributed to the Chinese state's capacity to realize the Three Gorges project, but paradoxically this enabling effect of globalization limited the Chinese developmentalists' pursuits, as the flow of knowledge and information, together with the circuits of cross-border networking, was also utilized by the environmental activists in their boycott strategies.

In the contemporary world, where small actions in local settings, such as buying bonds at a bank in the neighborhood or cutting up one's credit card in an apartment, have significant reverberations in the transnational context by pulling on infinite intangible strings of ideological, information, and capital exchange, political contestations transcend the national boundary of inside and outside and find venues of action on the global stage. The implications are particularly far-reaching for an authoritarian society in which political dissent is subject to domestic systemic constraints. The story of opposition to the Three Gorges project manifests the political dynamics of globalization, in which the struggle between developmentalism and environmentalism, particularist interests and universal values, and national sovereignty and global activism is played out in the interaction between an authoritarian state and transnational civil society, with global capital as the purpose as well as field of conflict.

Notes

1 An adapted version of this chapter was published in Yuen-ching Bellette Lee, "Global Capital, National Development and Transnational Environmental Activism: Conflict and the Three Gorges Dam," *Journal of Contemporary Asia* 43, no. 1 (2013). The author would like to thank Informa UK Limited, trading as Taylor & Francis Group, for its permission of publication.

2 Bing Bai, "Shuyu Zhongguo, ye shuyu shijie" [Belonging to China, (the Dam) also Belongs to the World], *Zhongguo sanxia gongcheng bao [China Three Gorges Project News]*, March 17, 1998.

3 According to a survey on China's rural and urban income disparity conducted by the Chinese Academy of Social Sciences, the per capita income of urban residents in 2002 was 3.1 times that of people from rural areas, up from the ratio of 2.8:1 in 1995, and 1.8:1 in the mid-1980s. If non-currency factors were considered, the report added, China's urban-rural income gap was the widest in the world. See Li Shi and Yue Ximing, "A Yawning Urban-rural Income Gap," *Caijing*, February 23, 2004.

4 "Fully Understand the Guidance Significance of Scientific Development Concept," *People's Daily*, March 23, 2004. http://en.people.cn/200403/23/eng20040323_138236.shtml; "Official Says China's Development Policy to be Adjusted," *People's Daily*, March 24, 2004; Menghui Wang, "Balanced Growth a Priority," *China Daily*, March 31, 2004. https://www.chinadaily.com.cn/english/cndy/2004-03/31/content_319339.htm; and "Hu's Speech on Development Strategies Issued," *Xinhua*, April 5, 2004. http://en.people.cn/200404/05/eng20040405_139432.shtml.

5 Hong Ma, "Jingji quanqiuhua yu women de duice" [Globalization and Our Coping Strategies], *Sanxia gongcheng bao [China Three Gorges Project News]*, November 23, 2000.
6 R. B. J. Walker, *Inside/Outside: International Relations as Political Theory* (Cambridge, England and New York: Cambridge University Press, 1993).
7 Bing Bai, "Shuyu Zhongguo," *Sanxia gongcheng bao*, March 17, 1998.
8 Rob Gifford, "China Dam Faces Cash Flow Crisis," *BBC News*, March 16, 1999.
9 James Kynge and John Ridding, "China Plans IPO to Fund Three Gorges Dam," *Financial Times*, March 12, 2002; "Giant China Dam Seeks Funds," *BBC (Business)*, March 12, 2002; "China 'to Float Three Gorges Dam'," *BBC (Business)*, September 30, 2002; "China Seeks Dam Project Cash," *BBC (Business)*, January 20, 2003; and Jian Yang, "Three Gorges: Dam Expensive," *CFO Asia*, May 9, 2003. http://www.cfo.com/printable/article.cfm/3009230?f=options.
10 "Giant China Dam Seeks Funds," *BBC (Business)*; and Yang, "Three Gorges: Dam Expensive," *CFO Asia*.
11 Yueqi Sun et al., "Chapter Five: Views and Suggestions on the Assessment Report of the Three Gorges Project – Written Statement Submitted to the Central Committee of the Chinese Communist Party by Ten Members of the Chinese People's Political Consultative Conference," in *Yangtze! Yangtze!*, ed. Patricia Adams and John Thibodeau (English translation), editor-in-chief Dai Qing, Chinese ed. (London: Earthscan Publications Ltd.; Toronto: Earthscan Canada, 1994).
12 The World Commission on Dams, *Dams and Development: A New Framework for Decision-Making* (London and Sterling, VA: Earthscan, 2000), 201.
13 The World Commission on Dams, *Dams and Development: A New Framework for Decision-Making*, 73–134.
14 B. McDonald, M. Webber, and Y. Duan, "Involuntary Resettlement as an Opportunity for Development: The Case of Urban Resettlers of the Three Gorges Project, China," *Journal of Refugee Studies* 21, no. 1 (2008): 82–102.
15 World Commission, *Dams and Development*, 206.
16 G. Heggelund, *Environment and Resettlement Politics in China: The Three Gorges Dam* (Aldershot, Hants, England and Burlington, VT: Ashgate, 2004); and Daniel Klingensmith, *"One Valley and a Thousand": Dams, Nationalism, and Development* (New Delhi: Oxford University Press, 2007).
17 B. McDonald-Wilmsen and M. Webber, "Dams and Displacement: Raising the Standards and Broadening the Research Agenda," *Water Alternatives* 3, no. 2 (2010): 142–161, www.water-alternatives.org.
18 Kari Huus, "More Dam Trouble," *Far Eastern Economic Review*, October 20, 1994, 70–72.
19 "Three Gorges Dam in China," *Export-Import Bank Press Conference*, May 30, 1996.
20 Author's interviews, August 1998.
21 The offering was criticized by Prof. Kazuo Sumi, a leading Japanese critic of the project, who complained to the Japanese Ministry of Finance that Nomura had violated Japanese securities law by not disclosing the connection between the State Development Bank of China and the Three Gorges Dam. The controversy led Nomura to drop the plan of making a second bond offering of another RMB 30 billion (US$3.5 billion) in 1997. "The Three Gorges Dam Update," *International Rivers Network*, November 1, 1997.
22 Karen Cook, "Dam Shame – Activists Target Global Financiers of Chinese Eco Disaster," *Village Voice*, March 28, 2000.
23 Kenny Hargrove, "China Development Bank Sells Bonds Amid Protests, Gitic Woes," *Bloomberg News*, May 12, 1999.
24 Cook, "Dam Shame," *Village Voice*.
25 Matt Forney, "Some Shareholders Protest the Role Morgan Stanley Played in Chinese Dam," *The Wall Street Journal*, April 20, 1999.
26 Cook, "Dam Shame," *Village Voice*.
27 David Harvey, *The Condition of Postmodernity* (Cambridge, MA and Oxford, UK: Blackwell, 1990), 284–307.

28 "China Sidesteps US Market for Potential Three Gorges Dam Financing," *Press Release, International Rivers Network and Friends of the Earth*, May 31, 2001; "Gorge Arrests Prompt Call for Morgan Pullout," *Financial Times,* April 5, 2001; and Julie Chao, "China Dams up Dissent of Three Gorges Project," *Cox Washington Bureau*, May 6, 2001.
29 Yi Ming, "An Investigation of Resettlement and Human Rights Problems in the Three Gorges Dam Project," *International Rivers Network*, January 2003.
30 Anthony Kuhn, "Going It Alone Downstream to China's Three Gorges," *NPR*, January 2, 2008.
31 Yuefang Duan and Shawn Steil, "China Three Gorges Project Resettlement: Policy, Planning and Implementation," *Journal of Refugee Studies* 16, no. 4 (2003): 422–443.
32 The central government sought to mitigate corruption in the resettlement program through auditing. See Dali Yang, *Remaking the Chinese Leviathan: Market Transition and the Politics of Governance in China* (Stanford University Press, 2004), 285–287. However, the efforts could not completely eliminate abuses at the local level.
33 Yi, "An investigation."
34 Heggelund, *Environment and Resettlement Politics.*
35 Haihui Shi, "Lainian shenghuo zenme guo?" [How Shall We Live on Next Year?], *Yi zhoukan [Next Weekly]*, September 20, 2001, 104–108.
36 J. Jing, "Rural Resettlement: Past Lessons for the Three Gorges Project," *The China Journal* 38 (July 1997): 77.
37 Charles Beitz, *The Idea of Human Rights* (New York: Oxford University Press), 8 (emphasis added).
38 IRN, "Resettlement Investigation Findings," *Media Advisory*, May 11, 2003.
39 IRN, "NGOs Decry Human Rights Crisis at Three Gorges as Officials Plan to Fill Reservoir," *Media Advisory*, April 3, 2003. In the media advisory, the IRN stated: "At the annual session of the UN Commission on Human Rights in Geneva this week, International Rivers Network and Friends of the Earth International have called on China to suspend submergence until the project's human rights problems have been resolved. They have also called on Western governments that fund the dam to ensure that the project comply with international norms."
40 IRN, "Eyewitness Report Documents Serious Human Rights Abuses in Three Gorges Project," *Press Advisory*, January 20, 2003.
41 IRN, "Eyewitness Report Documents Serious Human Rights Abuses in Three Gorges Project" (emphasis added).
42 IRN, "NGOs Decry Human Rights Crisis."
43 Yu-ping Gan, "Great Achievements of Thousands of Years Cannot Be Stigmatized," *China News Agency*, April 30, 2003. Translated by Kevin Li.
44 Quoted in Changhua Wu and Simon Wang, "The Emerging Nexus of Environment, Development and Human Rights in China: A Case Study of Foreign Waste Dumping," *The Earth Council*, March 1998.

Bibliography

Bai, Bing. 1998. "Shuyu Zhongguo, ye shuyu shijie" [Belonging to China, (the Dam) also Belongs to the World]. *Zhongguo sanxia gongcheng bao [China Three Gorges Project News]*, March 17.

BBC (Business). 2002a. "Giant China Dam Seeks Funds." March 12.

BBC (Business). 2002b. "China 'to Float Three Gorges Dam'." September 30.

BBC (Business). 2003. "China Seeks Dam Project Cash." January 20.

Beitz, Charles. 2011. *The Idea of Human Rights*. New York: Oxford University Press.

Cook, Karen. 2000. "Dam Shame – Activists Target Global Financiers of Chinese Eco Disaster." *Village Voice,* March 28.

Dai, Qing (Chinese edition), and Patricia Adams and John Thibodeau (English translation), eds. 1994. *Yangtze! Yangtze!* London: Earthscan Publications Ltd.; Toronto: Earthscan Canada.

Duan, Yuefang, and Shawn Steil. 2003. "China Three Gorges Project Resettlement: Policy, Planning and Implementation." *Journal of Refugee Studies* 16 (4): 422–43.

Export-Import Bank. 1996. "Three Gorges Dam in China." May 30. Press Conference.

Forney, Matt. 1999. "Some Shareholders Protest the Role Morgan Stanley Played in Chinese Dam." *The Wall Street Journal,* April 20.

Gan, Yu-ping. Translated by Kevin Li. 2003. "Great Achievements of Thousands of Years Cannot Be Stigmatized." *China News Agency*, April 30.

Gifford, Rob. 1999. "China Dam Faces Cash Flow Crisis." *BBC News,* March 16.

Hargrove, Kenny. 1999. "China Development Bank Sells Bonds Amid Protests, Gitic Woes." *Bloomberg News,* May 12.

Harvey, David. 1990. *The Condition of Postmodernity*. Cambridge, MA and Oxford, UK: Blackwell.

Heggelund, G. 2004. *Environment and Resettlement Politics in China: The Three Gorges Dam*. Aldershot, Hants, England and Burlington, VT: Ashgate.

Huus, Kari. 1994. "More Dam Trouble." *Far Eastern Economic Review,* October 20: 70–72.

IRN. 1997. "The Three Gorges Dam Update." November 1.

IRN. 2003a. "Eyewitness Report Documents Serious Human Rights Abuses in Three Gorges Project." January 20. Press advisory.

IRN. 2003b. "NGOs Decry Human Rights Crisis at Three Gorges as Officials Plan to Fill Reservoir." April 3. Media advisory.

IRN. 2003c. "Resettlement Investigation Findings." May 11. Media advisory.

Jiefangjun bao [People's Liberation Army Daily]. 1992. "An Exposition of the Three Gorges Proposal – a Speech Given by Vice-premier Zhou Jiahua in the National People's Congress." March 22.

Jing, J. 1997. "Rural Resettlement: Past Lessons for the Three Gorges Project." *The China Journal* 38 (July): 77.

Klingensmith, Daniel. 2007. *"One Valley and a Thousand": Dams, Nationalism, and Development.* New Delhi: Oxford University Press.

Kuhn, Anthony. 2008. "Going It Alone Downstream to China's Three Gorges," *NPR*, January 2.

Kynge, James, and John Ridding. 2002. "China Plans IPO to Fund Three Gorges Dam." *Financial Times,* March 12.

Li, Shi, and Yue, Ximing. 2004. "A Yawning Urban-rural Income Gap." *Caijing*, February 23.

Ma, Hong. 2000. "Jingji quanqiuhua yu women de duice" [Globalization and Our Coping Strategies]. *Zhongguo sanxia gongcheng bao [China Three Gorges Project News],* November 23.

McDonald, B., M. Webber, and Y. Duan. 2008. "Involuntary Resettlement as an Opportunity for Development: The Case of Urban Resettlers of the Three Gorges Project, China." *Journal of Refugee Studies* 21 (1): 82–102.

McDonald-Wilmsen, B., and M. Webber. 2010. "Dams and Displacement: Raising the Standards and Broadening the Research Agenda." *Water Alternatives* 3 (2): 142–61. www.water-alternatives.org.

People's Daily. 2004a. "Fully Understand the Guidance Significance of Scientific Development Concept." March 23. http://en.people.cn/200403/23/eng20040323_138236.shtml.

People's Daily. 2004b. "Official Says China's Development Policy to Be Adjusted." March 24.

Shi, Haihui. 2001. "Lainian shenghuo zenme guo?" [How Shall We Live on Next Year?]. *Yi zhoukan [Next Weekly],* September 20: 104–8.

Wang, Mengkui. 2004. "Balanced Growth a Priority." *China Daily,* March 31. https://www.chinadaily.com.cn/english/cndy/2004-03/31/content_319339.htm

Walker, R. B. J. 1993. *Inside/Outside: International Relations as Political Theory*. Cambridge, UK and New York: Cambridge University Press.

The World Commission on Dams. 2000. *Dams and Development: A New Framework for Decision-making*. London and Sterling, VA: Earthscan.

Wu, Changhua, and Simon Wang. 1998. *The Emerging Nexus of Environment, Development and Human Rights in China: A Case Study of Foreign Waste Dumping*. The Earth Council, March.

Xinhua. 2004. "Hu's Speech on Development Strategies Issued." April 5. http://en.people.cn/200404/05/eng20040405_139432.shtml.

Yang, Dali. 2004. *Remaking the Chinese Leviathan: Market Transition and the Politics of Governance in China*. Stanford University Press.

Yang, Jian. 2003. "Three Gorges: Dam Expensive." *CFO Asia*, May 9. http://www.cfo.com/printable/article.cfm/3009230?f=options.

Yi, Ming. 2003. "An Investigation of Resettlement and Human Rights Problems in the Three Gorges Dam Project." International Rivers Network, January.

Epilogue

A New Form of "Hydropower Discourse" in the 21st Century[1]

As revealed in the last chapter, in the polemics over global capital and human rights, we discern a largely dichotomous opposition between developmentalism and environmentalism. While one side sought to mobilize resources to assert its particularistic position and maintain its autonomy in defining the sociopolitical agenda for national progress, the other attempted to impose constraints with supranational protest strategies backed up by universal values established in relation to the human and natural worlds. But in the new century as Chinese technocrats responded to the environmentalists' challenge on dam building, they broke down the boundary between environmentalism and developmentalism with a new form of "hydropower discourse," which crossed over to the environmental field and appropriated some of its concepts.

Discourse here encompasses articulations, in spoken and textual forms, which enact, legitimate, and reproduce social relations that enable certain people or groups of people to exercise power over others by naturalizing the discourse's constituent ideology. In the case of hydropower discourse, the harnessing of rivers is conceptualized, debated, and discussed in such a way that a certain approach of hydraulic development appears to be natural and unobjectionable. The technocratic language of river development, expressed in the ethical terms of environmental protection in pursuit of renewable energy, eliminates the political content and socioeconomic implications from the practice of dam building. Removed in this depoliticizing act are, inter alia, people's rights, social justice, impacts on the natural environment, and economic distribution between citizens, geographical regions, and groups with disparate interests. The apparently apolitical character of hydropower discourse, in other words, conceals relations of dominance, in which people or objects in the lower end of the power hierarchy – be it nature, groups that have little or no share in the economic benefits, or rural villagers who are excluded from the decision-making system – are deprived of their voices in the development process by those who claim exclusive knowledge to set the energy agenda and formulate water policies.

But hydropower discourse in China does not only involve verbal articulations of hydraulic engineering. It is bound up with practices of dam building, oftentimes on a massive scale, the transfiguration of the natural landscape, and the transformation of people's ways of life. Such practices are made possible by the employment

DOI: 10.4324/9781003531494-8

of resources, such as technological knowledge, information, capital, and concepts that are prevailing in the global development structure. These practices instantiate the ideological propositions embedded in enunciations of river harnessing and are at the same time rationalized by the ideals of environmental sustainability in hydro development. Practice and ideology, in other words, support and reproduce each other, and are both wrapped up in the discursive formation of what I call hydropower discourse in China.

Hydraulic engineering is not a uniquely 21st-century phenomenon in China. Through millennia, harnessing waters for human use has been the task of ancient emperors and modern political leaders alike. From Dujiangyan built in Sichuan Province around 250 BC to the Gezhouba Dam on the Yangtze constructed under Mao, controlling floods and diverting rivers for productive use have been an important politico-economic agenda. Mao considered mastering nature as a means to express the communist might.[2] Karl Wittfogel goes as far as arguing that hydro development in China has historically given rise to oriental despotism, a form of total power that extends from water projects to the centralized organization of society in the social, economic, religious, and politico-military spheres.[3]

The hydropower discourse this epilogue addresses represents a part of the continuum of water conservancy history in China. But it differs from the Maoist and dynastic manifestations of hydraulic development in that it is coextensive with the neo-liberal structure of globalization and the emergent articulations of environmental sustainability. Unlike the agro-bureaucrats who, according to Wittfogel, had full control over resources and societal organization under the single-centered state, technocrats in reformist China do not have equivalent power. They work for the energy companies, which are state enterprises operating under the market mechanism with high autonomy in management and decision making. These energy companies, and the technocrats who staff them, control the mobilization of resources, including water and capital, and have access to the political leadership. But they do not hold centralized power, nor do they have absolute control of resources, and less so on society. Much of the hydraulic development is contingent on their negotiations with local authorities for a river to be exploited. Moreover, operating in the global arena of capital circulation, mechanical equipment transactions, and information exchange, the power companies and technocrats are subject to constraints in the global market and most of all, the scrutiny of transnational civil society and its challenge to the testability of their claim to environmental sustainability. In short, the Chinese hydropower discourse, despite its continuity, is marked with significant modifications in the 21st century. As calls for green energy to curb climate change have become ever more audible, it is important to examine the ideological propositions of this discourse, and the power relations that run through it.

Hydropower Discourse in Modification

In June 2003, the Three Gorges Corporation successfully installed world-grade hydropower generators with the help of Western companies. The river was completely blocked and the dam entered its first phase of electricity production. Two years later, the company developed its own generators with the knowledge they had obtained through technological transfer. With initial electricity generation having begun in 2003, China claimed success in conquering the world's third-largest river and building the biggest dam ever. A new form of "hydropower discourse" thus came into shape.

While this discourse was different from the Maoist mode of development based upon the ideology of communist supremacy, it was – and remains – distinct from the Dengist version of industrial progress embodied by the Three Gorges Dam. The 21st-century hydropower discourse was primarily subordinated to global development discourse, but it also crossed over into the environmental field to incorporate some of its concepts for rhetorical use. It appropriated for its ideological authority the idea of "sustainable development" first proposed by the United Nations in 1987 and later entrenched by the 1992 Earth Summit with the endorsement of Agenda 21, which is a blueprint for achieving sustainable development, and the establishment of the Commission on Sustainable Development to oversee its implementation.

In addition, the discourse operated in a set of institutions that presumed economic growth as a *natural* pursuit of the human world. Within the single year of 2004, various world-level meetings ranging from the International Conference of Hydropower and the International Symposium on River Sedimentation to the World Conference of Engineers were held at the Three Gorges and in Shanghai, celebrating the "exemplary" role of the dam and trumpeting the significance of harnessing hydropower as a way to alleviate the global energy crisis for continuous economic development.[4] Among these meetings, the most influential in precipitating China's emerging discourse was the United Nations Symposium on Hydropower and Sustainable Development, held in December 2004. In its Beijing Declaration on Hydropower and Sustainable Development, the more than five hundred participants from more than forty countries concluded that

> access to energy is essential for achieving sustainable development. . . . Noting with concern that two billion people do not have access to electricity, we call upon all stakeholders to work in concert to deliver energy services to all in a reliable, affordable and economically viable, socially acceptable and environmentally sound manner.[5]

Hydroelectricity, under this premise, was highlighted as a valuable renewable energy source that could "contribute to sustainable development, . . . to mitigating greenhouse gas emissions, . . . [and] to poverty reduction and economic growth through regional development and expansion of industry" in developing countries.

To the extent that the living conditions in certain parts of the world are in need of improvement, energy supply is considered a resource that enables local people to participate in economic development. But put in the light of the argument's sociopolitical implications and the effects it produces, the subjects – river, water, the two billion people, and developing countries – are rendered what Michel Foucault calls "objects" of a "discursive field."[6] They are examined under an "objectivist and empiricist" lens,[7] an operation that bears out the conclusion that for the "two billion people" to be pulled out of poverty and embark on sustainable development, hydroelectricity is the necessary and ultimate prescription. This argument resonates with the one put forward by the Three Gorges technocrats, who emphasized the connection of poverty alleviation, sustainable development, and hydropower generation while sidestepping the ramifications of human rights, social disruption, and ecological destruction. Without an exploration of the conceptual presumptions and implementation of river exploitation and without a more refined analysis of locally situated hydroelectricity production capacity, a well-intended resolution can be rendered a socioeconomic instrument of parties defending or pursuing specific power and interests.

In the context of the UN's Beijing Declaration, hydropower was brought to the top of the energy agenda in China – as a "clean, renewable, and environmentally sound" resource compatible with the principles of "sustainable development." At the UN conference in 2004, the deputy director of China's State Development and Reform Commission, Zhang Guobao, announced that hydroelectricity would be given priority in his country's energy policy. Pinpointing the existing opposition to any form of hydropower development, Zhang stated that an over-emphasis on protection rather than exploitation was a "violation of the human community's fundamental well-being."[8] Thereafter, the call for hydroelectricity production became increasingly audible in the Chinese media. The next fifteen to twenty years, as was noted in an article published in 2005, would be a golden period for China's hydropower development.[9] The success of the Three Gorges Dam, said one official, had pushed China's capability for hydraulic exploitation to the forefront of the world. "Right now," he asserted, "is the best time for China to embark upon hydroelectricity development and construction."[10] Having built nearly half of the world's dams, China had a plan to double its hydropower generating capacity by 2020 by erecting more dams.

The appeals came at a time when a convergence of circumstances pointed to an urgent need to tap into energy sources as alternatives to fossil fuels. It was a time when the world was wrestling with possible ways to curb the climatic change caused by excessive greenhouse gas emissions. Moreover, China was faced with the problem of an energy shortage in powering its expanding industries and sustaining its economic growth. These problems coincided with a worldwide shortfall in the supply of oil. With "environmental protection" as a supporting postulate, hydropower advocates in China sidestepped assertions of social disruption and human rights violations typically used in the anti-Three Gorges campaign and turned the tables on dam opponents with the proposition of environmental sustainability. Their argument gained further rhetorical vigor as the then Party General Secretary Hu Jintao propounded the concept of "ecological civilization" as a guiding principle of his government.

Under the premises of cutting carbon emissions and exploring clean energy, the hydropower sector consolidated under the lead of the Three Gorges Corporation. In August 2002, the company collaborated with five other major state-owned energy corporations and established the China Yangtze Power Company (hereafter referred to as Yangtze Power). The Three Gorges Corporation was the biggest shareholder, controlling 89.5 percent. Three other enterprises – Huaneng International Power, China Nuclear Industry Group, and China Petroleum and Natural Gas Group – each held 3 percent, while China Gezhouba Water Resources and Hydropower Project Group took 1 percent, and the Yangtze Surveying and Design Institute held 0.5 percent.[11] Later in 2003, Yangtze Power was listed in the mainland stock markets as a blue-chip company with a high profile – it was subsequently selected as one of the "ten best" listed enterprises in China, and Li Yongan, the president of Yangtze Power and general manager of the Three Gorges Corporation, was selected one of the "ten best" enterprise leaders.

With its collective capital and knowledge, Yangtze Power made plans to build a cascade of four dams on the Jinsha River, a part of the Yangtze river system upstream from the Three Gorges in southwestern China, which, nicknamed Double Three Gorges, would combine to generate twice as much power as the predecessor project. Construction on the first of the four projects, the Xiluodu Dam, began in 2005 and was completed in 2013. Its scale is second to the Three Gorges Dam: At its crest it is 600 meters high, more than three times that of the earlier dam, though at 700 meters it is less than one-third as wide. The capacity is 12,600 megawatts – compared to Three Gorges' 18,200 megawatts. It produces 57.1 to 64 billion kilowatt hours per annum – compared to 84.7 billion kilowatt hours at the Three Gorges. Xiluodu, with its upper stream position, claims to be able to supply water for Three Gorges' power generation in the dry season, reduce water flow in the rainy period, and seal off a substantial amount of silt.[12]

Water itself is undoubtedly a renewable source of energy with minimal environmental impacts. However, when it comes to damming the river, especially on a mega scale, the results go beyond what simple flowing water brings to the human world. At the Three Gorges, floating garbage amounts to 100,000 to 200,000 cubic meters per year and has posed a problem, particularly in the rainy season. It was recorded during a Yangtze flood in 2004 that the waste accumulated to a height of 4 meters behind the dam, exceeding the capacity of any garbage-clearing barge available at the time.[13] Besides water pollution, people in the reservoir area are also confronted with geologic hazards such as landslides, stone desertification, and riverbank slumps. In a report titled "Three Gorges Follow-Up Project," in 2010 the government revealed plans to relocate another three hundred thousand people – on top of the 1.2 million villagers already displaced – to make way for an "eco-screen" or "buffer belt" along the reservoir.[14] Without addressing the environmental and ecological defects, not to mention the social disruption, caused by river-damming, the advocacy of green energy can be a facade of what Yifei Li and Judith Shapiro call "authoritarian environmentalism."[15]

The neutrality of water as a clean, renewable resource also masks a complex web of social transactions in the politico-economic realm. Behind the champion of sustainability there lie the political interests of decision makers, the commercial striving of power companies, and the developmentalist vision of a state that is emerging as a world power. The four-dam cascade on the Jinsha, including the Xiluodu Dam, is a part of the grander scheme of the Great Western Development (*xibu da kaifa*), which China is actively pursuing as part of its national modernization drive. The campaign mainly covers the Sichuan and Yunnan Provinces in the southwest, which are among the most impoverished backwaters in China. It promises to achieve resource exploitation, energy production, and poverty alleviation. But its goal of development is not confined to the western terrain: it also aims to generate electricity for the power-deficient east coast, in particular Guangdong, to sustain its industrialization and enriched urban population.[16] Conceived to promote the development of the west, the hydraulic engineering projects are also meant to power the further reforms of the east; together the projects contribute to the overall modernization of China as a rising power.

The western hinterland carries the richest unharnessed hydropower resources in China. This region represents a good opportunity for hydraulic exploitation, but it is also a potential focus of controversy because of its richness in natural diversity and minority cultures. In the region there lies an area known as the Three Parallel Rivers, where the Jinsha (the upper Yangtze), Lancang (Mekong), and Nu (Salween) run almost parallel with one another before the latter two flow into Southeast Asia. It has been designated by the United Nations Educational, Scientific and Cultural Organization (UNESCO) as a World Heritage Site for being one of the richest temperate regions in the world: it is believed that over six thousand plant species and more than 50 percent of China's animal species live there. Chinese environmentalists fought to prevent developmentalists from encroaching upon the ecological system and ethnic minorities. Yet many local officials support the damming of rivers in the belief that hydropower generation will bring economic development, a supply of electricity, and capital investment to the area's communities.

The interests of local officials overlap with those of power companies, which see the rivers as renewable sources of profit. In an example of a process that Darrin Magee calls "corporatizing the electric power industry,"[17] in 2002 the state's energy sector was divided into five big power companies. Each of them went about claiming hydro territories under the banner of the sustainable development of non-polluting energy. Rivers in the southwest, the last frontier of the country's unexploited water resources, became a major target of competition. Among the corporate competitors were China Huaneng Group and China Huadian Corporation, which together generate about a fifth of China's electricity. The former established a hydro base on the Lancang River – known as the Mekong in Southeast Asia, while the latter gained development rights on the Nu River, known as the Salween downstream. In 2003, Huadian came to an agreement with the Yunnan provincial government on proposals to build thirteen dams along the Nu near the UNESCO-designated World Heritage Site. The projects were suspended by Premier Wen Jiabao in 2004 following vigorous opposition from Chinese environmental groups and were scaled back to four dams.[18] But Huaneng and Huadian also carved out hydraulic territories on the Yangtze. The two companies were planning a US$30 billion project to cascade eight dams on the middle reaches of the Jinsha in 2009, which together, it was claimed, would generate as much hydroelectricity as the Three Gorges Dam.

The commercial interests of the energy companies were entangled in the power relations that interpenetrated China's political structure. Huaneng, for example, has been controlled by the family of former Premier Li Peng, a water conservancy engineer who took an interest in hydropower generation. He was a steadfast supporter of the Three Gorges project throughout his political career. His son, Li Xiaopeng, also a trained engineer, headed Huaneng until June 2008, when he was appointed deputy governor of Shanxi Province. Li Peng's daughter, Li Xiaolin, was the CEO of Huaneng's most important subsidiary, China Power International Development, in Hong Kong.[19] Huaneng is a multinational corporation producing different kinds of energy. Its subsidiaries are listed on the Hong Kong, Shanghai, and New York stock exchanges. The other most powerful energy company, Huadian, which attempted to build the thirteen-dam cascade along the Nu, was established in 2002 as part of the power sector reform. Its first general manager, He Gong, was formerly a top leader of the Three Gorges Corporation. He had worked in Yunnan for fourteen years and had been the deputy chief of the province's Electric Power Bureau. Under him, the Manwan Dam on the Lancang River was built.[20] It was one of the major water projects in the province, but the resettlement was poorly managed and has left displaced villagers scavenging to this day. Almost immediately after He took office in Huadian, he approached the leading cadres of Yunnan with the proposal of exploiting the Nu. The thirteen-dam blueprint, conceived to generate 21,320 megawatts of electricity, surpassing the Three Gorges, emerged from those negotiations.

The hydropower discourse suffered an apparent setback in mid-2009 when the Ministry of Environmental Protection suspended the construction of two dams on the Jinsha (by Huaneng and Huadian) and another project on the Nu (one of the four by Huadian) on the grounds that they lacked prior environmental protection designs.[21] But the discourse resumed its stride within a year, as the government announced its determination to pursue a green energy policy. It entailed an increase in the proportion of non-fossil fuels in overall energy consumption to 15 percent by 2020 and a simultaneous reduction of carbon intensity – the amount of carbon dioxide per unit of gross domestic product – by 40 to 45 percent.[22] Hydropower, now prized for its lower costs compared to wind and solar energy because of technological innovation and the scale of production, was trumpeted as a prioritized green power in the 12th Five Year Plan (2011–2015).[23] The existing 200 gigawatts (GW) of national installed hydropower capacity, it was projected, would be raised to 380 GW by 2020. This means that for the Yangtze alone, the current 36 percent exploitation rate of the river's hydraulic resources (including the Three Gorges) would have to increase to 60 percent by 2030. The policy initiative came at a time when dam builders had already been invigorated by the government's US$586 billion economic stimulus package in late 2008, which allowed many localities including Yunnan and Sichuan to speed up their hydraulic projects.

The renewed momentum of dam building entailed a series of accelerated official endorsements from the middle of 2010. Over five months of that year – from July to November – the National Development and Reform Commission approved six large hydropower works. They included the 2.4-GW Jinanqiao Dam, which had been shelved by the environmental protection authority the previous year. Other endorsed proposals were the 8.7-GW Wudongde and 14-GW Baihetan projects, to be developed by the Three Gorges Corporation on the Jinsha, and the 2.6-GW Changheba, 2.4-GW Guandi, and 600-megawatt Tongzilin hydropower stations, all located in Sichuan Province.[24] More dams were planned or constructed on the upper reaches of the Yangtze's tributaries, including the Yalong, Dadu, and Wujiang.[25] The then Ministry of Environmental Protection, moreover, reversed its aforementioned suspension of the water projects undertaken by Huaneng and Huadian on the Jinsha. The green lights represented the ascendancy of nature exploitation through the use of a non-polluting resource under the banner of sustainability.

In tandem with the overarching development discourse, China's hydropower discourse reached out to other parts of the world, enabling the dam-constructing sector to establish a dominant position as a global builder and financier. In 2007, the Chinese government signed an agreement with Myanmar to construct a dam at Hutgyi on the Salween (Nu). The project would be partly financed by Chinese funds and was to be built by Sinohydro, a major Chinese hydropower company, to provide electricity for Thailand (90 percent) and Myanmar (10 percent).[26] Chinese dam builders were also involved in another eleven dams proposed for the mainstream Mekong (Lancang) – seven in Laos, two between Laos and Thailand, and two in Cambodia.[27] It was estimated that Chinese investment would make up to 40 percent of upcoming projects on the Mekong and its tributaries. These included four of the eleven proposed works – Pak Beng, Pak Lay, and Xanakham in Laos, and Sambor in Cambodia.[28] The Southeast Asian countries had been critical of China's efforts to dam the Chinese side of the Mekong (Lancang) for fear of impacts on the river's ecology and fisheries. Substantial concerns of this type lingered, but the cooperation deals indicated a more receptive attitude toward river exploitation.

Outside Asia, the Chinese hydropower discourse extended to the developing countries of other continents: in June 2004, the Three Gorges Corporation struck a pact with Brazil's Itaipu Dam, the largest river development scheme in the world prior to the Three Gorges. The two sides agreed to exchange experiences in personnel training, operations management, and reservoir tourism.[29] In Africa, as of May 2007, China was supporting at least ten dam projects in countries such as Sudan, Ethiopia, Zambia, Ghana, Nigeria, the Republic of the Congo, and Mozambique. Almost all of these schemes were financed through the China Exim Bank as part of bigger agreements in areas such as energy production and minerals extraction.[30] In February 2011, China Yangtze International, a subsidiary of Yangtze Power which is the mother company of the Three Gorges Corporation, established a joint venture with the Russian electricity firm EuroSibEnergo to develop hydro and thermal power in eastern Siberia. The new enterprise, named YES Energo Ltd., is registered in Hong Kong with a capital of US$6 million. The cooperation deal was further consolidated in June with an investment framework agreement on the construction of two hydropower stations and a natural gas-fired plant with a total capacity of 3 GW aiming to upgrade to 10 GW of new capacity. Apart from producing electricity for the Russian market, the energy generated will also be exported to northern and northeastern China.[31]

Conclusion

Modifications in the ideological practices of development at the Three Gorges illuminate the dialectical change of power exercised by the Chinese communist regime since the last quarter of the 20th century. In the aftermath of the Cultural Revolution, the Party emphasized instrumentalist scientific knowledge and the "socialist democratic" mode of decision making to relegitimize its power as the "savior" of its people. Facing the unintended consequence of popular protests for increased political transparency toward the end of the 1980s, the regime rolled back the reforms on inclusive politics and shifted to a depoliticized form of marketization in the 1990s with the promise of "common prosperity" while redefining the meanings of cultural icons such as the Yangtze River and the Three Gorges in accordance with the material value. Entering the 21st century, the Chinese developmental path saw another shift as the country's economy underwent a neoliberal turn along with the global trend. The high-modernist developmentalist ambition that the dam project embodies turned into a neoliberal aspiration for national development through the embrace of big corporations and global capital.

The adaptability of power stands out as a defining characteristic of the authoritarian mode of governance in China under reform. It provides an explanation for the durability of the regime despite crises and social discontent. The political theodicy of development, the ideology that is at once concrete and elusive, real and imaginary, resides in the everyday experience of gorge immigrants, which is connected with the productive activity of people in different sectors of China. Ideology as material practice produces political effects which feed back to and act on the ideological scenario of progress, which is itself the medium in which development activities transpire. Inasmuch as power cannot monopolize the interpretation of meanings, ideology by no means totalizes the political outcome of development policy. At each disjuncture and shift, sociopolitical consequences often unintended by the authorities challenge the existing prescription of modernization, forcing power to transmute into a form capable of adapting to the new economic situation and social tolerance. Change in the mode of governance thus comes into place, sustaining the Party's popular support and its claim to political validity.

Being a story of the Yangtze, the Three Gorges experience of modernization is also a story of Chinese society at large. The reformist state's governing tactics – the privileging of a particular kind of scientific knowledge, economic restructuring in the direction of market capitalism, the transformation of social relations in accordance with that systemic change, the production of new subjectivity through everyday practice, the transfiguration of the natural environment to make way for material reconstitution, and the cultural re-encoding of nonhuman objects in congruence with concepts underpinning the new socioeconomic order – take place all over China, in different ways and with varying intensities. The Three Gorges Dam, in other words, is exemplary of the modernization experience of China and its political implications in the reform era – the strategies employed, the mechanism of change, and the political effects with subsequent modifications of tactics which result in changes in the mode of governance.

In a broader sense, the Three Gorges tale of modernity is also the story of the world capitalist system in the late 20th and early 21st centuries. Debate and actual implementation of the project coincided with a period when China was industrializing itself to enter the world economy which was developing in a neoliberal direction. Itself an embodiment of the centralized, Fordist mode of production, the Three Gorges Dam was carried along and made part of the decentered structure of production, circulation, and exchange. In the Three Gorges story, we discern the transformation of the socioeconomic formulation of China along with that of the world, and the interaction as well as tension between nationalism and globalism. The enabling effects of globalization in the circulation of capital and information simultaneously act as constraints in terms of social activism for a project as statist and nationalist as the Three Gorges. The political significance of the engineering scheme, therefore, lies in not only the reform process of China but also the possibilities and inhibitions of socioeconomic interactions in the globalized world.

Notes

1 Adapted versions of this chapter were published in Yuen-ching Bellette Lee, "Global Capital, National Development and Transnational Environmental Activism: Conflict and the Three Gorges Dam," *The Journal of Contemporary Asia* 43, no. 1 (2013) and Yuen-ching Bellette Lee, "Water Power: The "Hydropower Discourse" of China in an Age of Environmental Sustainability," *ASIANetwork Exchange* 21, no. 1 (Fall 2013). The author would like to thank Informa UK Limited and *ASIANetwork Exchange* for their permission of publication.
2 Judith Shapiro, *Mao's War Against Nature: Politics and the Environment in Revolutionary China* (Cambridge University Press, 2001).
3 K. Wittfogel, *Oriental Despotism: A Comparative Study of Total Power* (New Haven and London: Yale University Press, 1957).
4 Xianghan Yu, "Erlinglingsi nian shuili fadian guoji yantaohui zai sanxia zhaokai" [The International Conference of Hydropower 2004 Held at the Three Gorges], *Zhongguo sanxia gongcheng bao [China Three Gorges Project News]*, May 28, 2004; Xianghan Yu, "Dijiuci heliu nisha xueshu taolunhui zuori bimu" [The Ninth International Symposium on River Sedimentation Drew to a Close Yesterday], *Zhongguo sanxia gongcheng bao [China Three Gorges Project News]*, October 22, 2004; and Bing Bai, "Shijie gongchengshi dahui zai Hu zhaokai" [The World Engineer Conference Convened in Shanghai], *Zhongguo sanxia gongcheng bao [China Three Gorges Project News]*, November 5, 2004.
5 United Nations, "Beijing Declaration on Hydropower and Sustainable Development," *CSD Documents*, E/CN.17/2006/10, Division for Sustainable Development, 2004.
6 Michel Foucault, "Politics and the Study of Discourse," in *The Foucault Effect*, ed. Graham Burchell et al. (Chicago: The University of Chicago Press, 1991).
7 Arturo Escobar, *Encountering Development: The Making and Unmaking of the Third World* (Princeton: Princeton University Press, 1995).
8 Bing Bai and Jian Han, "Zhang Guobao: Youxian fazhan shuidian shi Zhongguo nengyuan fazhan de zhongyao fangzhen" [Zhang Guobao: Giving Priority to Hydropower Exploitation Is an Important Policy Orientation of China's Energy Development], *Zhongguo sanxia gongcheng bao [China Three Gorges Project News]*, October 30, 2004.
9 "Shuidian kaifa shi shehui kechixufazhan de zhongyao tujing" [Hydropower Exploitation Is an Essential Way for Society's Sustainable Development], *Zhongguo sanxia gongcheng bao [China Three Gorges Project News]*, June 24, 2005.

10 Bing Bai and Jian Han, "Lu Youmei: youxian kaifa shuidian shi kechixufazhan de zhongyao duice" [Lu Youmei: Giving Priority to Hydropower Exploitation Is an Important Policy of Sustainable Development], *Zhongguo sanxia gongcheng bao [China Three Gorges Project News]*, October 30, 2004.
11 "Three Gorges Dam Ready for Listing in Shanghai," *Hong Kong Wen Wei Po*, August 25, 2002.
12 Aimin Xu, "Xiluodu dianzhan 26 ri kaigong" [Work on the Xiluodu Hydropower Station Started on the 26th], *Zhongguo sanxia gongcheng bao [China Three Gorges Project News Special: Jinshajiang Baodao]*, December 25, 2005.
13 Donghong Wang and Tingting Zhao, "Zuji ershiwan fang piaofuwu" [Tackling 200,000 Cubic Meters of Floating Garbage], *Zhongguo sanxia gongcheng bao [China Three Gorges Project News]*, October 16, 2004.
14 Jonathan Watts, "Three Gorges Dam May Force Relocation of a Further 300,000 People," *The Guardian*, January 22, 2010, http://www.guardian.co.uk/environment/2010/jan/22/wave-tidal-hydropower-water; Likun Zuo, "Three Gorges Reservoir Plagued by Hazards," *China Daily*, March 6, 2010, https://www.chinadaily.com.cn/china/2010-03/06/content_9548662.htm.
15 Yifei Li and Judith Shapiro, *China Goes Green: Coercive Environmentalism for a Troubled Planet* (Polity Press, 2020).
16 Darrin Magee, "Powershed Politics: Yunnan Hydropower under Great Western Development," *China Quarterly* 185 (2006): 23–41.
17 Magee, "Powershed Politics: Yunnan Hydropower under Great Western Development," 35.
18 Andrew Mertha, *China's Water Warrior: Citizen Action and Policy Change* (Ithaca and London: Cornell University Press, 2008), 110–149.
19 K. Pomeranz, "The Great Himalayan Watershed: Water Shortages, Mega-Projects and Environmental Politics in China, India, and Southeast Asia," *Asia-Pacific Journal* 7 (July 27, 2009): 11–22, https://apjjf.org/kenneth-pomeranz/3195/article.
20 Haidong Cao and Peng Zhang, "Nujiang daba turan gezhi muhou de minjian liliang" [Nongovernmental Strength Behind the Suspension of the Nu River Dam Proposal], *Jingji*, May 20, 2004, http://finance.sina.com.cn.
21 Malcolm Moore, "China Halts 20bn-Pound Dam Project," *Telegraph*, June 12, 2009, http://www.telegraph.co.uk/news/worldnews/asia/china/5513499/China-halts-20bn-dam-project.html.
22 "China Seen Quietly Opening Sluice for Mega Hydro Projects," *Reuters*, November 16, 2010, http://af.reuters.com/articlePrint?articleId=AFTOE6AE05G20101116.
23 "Hydropower Slowly Rows Upstream in China," *Caing*, December 10, 2010, http://english.caing.com/2010-12-10/100206366.html.
24 "China Seen Quietly Opening Sluice for Mega Hydro Projects," *Reuters*, November 16, 2010, http://af.reuters.com/articlePrint?articleId=AFTOE6AE05G20101116; "China Approves More Hydropower Amid Clean Energy Push," *Reuters*, November 29, 2010, http://af.reuters.com/article/energyOilNews/idAFTOE6AS06F20101129.
25 "Massive Chinese Hydro Project Moves Ahead," *Breakbulk*, January 27, 2011, http://www.breakbulk.com/traditioal-power-generation/masssive-chinese-hydrop-project-moves-ahead.
26 M. Osborne, "The Water Politics of China and Southeast Asia: Rivers, Dams, Cargo Boats and the Environment," *Japan Focus* 5 (June 4, 2007), https://apjjf.org/milton-osborne/2448/article.
27 M. Osborne, "The Mekong River Under Threat," *Asia-Pacific Journal* 8 (January 11, 2010), https://apjjf.org/milton-osborne/3286/article.
28 P. Hirsch, "Cascade Effect," *China Dialogue*, February 8, 2011, http://www.chinadialogue.net/article/show/single/en/4093.
29 Bing Bai and Yuanhua Wang, "Sanxia, Itaipu liangda shuidianzhan xieshou" [Cooperation of Two Biggest Hydropower Stations – Three Gorges and Itaipu], *Zhongguo sanxia gongcheng bao [China Three Gorges Project News]*, June 4, 2004.

30 "China – New Promoter of Mega Dams," *IPS News Agency*, May 23, 2007, http://www.ipsnews.net/print.asp?idnews=37844; Deborah Brautigam, *The Dragon's Gift: The Real Story of China in Africa* (Oxford and New York: Oxford University Press, 2009).

31 "EuroSibEnergo and China Yangtze Power Announce Siberian Project JV," *EuroSibEnergo*, February 24, 2011, http://www.eurosib.ru/en/press/news/456/; "EuroSibEnergo, Yangtze Power Sign Investment Framework Pact," *Bloomberg*, June 17, 2011, http://www.bloomberg.com/news/2011-06-17/eurosibenergo-yangtze-power-sign-investment-framework-pact-1-.html; and "EuroSibEnergo, Yangtze Power to Develop Hydro Projects in Siberia," *HydroWorld*, June 24, 2011, http://www.hydroworld.com/articles/2011/06/eurosibenergo--yangtze.html.

Bibliography

Bai, Bing. 2004. "Shijie gongchengshi dahui zai Hu zhaokai" [The World Engineer Conference Convened in Shanghai]. *Zhongguo sanxia gongcheng bao [China Three Gorges Project News]*, November 5.

Bai, Bing, and Han, Jian. 2004a. "Zhang Guobao: Youxian fazhan shuidian shi Zhongguo nengyuan fazhan de zhongyao fangzhen" [Zhang Guobao: Giving Priority to Hydropower Exploitation Is an Important Policy Orientation of China's Energy Development]. *Zhongguo sanxia gongcheng bao [China Three Gorges Project News]*, October 30.

Bai, Bing, and Han, Jian. 2004b. "Lu Youmei: youxian kaifa shuidian shi kechixufazhan de zhongyao duice" [Lu Youmei: Giving Priority to Hydropower Exploitation Is an Important Policy of Sustainable Development]. *Zhongguo sanxia gongcheng bao [China Three Gorges Project News]*, October 30.

Bai, Bing, and Wang, Yuanhua. 2004. "Sanxia, Itaipu liangda shuidianzhan xieshou" [Cooperation of Two Biggest Hydropower Stations – Three Gorges and Itaipu]. *Zhongguo sanxia gongcheng bao [China Three Gorges Project News]*, June 4.

"Beijing Declaration on Hydropower and Sustainable Development." 2004. CSD Documents, E/CN.17/2006/10, Division for Sustainable Development., United Nations.

Bloomberg. 2011. "EuroSibEnergo, Yangtze Power Sign Investment Framework Pact." June 17. http://www.bloomberg.com/news/2011-06-17/eurosibenergo-yangtze-power-sign-investment-framework-pact-1-.html.

Brautigam, Deborah. 2009. *The Dragon's Gift: The Real Story of China in Africa*. Oxford and New York: Oxford University Press.

Breakbulk. 2011. "Massive Chinese Hydro Project Moves Ahead." January 27. http://www.breakbulk.com/traditioal-power-generation/masssive-chinese-hydrop-project-moves-ahead.

Caing. 2010. "Hydropower Slowly Rows Upstream in China." December 10. http://english.caing.com/2010-12-10/100206366.html.

Cao, Haidong, and Zhang Peng. 2004. "Nujiang daba turan gezhi muhou de minjian liliang" [Nongovernmental Strength behind the Suspension of the Nu River Dam Proposal]. *Jingji*, May 20. http://finance.sina.com.cn.

Escobar, Arturo. 1995. *Encountering Development: The Making and Unmaking of the Third World*. Princeton University Press.

EuroSibEnergo. 2011. "EuroSibEnergo and China Yangtze Power Announce Siberian Project JV." February 24. http://www.eurosib.ru/en/press/news/456/.

Foucault, Michel. 1991. "Politics and the Study of Discourse." In *The Foucault Effect*, edited by Graham Burchell et al. The University of Chicago Press.

Hirsch, P. 2011. "Cascade Effect." *China Dialogue*, February 8. http://www.chinadialogue.net/article/show/single/en/4093.

Hong Kong Wen Wei Po. 2002. "Three Gorges Dam Ready for Listing in Shanghai." August 25.

HydroWorld. 2011. "EuroSibEnergo, Yangtze Power to Develop Hydro Projects in Siberia." June 24. https://www.renewableenergyworld.com/energy-business/new-project-development/eurosibenergo-yangtze/.

IPS News Agency. 2007. "China – New Promoter of Mega Dams." May 23. http://www.ipsnews.net/print.asp?idnews=37844.
Li, Yifei, and Judith Shapiro. 2020. *China Goes Green: Coercive Environmentalism for a Troubled Planet.* Polity Press.
Magee, Darrin. 2006. "Powershed Politics: Yunnan Hydropower under Great Western Development." *China Quarterly* 185: 23–41.
Mertha, Andrew. 2008. *China's Water Warrior: Citizen Action and Policy Change.* Ithaca and London: Cornell University Press.
Moore, Malcolm. 2009. "China Halts 20bn-Pound Dam Project." *Telegraph,* June 12. http://www.telegraph.co.uk/news/worldnews/asia/china/5513499/China-halts-20bn-dam-project.html.
Osborne, M. 2007. "The Water Politics of China and Southeast Asia: Rivers, Dams, Cargo Boats and the Environment." *Japan Focus*, June 4. https://apjjf.org/milton-osborne/2448/article.
Osborne, M. 2010. "The Mekong River under Threat." *Asia-Pacific Journal,* January 11. https://apjjf.org/milton-osborne/3286/article.
Pomeranz, K. 2009. "The Great Himalayan Watershed: Water Shortages, Mega-projects and Environmental Politics in China, India, and Southeast Asia." *Asia-Pacific Journal,* July 27. https://apjjf.org/kenneth-pomeranz/3195/article.
Reuters. 2010a. "China Seen Quietly Opening Sluice for Mega Hydro Projects." November 16. http://af.reuters.com/articlePrint?articleId=AFTOE6AE05G20101116.
Reuters. 2010b. "China Approves More Hydropower Amid Clean Energy Push." November 29. http://af.reuters.com/article/energyOilNews/idAFTOE6AS06F20101129.
Shapiro, Judith. 2001. *Mao's War against Nature: Politics and the Environment in Revolutionary China.* Cambridge University Press.
Wang, Donghong, and Zhao, Tingting. 2004. "Zuji ershiwan fang piaofuwu" [Tackling 200,000 Cubic Meters of Floating Garbage]. *Zhongguo sanxia gongcheng bao [China Three Gorges Project News],* October 16.
Watts, Jonathan. *The Guardian.* 2010. "Three Gorges Dam May Force Relocation of a Further 300,000 People." January 22. http://www.guardian.co.uk/environment/2010/jan/22/wave-tidal-hydropower-water.
Wittfogel, K. 1957. *Oriental Despotism: A Comparative Study of Total Power.* New Haven and London: Yale University Press.
Xu, Aimin. 2005. "Xiluodu dianzhan 26 ri kaigong" [Work on the Xiluodu Hydropower Station Started on the 26th]. *Zhongguo sanxia gongcheng bao [China Three Gorges Project News Special: Jinshajiang Baodao],* December 25.
Yu, Xianghan. 2004a. "Erlinglingsi nian shuili fadian guoji yantaohui zai sanxia zhaokai" [The International Conference of Hydropower 2004 Held at the Three Gorges]. *Zhongguo sanxia gongcheng bao [China Three Gorges Project News],* May 28.
Yu, Xianghan. 2004b. "Dijiuci heliu nisha xueshu taolunhui zuori bimu" [The Ninth International Symposium on River Sedimentation Drew to a Close Yesterday]. *Zhongguo sanxia gongcheng bao [China Three Gorges Project News],* October 22.
Zhongguo sanxia gongcheng bao [China Three Gorges Project News]. 2005. "Shuidian kaifa shi shehui kechixufazhan de zhongyao tujing" [Hydropower Exploitation Is an Essential Way for Society's Sustainable Development]. June 24.
Zuo, Likun. 2010. "Three Gorges Reservoir Plagued by Hazards." *China Daily,* March 6. https://www.chinadaily.com.cn/china/2010-03/06/content_9548662.htm.

Index

Page numbers in *italic* indicate a figure and page numbers in **bold** indicate a table on the corresponding page.

For Product Safety Concerns and Information please contact our EU representative GPSR@taylorandfrancis.com
Taylor & Francis Verlag GmbH, Kaufingerstraße 24, 80331 München, Germany

www.ingramcontent.com/pod-product-compliance
Ingram Content Group UK Ltd.
Pitfield, Milton Keynes, MK11 3LW, UK
UKHW022042061126
477531UK00009B/487

* 9 7 8 1 0 3 2 8 7 2 1 9 3 *